the context of
FOREIGN LANGUAGE TEACHING

the context of
FOREIGN LANGUAGE
TEACHING

Leon A. Jakobovits
Professor of Psychology
University of Hawaii

Barbara Gordon
President, Transactional Engineering Corporation
Miami Beach, Florida

NEWBURY HOUSE PUBLISHERS Inc / Rowley / Massachusetts

Newbury House Publishers, Inc.

Language Science
Language Teaching
Language Learning

68 Middle Road, Rowley, Massachusetts 01969

ISBN: 0-88377-010-5 (Paper edition)
      0-88377-011-3 (Cloth edition)

Printed in the U.S.A.   First printing: March, 1974

Education

CONTENTS

*This book is dedicated
to the warm creative genius
of Carl Rogers
whom we hope to meet one day.*

Part One: The Pedagogical Context

1 The Psychology of FL Learning

Many factors, conditions and situations in the educational system at all levels conspire to concretize and reify divisions in learning topics which originate from considerations that are separate from and irrelevant to the learning process itself. It is our feeling that the reasons that maintain curricular compartmentalization are either unrelated or actually detrimental to the student and the process of education. Disciplinary specialization has distinct advantages for certain purposes: for conducting research of a certain kind; for becoming a so-called expert in the field, and the social, intellectual and economic advantages that go along with having the status of an expert in our society; for professional and sociopolitical reasons having to do with influence and power; and so on. But it seems to us that too often considerations of this kind are allowed to interfere with the best interests of the student and his education.

Consider the trappings that surround the academic subject of second language learning, professional, educational, academic, and political: the FL profession with its organizations, conventions, journals, licensing procedures, and career opportunities; the FL literature and research, themselves subdivided into areas of specialization and methodological applications; the sociopolitical activities that revolve around the maintenance of ethnic identity; the specialized laws enacted with these interests in mind; and so on. These various divergent lines of interaction are somehow expected to converge into a meaningful topical unit of a classroom subject. But do they?

"Second language learning" as a classroom subject is one thing, and being a bilingual person is another thing, and these two things have often very little to do with one another. We believe that both of these can have valid educational objectives, but to confuse them is to neutralize the advantages that either may have to offer. When we went to high school we took Latin and Ancient Greek as school subjects, and it was clear to us, and it seemed so to the teacher as well, that the objective was not that of producing a bilingual individual. But when one of us took Flemish, and Spanish, and

German, and French, and Hebrew, a confusion existed: the objective was ostensibly to produce a multilingual individual, but the educational activities surrounding these subjects did not differ much from those involving Latin and Greek.

This was over twenty years ago, and it is now a matter of historical interest in FL education how this kind of confusion was supposedly eliminated. We speak of the advent of the audiolingual age in FL teaching, and we even have dates associated with the inauguration of this new era. The last generations of high school and college students are products of the language laboratory and of pattern practice, and the activities that these imply are supposed to attest to the changing educational objectives of second language learning. The objective of the current "modern" era in FL education is to produce a living viable bilingualism which is involved in talking, reading, and writing in two or more languages.

For a new perspective on FL learning, let us state a number of premises that need prior discussion and some subsequent agreement:

1) Bilingualism entails biculturalism.

2) Bilingualism cannot as a rule be achieved in the FL classroom alone.

3) There are valid educational objectives in learning a second language that are other than the attainment of bilingualism.

4) Learning a second language has associated with it factors and considerations that are unique to it and are different from learning other school subjects.

5) When a large proportion of students fails to learn a second language in school, their "failure" is not a reflection of the teacher's competence or the method he uses.

6) The conditions that hold under a mass educational system are unfavorable to the development of an effective FL curriculum.

We would like to take up each of these points in turn.

1. Bilingualism and Biculturalism

We suppose it would be possible to define bilingualism in a way that would invalidate the proposition that bilingualism entails biculturalism. In fact, people's use of the term, both academic and other, varies considerably from one extreme that defines bilingualism as a state of linguistic interference involving two or more languages, to the other extreme that reserves the term to describe the state of an individual who is equally at home in two or more languages under all conditions of usage and in addition sounds indistinguishable from native speakers of either language. Actually, one can argue with some merit that the proposition that bilingualism entails biculturalism holds true for both of these extreme definitions, as well as all those in between. In that case, we need to discuss what it is to be bicultural.

We are faced here with exactly the same problem as that of bilingualism. We find it useful to think of biculturalism in terms of the sharing of two cultures that have some identifiable identity of their own. This is ultimately a matter of classificatory convenience. Thus, in the case of political or national reasons, cultural boundary lines are set up that may or may not overlap with the boundaries set up on the basis of economic, religious, ideological, or historical reasons. Thus, we, along with many of our fellow Canadians, consider Canada a bilingual and bicultural country, meaning English and French, and this is a matter of historical classification. In fact, the Canadian population is made up of a number of other ethnic-linguistic groups as well, and this has become on the part of the latter groups a point of contention vis-à-vis the work and official designation of the Royal Commission on *Bi*-lingualism and *Bi*-culturalism.

It is clear, then, that biculturalism can be defined on the basis of a number of different and equally relevant criteria. Therefore, it is important to be always clear as to the particular criteria used in any discussion.

We would like for our present purposes to define biculturalism in terms of a transactional criterion. Transactions between two individuals are made possible as a result of their sharing certain types of knowledge and certain types of inferential reasoning behavior. The shared knowledge includes a linguistic code, semantic structures, certain attitudes, rules of conversation, and rules of the social and physical order of things. The shared inferential reasoning behavior includes expectations of what leads to what under particular conditions. When people interact on repeated occasions and do so for mutual benefit, they will learn each other's transactional premises. Thus, subgroups of habitual transactants form cultural or subcultural identities. When a member of one subgroup interacts with a member of another subgroup he has to readjust his transactional premises. It is at this point that he begins the process of becoming bicultural.

Now, if we look at the nature of this readjustment process, we note that it involves acquiring new knowledge, new expectations, and new ways of making inferences. A new linguistic code or changes in the linguistic code may or may not be involved. Thus bilingualism is not a prerequisite for biculturalism. Or to put it another way, while bilingualism always entails biculturalism, biculturalism entails bilingualism only in the special instance where a new linguistic code is to be acquired when interacting with a member of the second culture. It is this special case that we are faced with in learning a second language, but the properties of the general class of which it is an instance should always be kept in mind. Unless this is done it would be difficult to distinguish the learning of a second language from the learning of an alternate code for "communication" within a subculture, such as the language of the deaf or the Morse Code. For instance, if two friends decided one day to learn finger spelling and started interacting that way, this would not be an instance of biculturalism. We suppose one might call this an instance of unicultural bicodalism. Bilingualism, on the other hand, is more than bicodalism, since the second language is not intentionally patterned on the first. It includes a reorganization of knowledge as embodied in the phonological, syntactic, lexical, and semantic structures of that language as well as certain sociolinguistic rules. This reorganization of knowledge contains different transactional premises and constitutes biculturalism. It is for this reason that we stated that any degree of bilingualism entails some degree of biculturalism.

This way of looking at second language learning allows a different perspective on FL teaching. The latter thus becomes a question of training in biculturalism. Once this premise is accepted, the problems involved in FL teaching methodology take on different dimensions. We believe that the issues involved in bicultural training are more productive than those involved in bilingual training. Let us simply sketch some of the parameters that we think might be involved in such an investigation.

To begin with, a focus on bicultural training would give a more appropriate status to the role of language training per se. There is a widespread attitude among teachers and educators involved in FL training, which is shared also by students and their parents, that mastering the elementary mechanics of language is a necessary prerequisite for getting to the subsequent stage of some degree of bilingualism, this latter stage being the really worthwhile aspect of the experience because it then allows the incipient bilingual to come into contact with the culture of the people either directly through oral communication or indirectly through reading and exposure to the mass media. The assumption that lies behind this attitude seems to us to give an unwarranted amount of weight and importance to a particular form of bicultural "communication," that which is directly mediated by the second code. Yet it seems to us that other forms of bicultural transaction are equally worthwhile for various purposes and under many conditions. For instance, the amount of bilingualism gained through a few weeks travel in Japan is fairly negligible when unsupported by prior or concurrent language training, yet the degree of biculturalism one might absorb during the same time may have very lasting consequences for the individual. Similarly, a serious interest in Oriental art, or Eastern philosophy, or even the regular practice of karate, may transform an ethnocentric unicultural individual into a culturally more sophisticated person, who, even though he may know nothing of a second language, is well on his way to bicultural and multicultural competency. On what bases can it really be claimed that mastering the mechanics of a second language is a superior educational objective to these other forms of biculturalism, especially when that kind of demand actually stands in the way of bicultural experiences, as we believe it does for the majority of students in our FL programs? We think educators must face this issue head on and reexamine their attitude towards the universalization of the FL curriculum in its current manifestation. We have grave doubts about the value of cramming knowledge down the throat of anyone, whether it be a FL, or Oriental art, or trigonometry. We believe that expending massive educational efforts in teaching FL's in the absence of a genuine interest in that type of knowledge is not only futile but harmful. It seems to us that for the educational process to be effective it ought to be dispensed in a miserly fashion: give only as much as is demanded. To feel comfortable with this kind of educational philosophy, the teacher must have two prior beliefs: (one is that merely acquiring facts in the absence of an intrinsic interest is not ultimately very useful, hence to attempt it is futile; the other is a belief in the intrinsic worth of the individual, that what matters is the process of satisfying his creative and intellectual needs that in fact exist, rather than needs defined for him by others. Are FL teachers prepared to take off the colored glasses of their provincial perspective and view the problem in its wider educational implications?

2. Can Bilingualism Be Achieved in the Classroom?

When FL teachers and administrators are faced with the fact that the vast majority of their students do not attain a state of functional bilingualism at the end of their training, their most common reaction is to look around for more effective methods of teaching. This is not an irrational or surprising reaction. But if repeated searches for the best method fail to graduate a greater proportion of bilinguals, another conclusion should be seriously considered, namely that bilingualism cannot as a rule be achieved in the classroom alone. There are a number of considerations that can serve to rationalize this conclusion. Let us mention a few:

(a) Developing communicative competence in a language requires conditions in which communicative needs exist. One can put this in a slightly different way which might be more useful: the degree of communicative competence acquired by an individual is proportional to the extent of his communicative needs. Now, what are the communicative needs of an American student in the classroom taking French, say? We can't think of very many which cannot be satisfied in English, short of the case of the pupil who falls in love with his pretty unilingual French teacher. While being present in FL classes where the use of English was forbidden, we have repeatedly noted that whenever a genuine communicative need arose, the students automatically and insistently lapsed into the use of English. Carrying on a classroom discussion on some topic did in a few instances create genuine communicative needs when the students got involved in the subject, but the requirement of using the second language was purely artificial, and by the time the painful process of constructing a reasonably correct sentence was achieved, the need had come and gone and the discussion turned into an artificial language exercise. We are not knocking the usefulness of discussions in the FL classroom; in fact, we believe they are distinctly more advantageous than pattern practice exercises. But we are drawing your attention to the difficulty of creating genuine communicative needs in the classroom setting, and hence, according to the proposition we stated above, to the difficulty of developing functional bilingualism.

(b) Achieving functional bilingualism in the classroom requires a fairly high degree of FL aptitude. We take aptitude to be an inverse function of time required to achieve a set criterion. Thus, even though it may be the case that almost all adults are capable of becoming bilingual, only a small proportion of them could achieve that status given the time limitations that hold in the school setting.

(c) Achieving functional bilingualism in the absence of extensive contact with unilingual native speakers requires an integrative orientation on the part of the learner. By "integrative orientation" we mean an attitude whereby the learner identifies with native models and perceives an intrinsic value in acquiring cultural characteristics that the native models possess, including their language. It is simply a fact that the vast majority of American students do not have such an integrative orientation towards foreign models.

In the absence of any of the three conditions that we stated, namely, genuine communicative needs, high aptitude, and integrative orientation, let alone their combination, it is then unrealistic to expect that the classroom can produce very many functional bilinguals.

3. Are There Valid Objectives in Learning a Second Language Other Than Bilingualism?

Earlier we stated the answer in the affirmative. (And here we can almost hear the sigh of relief on the part of FL teachers whom we have not as yet totally alienated and who are still reading.) What are some of these objectives?

Let us start with the extrinsic ones. American culture seems to attach value to FL learning. While this attitude is neither simple nor universal, it has been strong and pervasive over the years and has made possible the recent drive towards universalization of the FL curriculum in our schools. Language loyalty and maintenance activities on the part of ethnic groups in this country have remained very strong and active. We would guess that no less than half of

Americans living today can count in their parental or grandparental generation an individual whose first language is other than English. In addition, there still lingers today the traditional European value whereby one is not fully educated unless one "knows" a second language. Furthermore, many Americans have come to believe that international peace requires greater understanding and contact between the peoples of the world, and thus by taking a FL course in school they feel that they are somehow contributing to world peace. Finally, many more Americans today travel abroad, or at least consider traveling abroad, and this fact is consistent with the study of FL's.

It should be noted that some of these extrinsic motivations to FL study may not in fact be valid from the point of view of an impartial observer. That is, one may be considered to be an educated person even though one is unilingual in English; one may not actually contribute to world peace by enrolling in a FL course; one may not make use of Spanish while traveling in France and Italy; and so on. But this is not the point. Given a prevalent cultural value for FL study, it can be considered a valid educational objective to have a strong and active FL curriculum.

Now, to mention some other objectives that might be more intrinsic in nature. Exposure to a FL constitutes bicultural training. The teacher may be a foreigner. The content of the day's lesson may offer a new perspective on a different social order. Or it may be a foreign magazine, or a movie, or a book, or a meal. A new insight may be gained on the neighbors next door or on the foreign dignitaries that the president is seen meeting on the White House steps. History, geography, and anthropology may take on a slightly different perspective, one that might be closer and more relevant to personal experience. Language, as a device for transactions, becomes more concretized as the individual leaves the automatic, unthinking facility of his native language and moves into the painful, halting hesitancies of a foreign tongue as he deliberately tries to place the adjectives and verbs in their proper order. For the first time, the artificial structuredness of human language enters his awareness and becomes a living reality. There are undoubtedly rare, but recurrent moments, when he feels the architect's elation when viewing the finished product of his imagination as he beholds that rare phenomenon of a novel well-formed sentence in the second language for which he himself is responsible. Then, for the very few, there is that supreme satisfaction that comes from viewing a French movie without having to bother to read the English subtitles, or settling down with a novel without pencil and dictionary. The mere contemplation of these two delights is sufficient to drive many a student to one more hour of a boring language laboratory session.

Finally, let us mention along with these intrinsic values, a more esoteric argument that comes out of the psycholinguist's bag. In this view, unilingual speakers are compared to the egocentrism of young children who innocently believe that the word is the thing, and the concept is the word. The semantic structure of a language reflects the conceptual framework of speakers of that language, a notion that has led to the development of such serious disciplines as ethnolinguistics and cognitive anthropology. Learning a second language requires the acquisition of a new semantic structure that reflects a new order of things in the world. The learner makes the momentous discovery that lo and behold the world isn't as it is, and the cognitive dissonance that this realization creates may very well transform him into a more understanding, more humble, more compassionate, more flexible-thinking human being.

These, then, are some of the values of FL study other than functional bilingualism, and we submit that they are not unimportant. Let no FL teacher, contemplating the so-called failure of the FL curriculum, feel defensive or sheepish about his contribution to the educational development of our youth. The attainment of bilingualism is by no means the only justifiable value of a FL program.

4. Learning a Second Language Is Unlike Learning Other School Subjects

We have already referred to some of the particular attitudes that revolve around the study of FL's, and these attach to it a cultural significance that is distinctly different from that of other school subjects. But now we have in mind another sort of difference which is related to the developmental learning steps involved in studying a second language and their attitudinal consequences. That "mathematics is difficult" is a common piece of folklore that most students and parents hold with unshakable conviction. Not to run into trouble there is no mean achievement, let alone be good in it. That "Spanish is a cinch" while "German is for the brainy people" are also interesting little bits of knowledge that you can discover when you spend your time administering opinion surveys to high school students, as some of our academic colleagues and I are fond of doing. But very few students enrolling in a second language course have any inkling of the pain they have let themselves in for by that action. Imagine how difficult it is to learn how to talk! This can't be! There must be something wrong somewhere! Either the teacher is no good, or I have no aptitude for languages. And there goes another lost cause.

There are three kinds of problems that face second language learners that we feel are unique: the self-evaluations concerning rate of progress and degree of achievement; the peculiar cumulative nature of their developing competence; and the psychological resistance to free expression. Let us discuss these in reverse order.

There appears to be a qualitative difference for many learners in the significance they attach to making errors while speaking in a FL versus getting an answer wrong in another school subject. Getting the wrong answer for a problem in algebra or the wrong date for an historical battle is a pity because of the grade missed, but there is something either sacrilegious or idiotic in unintentionally murdering a sentence. There is an interesting psychological phenomenon here that would surely be worth further investigation, but for the moment, let us simply note that this attitude serves to inhibit and retard the expressive leap in a second language. Teachers too, we might add, share this attitude with their students and although their rationalization for it might be different (for instance, "it is more difficult to unlearn errors later on") their low tolerance for phonological distortions and syntactic irregularities no doubt serves to maintain the students' resistance to communicative speech. We have no doubt that error analysis would show up developmental patterns that necessitate intermediary forms of speech for which correction is futile and attitudinally harmful.

Next, another second language learning problem is that so much of it is initially in the form of latent knowledge and progress seems so uneven to the learner. For instance, the so-called "active" skills—speaking and writing—are far behind the "passive" skills of listening and reading, and while the latter proceed in noticeable steps, the former seem never to get off the ground. Actually, "active" and "passive" are misnomers here because the deep structure analysis of a sentence is similar whether you generate it or someone else does it for you. The only passive thing about listening is that your peripheral vocal apparatus creates less disturbance in the air than when you talk, but syntactically you are equally active in both situations. This is not to say that the processes are identical—otherwise they would develop at comparable rates—but the nature of the difference might not be what we suppose it to be.

There are furthermore problems associated with diagnosing areas of difficulty. A mistake in an algebra problem can be traced to a forgotten formula (that can then be relearned) or an error in subtraction (that can be shrugged off). Not so when an expression in the FL is misunderstood or when a sentence fails to materialize in the quivering throat of the student. When second language learners are asked to list their major problems, one that is high on almost everyone's list is vocabulary. This is a doubtful assessment, and experienced teachers know this. Other common candidates are gender and verb tense. But here too there are reasons to believe that the problems are more complex than that. There is room here for a great deal more systematic observation than we now have available.

Finally, the third kind of problem that seems to be peculiar to second language learning, one that is not unconnected to the other two, is the student's self-evaluation of the rate of his progress and the extent of his achievement. He seems to share with many a teacher and parent the delusion that he ought to know more than he does at any one point and that unless he ultimately achieves functional, easy going, nativelike fluency in his expressions his efforts have been in vain. As we have pointed out earlier, not only is bilingualism not the sole valid objective of FL study, but that objective is quite unrealistic for many learners within the school system, and perhaps teachers could play a more active and constructive role in the formation of more realistic self-evaluations on the part of their students.

5. The Relation Between Student "Failure" and Teacher "Failure"

There is a very pernicious sort of argumentation whereby some unjustified goal is set for a program, then, when it is not attained, the program is dubbed a failure. We believe this is the type of argument that is responsible for the crisis atmosphere in FL education today and the ensuing frantic search for better methods, better bilingual programs, better manipulative techniques for motivating students to learn, and so on. Naturally, our remark is not intended to license another kind of extreme attitude whereby all is well under the sun and we need not worry about continuing excellence in education. The point is that the setting of goals for a program ought not to be done very lightly and in the absence of careful justification.

The other day a graduate student in linguistics dropped in to see one of us in the office, and being from Thailand he wanted me to tell him why their ESL program over there was a failure. "Is it true," as he had heard, "that you are against the audiolingual method, and if so, which method would be better?" I asked him what the purpose of their ESL program was and he told me, "Why, of course, so that the Thais can learn the two active and the two passive skills in English." Undaunted, I asked, "What for, why do the Thais want to know the four skills in English?" upon which he said, "In order to be able to read English textbooks." Several minutes of silence ensued, whereupon he said "I see what you mean; you mean, what's the use of learning the four skills in English when what they want is to learn how to decode English textbooks."

We relate this episode—and we hope we are not doing the student an injustice—because it so clearly points up the excesses of goal setting for many existing programs, excesses that we believe are quite habitual in the second language teaching field. Perhaps one explanation for the acuteness of this problem is that few people in this field actually believe that it is either possible or useful to develop specialized skills in the use of a second language. It is as if they treated language learning as a monolithic block to be digested in toto or not at all. This appears to be indeed a matter of belief for we have been unable to find any serious attempt that has investigated the problem. And yet, it seems to us, that there are cogent arguments against the monolithic theory. We know that reading in one's native language is a specialized skill, and, particularly when it comes to reading textbook English, the variance to be found there in individual differences in competence does not seem to match the much smaller variance in competence we can note in the daily use of native English speakers. Similarly, the skill with which the French Canadian bus driver in Montreal handles customers in English, when the need arises, totally belies his English competence as soon as they engage him in a political discussion. The same noncommunicative situation arises with the English salesclerk with whom we make conversation in French after she has sold us the piece of merchandise in very competent French.

Thus observation supports the separateness of various communicative skills in a language. There remain then two problems in this connection. First, is there not a minimum common core of linguistic knowledge that transcends specialized communicative settings and that should be taught to all language learners? And second, is the teaching of specialized goals justifiable and feasible given a great deal of heterogeneity in need and unpredictability in later use?

Neither of these questions, it seems to us, is amenable to a pat answer, but we believe that it is possible to set guidelines that apply differentially to particular situations.

In the first instance it ought to be recognized that the resources available to any particular language training program, be it in a high school setting or a special language school, are limited. Certain decisions have to be made about the priority of needs to be met. Then one must examine whether the learning conditions in that school and the larger community are favorable for meeting the priority needs. For instance, offering a conversational course in Russian in a high school and community where there is one living speaker of Russian is asking for trouble, unless it is made quite clear to all concerned that bilingualism is not the goal of the course. Offering an audiolingual course in German to chemistry majors in college whose sole interest is to decipher journal articles, can only be done if the students are not expected to be happy and the teacher is careless of his life. And to teach the "two active skills and the two passive skills" to Thai college students who only wish to get through their engineering texts is not only futile, as experience shows, but positively heartless. Obviously, we have to proceed with deliberate planning in the specialization of second language courses, but equally obviously a process of unfreezing the current monolithic programs is long overdue.

6. Toward Compensatory or Individualized FL Instruction

The last of our six premises stated that an effective FL curriculum is not possible under present conditions of mass education. There is nothing so peculiar to FL instruction that this should be true only of it and not of other school subjects, and so our premise here is but an expression of the more general thesis that effective education and mass teaching do not go together.

This completes our discussion of the six premises we stated at the beginning. We'd like to summarize briefly. There are valid educational objectives in learning a second language that are other than the attainment of bilingualism. Bilingualism is a process of enculturation, and although the acquisition of some forms of biculturalism represents a realistic and worthwhile goal, the achievement of a state of bilingualism is not to be expected for the majority of students. Learning a FL in school has associated with it certain unique aspects, and whatever the student learns or fails to learn is not a reflection of the teacher's competence or the language teaching method he uses. Instead, they are a joint function of the student's attitudes, needs, and aptitude, the quality of the existing relationship between the teacher and the student, and the specific objective of the course in terms of the specialized language skills the teacher and the student agree upon to pursue.

These, to us, are the major premises that define the psychological bases of second language learning.

REFERENCES

Jakobovits, L. A. *Foreign Language Learning: A Psycholinguistic Analysis of the Issues.* Rowley, Mass.: Newbury House Publishers, 1970.

Savignon, Sandra. *Toward Communicative Competence: An Experiment in Foreign Language Teaching.* Philadelphia: The Center for Curriculum Development, 1972.

2 How To Individualize FL Teaching

Discussions on FL teaching methodology usually consist of partisan statements and arguments in which the purported advantages of one method are juxtaposed to the alleged disadvantages of another, with a view to convincing the reader or listener to adopt one and abandon or stay away from the other. This procedure is considered acceptable and ordinary, and we in turn, have often engaged in this kind of polemics (e.g., Jakobovits, 1970 a, b).

We feel that in the past year or so the polemical climate in FL education has begun to change somewhat, and we would like to attempt a different approach to this perennial problem that concerns us so much. Although there remain amidst us staunch method adversaries enlisted in one cause or another, our impression is that a great number of FL teachers hold a pragmatic view that is both eclectic and sound: they are not committed to a particular theoretical point of view and are willing to experiment with "whatever seems to work." We consider this an encouraging development which is more likely to benefit the students than is the rigid adherence to a particular paradigm. Consequently, we would like, in this chapter, to present a comparative analysis of FL teaching procedures that might help delineate their major characteristics and show us a new approach. Our attitude in this presentation can be characterized by the statement that no one approach is in and of itself superior to any other, but that some might be more suitable than others depending on the circumstances. Our analysis will try to specify the relationship between the features of the teaching procedures and these teaching circumstances. What we are aiming for, then, is a *context dependent* analysis of FL teaching procedures.

The EBTA Cube

We would like to begin by proposing three basic distinctions that characterize the various FL teaching procedures: non-programmed versus programmed instruction, mass versus individualized instruction, and traditional versus compensatory instruction. Let us take up each of these in turn and examine their characteristics, the major assumptions and premises that underly them, and some of their implications.

Nonprogrammed vs. Programmed Instruction

To us the most salient differentiating feature between programmed and nonprogrammed instruction is the extent to which the content of a "lesson" is broken up into small unitary "steps" each to be acquired separately and sequentially. Programmed instruction often has associated with it special "hardware" paraphernalia (e.g., "teaching machines"), but we consider these coincidental (not, however, unimportant or irrelevant). There also exist programmed courses which use textbook-type materials for the presentation of the program. "Self-pacing" is often a built-in feature of programmed courses, but in most cases individual differences in rate of learning are not directly taken into account by the internal structure of the program and translate instead into how long it takes an individual to complete a "lesson" and consequently the overall course. Individual differences in learning style are usually not taken into account. Some programs, for instance, will provide shortcuts for the fast learner and elaborations of some steps for the slow learner, while using the same principle of presentation in both instances. Programmed instruction insures acquisition by the very act of completion of the program by the student, and special achievement and performance tests for the course are thus not required. Every student who *completes* his programmed course or "module" is automatically considered to have been "successful." Finally, although programmed instruction constitutes "individual" instruc- tion par excellence, in the sense that the student is alone with his mechanical or textual "teacher," it does not necessarily represent "individualized" instruction as characterized below.

The traditional justification for programmed instruction is the assumption that it is easier to learn small, clear, isolated steps, one at a time, than more or less large, inductively obscure principles. The major problem in programmed instruction has been the difficulty of breaking up the overall content of a skill or course into such specific steps ("frames"). Programmed courses thus vary in validity (the relationship between the steps in the program taken as a whole and the ultimate competence to be achieved), in efficiency (the relationship between how fast and with how many errors an individual acquires competence and his theoretical aptitude or ability), and in interest (the attitudinal and motivational "cost" to the student).

The implications of the development of programmed instruction for education are quite serious and significant, although not necessarily in all aspects of education. Competencies associated with some particular "school subjects" may be more amenable to handling with programmed instruction than others, and they may be more significant with certain types of students than others (e.g., the slow and fast learners versus the "average" student). In our opinion, programmed instruction today faces the same kind of challenge that nonprogrammed instruction has faced for a long time, which is to combine it with compensatory and individualized principles of instruction (see below).

Mass vs. Individualized Instruction

The fact of mass education, its existence and presence in our, and other technological societies, is not a result of merely the emergent need of educating large numbers of people. In its present form, it is no less a result of certain specific assumptions about the learning process and the intended educational objectives. We think this observation is notable because too often educators attempt to rationalize many recognized shortcomings of the educational system by saying that they are the result of an overflow of student population in our schools (or, alternately, an underflow of "qualified" teachers). Certainly it is understandable that overflows and underflows reduce the efficiency of a system. But an increasing number of people have come to believe that some of these shortcomings are to be attributed to the assumptions and principles of the learning-teaching process, and have advocated different, often contradictory assumptions and principles. We would like to refer to this difference as the "mass vs. individualized contrast."

Mass instruction assumes that effective teaching is possible when a group of individuals are brought together in a classroom or laboratory and treated as multiple copies of one ("average") individual ("lockstep"). A relatively pure instance of this approach is basic army training; a contaminated instance is the typical large American graduate school—and there are shades in between. This basic assumption has several corollaries, the most important ones being the following: graduates of the training program have similar minimal competencies, and they can be made to learn in similar sequential and cumulative steps.

The major assumption of mass instruction is contradicted by the individualized approach which treats each individual as a different species of learner. This difference is analogous to the contrast between mass produced and custom-built automobiles. Note that the principles and opportunities of mass production constitute a technological and economic reality which is what makes it possible to have custom-built automobiles. Similarly, the reality of a public educational system, with its software of teachers and curricula, and its hardware of classrooms and laboratories, makes it possible to have individualized instruction (which should not be confused with one-to-one teaching).

As with orders for custom-built cars, each individual learner is considered a unique and separate problem: graduates of a training program do *not* have similar minimal competencies and they can *not* be made to learn in similar sequential and cumulative steps. These beliefs lead to very different decisions about curricular content and development and to very different expectations about achievement, performance, and competence. [1] Here, the notion of self-pacing assumes less trivial, more critical importance than in many current programmed instruction courses. Here, examinations and tests are not geared to the school year and "grade level" is not synonymous with age. The conception of "teacher," "classroom," and "homework" become less neat and well defined; instead we may speak of "tutor" or "facilitator" and more simply "work" rather than "class work" or "homework."

Traditional vs. Compensatory Instruction

We come here to a distinction we wish to make that is likely to create more difficulties than the other two, partly because the word "traditional" ordinarily includes such a broad range of things, and partly because we have previously used the phrase "compensatory instruction" (Jakobovits, 1970a, Chapter 3) where, according to the more refined terminology presented here, we would use "compensatory-individualized instruction." We believe that the additional differentiation is useful and worth the effort.

Traditional instruction makes the following traditional assumptions: that formal education prepares the individual for the "real life" problems outside school; that courses and curricula provide specialized knowledge and skills which, in their aggregate, constitute professional or work-setting competence; that the discrete skills and knowledge which make up the content of courses and textbooks are to be selected on the basis of some sort of sampling distribution (in terms of their "importance," "frequency," "usefulness," "prerequisiteness," etc.), since they are too numerous to be taught in their entirety; that acquisition of a minimum specified number of such facts and skills constitutes ipso facto evidence of the acquisition of the specialized competence; that the specialized competence which is the purported goal of the instruction process can be adequately defined in terms of these discrete skills, which is to say, independently of the performer and the context of his performance.

Compensatory instruction specifically denies the validity of these assumptions of discreteness, of sampling, of sequential accumulation, of the *quid pro quo* of formal instruction and competence. The school is not considered as either a substitute or a preparation ground for society "out there," but is taken for its face value as a place *in* society, like the home, or the work setting, which individuals of a certain age are forced to attend, in which they must work and cope to survive as a part of their social and human condition. The school is thus a training and preparation ground only in the trivial sense that the home, the church, the neighborhood, the Boy Scouts, or whatever, are training grounds. This is a trivial sense since every decade of an individual's life can be looked upon as preparation for the decades that come afterward.

If you look upon the school in this latter way, then the courses and curricula you encounter there would no doubt still provide specialized knowledge and skills, but whether in their aggregate they constitute professional or civic competence is an open question to be carefully assessed rather than granted by definition. Similarly, it becomes a problem for demonstration whether professional or civic competence can develop in any other way but by doing and living in a professional way and a civic way. Furthermore, since our specific understanding of real life situations has always been immeasurably less than our understanding of abstract, theoretic, and artificial systems it remains to be shown that an effective formal instruction process, which requires specificity of knowledge, is at all possible under such conditions. Thus, that people can learn, is an undeniable fact of life; that people can teach, is an interesting hypothesis, but an uncertain one.

We have now completed our elaboration of the three binary distinctions of basic approaches to teaching. Since each dimension has been independently defined, we have a possible total of eight basic approaches to teaching. These can be arranged in a three-dimensional cubic figure, as in fig. *1a,* or a two-dimensional figure, as in fig. *1b.* We would now like to discuss the characteristics of a FL curriculum within such a model.

FL Instruction Within the EBTA Cube

We are now going to adopt a more argumentative style because we believe that fundamental changes are needed in the approaches to FL teaching which characterize many FL curricula in our public educational system at all three levels. Programmed instruction is not yet widespread in education, generally, and in FL instruction it is used very infrequently, as far as we are aware. Individualized instruction in FL teaching is even more recent a development, although there are signs that an increasing number of individual teachers have taken upon themselves the task of implementing some of its principles in their classrooms (see Altman, 1971; Rogers, 1969). Compensatory instruction is not yet a reality anywhere in the public educational system, but we shall try to argue that we have the knowhow to start implementing many of its principles. That leaves the nonprogrammed-mass-traditional approach (type 4 in Fig. 1) as the standard prototype practically everywhere. This approach, as defined in the first half of this chapter, makes the following assumptions (in this, we are going to restrict our focus to the learning and teaching of a second language):

1. The teaching objectives of the language course are stated in very general terms such as "a speaking knowledge" or "a knowledge of

'the four' basic skills," rather than in specific terms as defined by a learning program. Furthermore, there is no need to break up the knowledge that is to be acquired into the strictly unitary steps of a programmed sequence.

2. With some exceptions (such as remedial classes), learners are treated alike in the overall instructional process.

3. Graduates of a FL course or program have similar minimal competence in the second language as attested by the obtention of at least a passing grade.

4. Individuals can learn a second language by going through similar sequential and cumulative steps as defined by the content of a set of lessons variously organized depending on the particular text or method being used.

5. The FL course prepares the individual for the use of the target language outside the classroom or laboratory.

6. Communicative competence can be broken up into discrete skills and "pieces" of knowledge for more efficient learning, and these discrete elements constitute the content of lessons, laboratory exercises, and homework.

7. The degree of communicative competence acquired is directly related to and assessed by the quality of performance on achievement tests (standardized or examination type) which sample attained knowledge of discrete elements presented in the lessons.

8. Communicative competence or knowledge of the language is defined in abstract, generalized, context-free terms.

Assumption (1) derives from the earlier discussion on nonprogrammed vs. programmed instruction. Assumptions (2) to (4) relate to the distinction we have made between mass and individualized instruction, and (5) to (8) derive from the traditional-compensatory contrast. On the basis of our evaluation of the language learning process or the development of communicative competence (see Jakobovits, 1970 a, c), we have come to believe that, with the possible exception of the first (see discussion below), the assumptions associated with the mass-traditional approach are unsound. The following arguments substantiating our impression can also be looked upon as a characterization of the individualized-compensatory approach to language teaching (nonprogrammed or programmed).

We start with the general premise, often stated by Carroll (e.g., 1965, p. 22) that students in a FL class learn, if anything, precisely what they are taught. This assertion can be interpreted at two different levels, both of which we believe to be valid. At one level, an audiolingual course that emphasizes "oral skills" will show higher achievement scores on tests of listening and speaking performance than a "traditional" course that emphasizes reading and writing, and at the same time, it will show lower scores on tests of reading and writing as compared to the "traditional" course. At another level, one that is not discussed to the same extent in the FL teaching literature, the language skills acquired in the classroom or laboratory will be different from the language skills needed for communicative competence outside the school. That these represent different skills is proved by the common observation that the relationship between success on language achievement tests or course grades and the success in communicating in the target language in real life situations is weak. This weak relationship also holds in the reverse situation where individuals who have learned a second language "in the streets" and have success in communicating in it do not necessarily obtain high scores on standardized achievement tests.

A corollary to this basic assumption is that the development of communicative competence occurs only in learning situations where there is a real communicative need and in response to it. The classroom and the laboratory in the context of formal education constitute a social setting where the communicative needs are different from those in non-school settings. This means that the school achiever will develop a pattern of communicative competence that is different from and not suitable for meeting the communicative needs outside the school. We are not arguing here that the school context is irrelevant; only that it is irrelevant to a significant number of non-school contexts. For instance a formal course in history may be relevant to contributing to our understanding of the historical process as viewed within an academic frame of reference, but its relevance to understanding the daily events reported on the front page of a newspaper is unconvincing. The study of Latin may be relevant to an understanding of Latin and Ancient Roman civilization, but its relevance to anything else is a moot point. Similarly, the study of a FL in the classroom may develop certain worthwhile knowledge, but its relevance to the use of that language for communicative purposes outside the school appears to be small (e.g., see Carroll, 1968).

Let us argue now in more specific terms. It is generally accepted in FL education today that the development of listening comprehension skills is a highly specific affair and that students must be exposed to fluent nativelike speech to be able to understand a native speaker of the target language (as, for instance, a foreign movie or radio broadcast). But this principle is overlooked in most of the other communicative functions of language. For instance, it is generally assumed that asking and answering questions in a pattern practice exercise or a simulated dialogue on the content of a lesson serves to develop the skills needed in asking and answering questions in a real conversation or communicative setting. This expectation is contradicted not only by the daily experience of the FL teacher, but as well by a theoretical analysis of simulated classroom dialogues and real ones. The ability to ask and answer questions is dependent not only on the knowledge of the relevant vocabulary and syntactic patterns, but also on background knowledge about the social rules or conventions of conversational interaction and on inferences about intent, appropriateness, and the like. For instance, one does not ask a stranger's name when he has just identified himself to another speaker in our presence. Consider the following conversational sequence:

A1. How long have you been in Montreal?

B1. Three months. And you?

A2. Ah, I'm an old resident of Montreal. We moved here when I was a child. And how do you like it so far?

B2. Well, it's different. I never lived in a large cosmopolitan city before. I imagine it takes people a while to get used to the hustle and bustle . . . .

A3. Well, yes. Where have you lived before?

B3. In Quebec City. It's much quieter there, and the population is more homogeneous. Mostly French Canadian, you know.

A4. I don't know Quebec very well . . . . Do *you* have any children?

B4. Two boys and a girl. They all go to Gardenview Elementary.

Note that the question in *A1* is appropriate only if *A* has reasons to believe that *B* is a newcomer to the city. The question in *B1* has no such implications, yet it is appropriate in response to *A's* question. The question in *A2* is permissible as a retort to the earlier answer in *B1*. Had *A1* and *B1* not preceded it, this question would have been phrased differently and in such a way as to refer to the missing part by means of some sort of elliptical reference to the missing part (e.g., "Well, I understand you are a recent arrival to our city. How do you like it so far?"). Note that *A3* contains an assent to a question that is only implied, not stated, in *A2* (e.g., "I imagine . . .bustle . . .Don't you think so?"). And so on for the rest of the sequence.

Now consider an analogous conversational sequence in a simulated classroom dialogue.

    A1. How long have you been in Montreal?
    B1. Three months.
    A2. How do you like it so far?
    B2. I like it very much.
    A3. Where have you lived before?
    B3. In Quebec City.
    A4. Do you have any children?
    B4. Yes.
    A5. How many?
    B5. Three.
    A6. Boys or girls?
    B6. Two boys and one girl.

This second sequence is not merely more stilted, more unnatural, more forced; a different organizational sequence underlies the conversation, one that is appropriate in another communicative context (e.g., interview situations where *B* "submits" to *A*'s questioning for whatever particular reason).

We have given a fairly trivial example, but we hope it illustrates our point. We shall not go into any further details here, but think of the wide range of conversational encounters where differences of this sort become evident: asking for information, expressing an opinion, reporting an event, elaborating a statement, justifying an assertion, explaining, making smalltalk, joking, complimenting, subtly disagreeing, appearing unprejudiced, and so on, to the full range of everyday, ordinary, commonplace conversational interaction.

FL educators, when presented with arguments such as these, often reply that "liberated expression" is only to be expected at more advanced stages of language learning, that in elementary language training one must first go through the admittedly artificial exercises of pattern practice and classroom dialogues. We question the soundness of this sequential hypothesis that considers the elementary exercises either a prerequisite to "liberated expression" or, a simpler, more basic, more elementary form of it. We are confident that a communication analysis of the typical classroom interaction will show it up as being no less complex than ordinary conversational interaction, but different from it. Certainly it is the case that the "street produced" bilingual learns the rules of ordinary conversation without going through the so-called elementary, nonordinary classroom conversational patterns.

Let us summarize our argument thus far. The classroom represents a nonordinary, specialized communicative setting, with its own complex rules of conversational interaction and specialized functions for language use (e.g., instruction and problem solving). Ordinary commonplace conversational interaction has its own and a different complex set of rules, and it cannot be replicated or simulated in the classroom. The communicative competence that underlies it can only be developed in real life situations.

The FL educators and teachers who become convinced of the validity of this argument will be faced with the necessity of making certain difficult, exploratory, but, we think exciting, decisions that will radically change the contemporary spectrum of the FL curriculum. It will be a change away from the mass-traditional approach to the compensatory-individualized approach. The extent of displacement they may achieve as a result of these new policy decisions will no doubt vary with the existing social, political, and administrative conditions of each school community. This is as it is—but the crucially important point is that each decision that is made, no matter how small in consequences, be of such character as to move the spectrum of FL instruction away from type 4 in the EBTA cube (mass-traditional) to types 1 and 5 (compensatory-individualized). We would like to suggest some major policy decisions that have this character.

1. *The diversification of the FL curriculum while simultaneously restricting the instructional objectives of particular courses within the curriculum* (see also the discussion in Jakobovits, 1970*b* and

1970*a*, Chapter 5). Traditionally stated objectives such as "a knowledge of the language" or "a knowledge of 'the four' basic skills" are euphemisms for having no goal and confusion. Instead, objectives ought to be stated within three major functional types, (*a*) ordinary commonplace conversational use; (*b*) monadic language use; and (*c*) nonordinary specialized language use. Specialized courses with restricted focus may be offered within each of the three major types. Thus within the type of ordinary commonplace conversational use there will be courses or sections with "how to . . . " titles in the following form: How to Speak to Strangers in French; How to Shop in Japanese; How to Make Friends in Russian; How to Travel in Spanish; and so on. Within the monadic language use type, courses having rather solitary objectives can be specified in the following form: How to Read Classical Literature in Arabic; How to Write Business Letters in Hebrew; How to Enjoy Indian Movies; How to Listen to French Canadian News Broadcasts; How to Decode Chinese Propaganda Leaflets; How to Pray in Tibetan; and so on. Finally, within the type of nonordinary specialized language use we would have the following: How to Study Chemistry in German; How to be an English-Albanian Simultaneous Translator; How to Talk to Your French Teacher; How to be a Comedian in Italian; How to Give the Impression of Being a Multilingual Person; and so on.

We hope these rather comical titles do not discourage the serious FL teacher who is contemplating a move toward compensatory-individualized instruction. We allow ourselves a little bit of humor in an area too devoid of it. Why does FL learning and teaching have to be such a grimly serious and painful enterprise? Think of how much fun students would have in a course entitled "How to be a Comedian in Italian." And think how much of the Italian language and culture they would learn in such a course even if they failed the Italian Cooperative Listening Comprehension Test. Naturally, the FL teacher would be hard pressed to find a textbook on Italian Humor for Second Language Learners, Level 1. But who needs it? We would much rather trust the intuitions of the Italian FL teacher who appreciates Pasta, Mamma, and *Don Giovanni.*

2. *Grades in FL courses ought to be based more on the individual student's involvement than on his performance on achievement tests.* By student involvement we mean to refer to the extent to which he

engages in the following activities: helping to determine the nature and objectives of the course, both in content and procedure; helping to determine assessment procedures and evaluation criteria for progress and substantive achievement; assuming responsibility for his own learning and course-related activities; making decisions about the languages taught and the overall shape of the FL curriculum; and so on. This type of student involvement gets us away from the perennial and unproductive problem of "How to motivate the FL student" for the simple reason that unmotivated students under the conditions we are describing would not be caught alive in a FL course. Carl Rogers, the famous clinical psychologist-educator, has described in moving terms the beautiful relationship that a teacher can have with his students under conditions which we would describe as compensatory-individualized. In his recent book *Freedom to Learn* (Rogers, 1969) he describes various "contracts" which the teacher-facilitator and the students can draw up at the beginning of the course to insure this type of student involvement. It is a text that we recommend to all educators, parents, and students in any educational field of endeavor.

3. *Student counselling ought to form an integral part of the FL curriculum.* In Chapter 1 we have elaborated six premises which form the psychological bases of second language learning. With these six premises in mind, we know that learning is a sacred and sublime activity and ought to be respected for what it is, namely, a very personal and intimate affair. Language learning is particularly important and special because it is the contact point between the individual and his social and physical environment. The school ought not to be a place where the individual merely learns, but also a place where the individual discovers why he learns and how he learns. This cannot be accomplished in our present classrooms where students are treated as mechanical pawns in a giant educational factory. We would advocate the establishment of small encounter groups within the FL curriculum which would provide them with the opportunity to examine their attitudes and learning styles in the study of a second language. These encounter sessions can serve to establish a personal and human relationship between the FL teacher and student, can serve as the occasion for drawing up the course contract, and can create a greater awareness of the self as a learner and the

psychological implications and consequences of bilingualism and biculturalism. The educational commitment, as we see it, must always be centered in the development of the individual rather than in the acquisition of a predetermined body of knowledge or set of skills.

Educational Slogans and the Sequential Hypothesis

The field of education ordinarily operates within and by means of educational slogans (see Gordon, 1971). These slogans are represented by folk-theoretic explanations given by teachers and other educators for existing practices and diagnostic activities. Here are some examples: "Students are not working up to their abilities"; "FL instruction is designed to teach the students to communicate in a second language"; "The problem is how to motivate the students"; "I use method x to teach"; "Basic patterns and vocabulary must precede free expression" (the sequential hypothesis); and so on. The justification of educational slogans (their rationality vs. their superstitious application) is a topic not unlike that of the emperor's clothes in the children's story: there is a conspiracy (negative contract) to remain silent about it. We are particularly interested here in the sequential hypothesis. This hypothesis has become so ingrained in the very conception of language teaching that it is seldom remembered that this is a *hypothesis* rather than a self-evident truth, so much so that questioning its implications strikes many teachers as odd. But consider.

A child learning a first language is ordinarily exposed to the full range of syntactic patterns of the language of adults and although there is such a thing as "baby talk" that some adults use in interacting with young infants, there is no evidence that this adjustment pattern or anything else that anxious middle-class parents do to "speed up" language development has any significant effect on the child (see Smith and Miller, 1966; Lenneberg, 1967). This experience shows that language *can* be learned contrary to the sequence hypothesized in the basic patterns and vocabulary hypothesis. If you think that second language learning is different from first language acquisition in this respect, then think of the common fact that many individuals who are immersed in a culture (e.g., immigrants) come to develop communicative competence in the second language in the absence of a formal instruction procedure that is guided by the sequential hypothesis.

In the light of these two common observations, you might wish to change the sequential hypothesis such that it is a hypothesis about the most effective procedure of learning a second language *in school*. But what evidence do you have that this is indeed so? What is an alternative hypothesis? You might say, for instance, that students will learn, if anything, precisely what they are being taught. If they are taught basic patterns and vocabulary in artificially structured verbal interactions, they will be able to perform under those conditions, but they will not be able to interact in ordinary communicative interactions. The expectation of transfer from the first to the second communicative setting has too often remained unfulfilled to deserve continued faith. Why not *begin* the teaching of a language at the second level, in those cases where communicative competence in free conversational interaction is the goal, rather than hope it will materialize by itself in later stages or reserve the practice of it for "more advanced" language learning stages?

Note that the very notion of "basic" patterns and vocabulary is a weakly defined one. Anyone who has transcribed tape-recorded versions of free speech must be convinced that we do not ordinarily speak in alternating "sentences" of the type one practices in classroom exercises and simulated dialogues. It is possible, of course, to write an elementary text in such a way that it contains x number of patterns and y number of words and to practice artificial dialogues containing no more than the particular patterns and words in the "basic" text. But this is possible only because what is being said and how it is said is artificially restricted *in advance*. Even the simplest of free communicative interchanges, however, do not subscribe to this artificial restriction, and it is not a source of much satisfaction to realize that, say, 80% of what is ordinarily done in free speech will be subsumed under the "basic" patterns and vocabulary since it takes the other 20% to successfully transact any conversation.

Rejection of the sequential hypothesis does not necessarily imply the absence of any structure in teaching, even though it is true that, at the moment, we do not know precisely how to systematize the instruction of free conversational competence. This is not because the latter type of structured instruction is inherently more complex and difficult to achieve, but because we have not focused in our past research and teaching on the systematic organized nature of ordinary conversations, and until we do so we shall remain hesitant and ineffective in our teaching of it (for a start in this, see Sacks, 1971; and the discussion in Chapter 9.)

Anyone who cares to think about it would realize that language is used for many different purposes and in many varieties and registers. These different functions and varieties have different, partially independent, underlying skills and competencies and it is naive to think that the same basic hypothesis about teaching procedures can effectively meet the various learning needs in their development. The traditional classification of the "four basic skills" into listening, speaking, reading, and writing categories seems totally inadequate in the light of recent discoveries in sociolinguistics and ethnomethodology (Ervin-Tripp, 1967; Garfinkel, 1968; Sacks, 1971; Searle, 1969). A more realistic approach would take into account the functions and varieties of language as defined by the context in which the language is to be used: ordinary conversational interaction, using language for instructional purposes, reading for pleasure, writing business correspondence, and so on. A realistic goal for our current educational objectives in FL instruction would be for the curriculum to establish three separate and independent "tracks": one track for ordinary conversational interaction, another for reading, and a third for instructional use. Each track would be made up of a flexible package of mini-courses or modules, each worth a certain amount of credit points upon completion. Students should be counseled which track to take on the basis of diagnostically evaluated assessment procedures including aptitude, time and opportunity available for study, interest, learning style and perceived goals (see the discussion in Jakobovits, 1970a, Chapter 3). The procedures and materials to be used with each track ought to be developed by the FL teacher in accordance with a specification of the skills to be acquired. It is important to choose fairly specific terminal behaviors, defined by communicative context and setting, and begin training under those conditions *at the outset* rather than under some allegedly prior or basic but artificial conditions.

The FL teacher is the person who must implement these changes. The prevailing hesitancy of the FL teacher in implementing changes and his dependence on methods and commercially available courses must be actively discouraged by FL administrators and supervisors. For over twenty years now, the FL profession has encouraged this kind of dependence, and if it had been effective it should have been more successful than it has in fact been (see Carroll, 1968). It's time for a swing of the pendulum in a totally different direction, in the assertion of the teacher's role as the one who makes the instructional decisions. Nothing short of this is compatible with the professional responsibility and personal integrity of the teacher.

Programmed FL Instruction

The role which programmed instruction can play in FL teaching needs careful evaluation. We stated earlier that the programmed-mass-traditional approach (type 8 in the EBTA cube) can involve the same difficulties and shortcomings that we find in the nonprogrammed-mass-traditional approach (type 4). The challenge of developing programmed FL courses lies in the application of programming principles to those of individualized and compensatory instruction. If that can be done, we would gladly relabel the sides of the EBTA cube in such a way as to make type 5 into "number one." At first blush it would seem that nothing could be more antithetical to individualized and compensatory instruction than the image of a student sitting in a solitary cubicle pressing the buttons of a teaching machine or computer console. We would hate to elaborate such an Orwellian scene. However, it is the case that even within the context of our present impersonal educational institutions some students seem to be functioning well with programmed courses. Hail to them! It seems to us that within the context of individualized and compensatory instruction the principles of programmed teaching can serve a useful and unique function. Where there is a need for brute force rote memorization, programmed materials can be very handy and efficient. A learning program consisting of small conversational subroutines can be both interesting and helpful. Furthermore, teaching programs can serve to diagnose learning problems through error analysis and can provide additional individual practice when needed. Finally, in the absence of other educational opportunities (such as a FL teacher in a particular language) the programmed laboratory can play an essential function in strengthening the FL curriculum.

We are restating with the above comments some of the ordinary things we say today about teaching machines and programmed instruction. It might be worth exploring some nonordinary things we can say about a programmed FL curriculum. We might start with the following statement: a program is a theory about the structure of knowledge and the process of its apprehension by the human mind. A language learning program would thus be made up of three sorts of things. One will be a descriptive grammar of the language laid out in a matrix that can form the blueprint for a sequence of linear and branching frames and modules. The second will be a set of specific hypotheses about a learner's inferential and problem solving activities. And the third will be a set of general principles concerning the storage and retrieval mechanisms of the mind. The total number of frames is likely to be a very large number although the number of frames used by any individual learner would be a much smaller number, the actual size varying greatly from one learner to another. The construction of frames would be guided by aspects of the three sets of things just mentioned: the descriptive grammar in matrix form will guide the areas to be covered, one or more frames for each rule or point of grammar; the content and form of each frame will additionally be influenced by the programmer's hypotheses about how various learners apprehend grammatical inferences, inductively and deductively. At this stage a number of alternative frames arranged in branching sequence will be constructed for each point of grammar, these alternative forms being guided by expected variations in style of inferential behavior. These alternative branches will serve as remedial or compensatory devices during the execution of the program by individual learners. Finally, the frames will be arranged in a structured grid of interconnecting access points in such a way as to provide sufficient practice for storage and retrieval in the mind of the learner while simultaneously excluding unnecessary steps. If you look at the program steps from the first frame to the last as an inferential maze, then the actual route taken by each individual learner will be potentially different from that of any other learner, being determined exclusively by learner characteristics in congruence with the principles of compensatory and individualized instruction.

Now let us return to the Orwellian image once again. Would such a program be equivalent to having a language teacher or could it possibly replace the language teacher altogether? This question reminds us of the robot stories in science fiction literature. In one of these, as we recall, humanlike robots were constructed, and their outward physical similarity to humans was so perfect that they were actually indistinguishable from real humans. Furthermore, their artificial "positron" brains were functional duplicates of human brains. Is a robot that is indistinguishable from a human a robot, or is it another human? Is a program that can duplicate the environment a teacher can provide, a program, or is it a teacher? Posing the problem in these terms makes it obvious that we are not asking a for-real question. Perhaps we should ask, more profitably, what is it about the environment a teacher can provide that is different from the environment the program can provide, and is this difference relevant for the competence that the learner is to acquire? Here we must distinguish between two sorts of programs: if we are thinking of a "fantastic" program, by which we mean one that can talk and think like a human, then it is obvious that the program will be at least equivalent to the teacher, and probably much better. But at this stage of our knowledge this kind of program remains truly a fantasy, even to the point where it is not at all clear whether it could ever become a reality. If we are thinking of "real" programs, by which we mean not only those that our present technology might generate, but as well, future foreseeable technologies, then what such a program would be lacking would be that which any ordinary speaker could provide, namely the opportunity of carrying out an ordinary conversation. Thus, it is now conceivable that a programmed FL course in combination with exposure to ordinary speakers of the language could be at least equivalent to and possibly better than the FL teacher. Now this conclusion is obviously not satisfactory, since experience shows that a FL can now be learned solely as a result of exposure to ordinary speakers of the language in the absence of either a programmed FL course or a FL teacher. So the question of the machine versus the teacher remains unresolved. And maybe this is as it should be.

No doubt a more practical question is, what can the program do for the FL teacher and the FL learner? We think the usual answer which says that the program can free the teacher from routine tasks involved in rote memorization and practice drills, while probably true and not inconsequential, is nevertheless selling the program short. It overlooks the fact that programmed modules of limited scope can facilitate the learning process in ways that are completely beyond the capacity of the human teacher. Individualized, compensatory and remedial instruction must be responsive to individual differences in style and rate of learning in such a way as to provide the opportunity for exposure to a sufficient number of alternative branching sequences of frames that is far beyond the attention span and control of a human teacher, yet it provides no special problem for even our presently available hardware in computer assisted instruction. It is true that we do not have many comprehensive programs available at the present time, but we think this is less because of an absence of knowhow than the absence of practice and development. For one, the hardware associated with computer-assisted instruction is very expensive and beyond the range of most educational establishments. For another, most teachers have not shown any interest in contributing to the development of such instructional programs, not even the simple kind that need no special hardware or expensive hardware. It is here that we feel that a change in attitude on the part of FL teachers would be most useful and productive (see Howatt, 1969, for useful hints).

There are two large areas of the EBTA cube with which we have not dealt so far, namely the individualized-traditional (type 2 or 6) and the mass-compensatory (type 3 or 7) approaches. As individualized instruction gains in prominence and popularity, we will see interesting attempts to apply it within the context of traditional objectives: the teaching of a predetermined package of discrete elements of knowledge tailor-made to the individual learner, particularly in the form of programmed instruction (type 6). We suspect that the majority of FL teachers today could see themselves working under such conditions. The mass-compensatory combination is more problematic. It is the typology that some so-called "free schools" follow today: the exposure in school to a set of predetermined uniform conditions with the expectation of similar minimal attainment and similar sequential cumulative acquisition steps, but not defining these conditions in terms of the usual course content. It retains the age-graded promotion idea, while at the same time rejecting textbooks and traditional subject area divisions.

We have now completed our journey through the EBTA cube, and we hope it has served a facilitating, rather than a befuddling function, a new way perhaps of discussing the problems and challenges that face FL education today.

Initiating Change: The EBTA-mobile Trip

In this final section we would like to make more specific suggestions as to the kind of changes in FL instruction that we think are desirable. The EBTA cube represents a way of talking about the philosophy of teaching that is basic and general. How does movement take place within the EBTA cube, say if we wish to move from the top righthand corner (type 4) to the bottom lefthand corner? A method of translocomotion occurs to us which we shall briefly describe, but given its presently unrefined character, we hope it will be taken not as a method to be applied, but rather a method to be discussed. We shall call this proposed solution to the problem of initiating change in basic approaches to teaching the Triadic Method of Least Resistance, and the ensuing profile of the instructional changes as the EBTA-mobile Path.

Step 1. List the instructional areas in which you believe you have some degree of control. We would like to suggest the following seven general headlines:

A. The shape of the overall curriculum
B. Course content and materials
C. Classroom activities and assignments
D. Type of tests and their timing
E. Nature of grading system
F. Distribution of time and work modules
G. Opportunity for diagnostic and remedial activities

Step 2. Get together with administrators and supervisors and discuss all alternatives that occur to you in these instructional areas in connection with the following four directions of change:

1. Ratio of student/non-student initiated acts
2. Specificity of student contract
3. Degree of self-pacing
4. Nature of student/teacher interaction

Theoretically, you have a 7 x 4 matrix of 28 boxes each of which are independent of one another (see Table *1*). For instance, for area *A* (the shape of the overall curriculum), the ratio of student-initiated acts may be quite low, whereas it may be quite high in areas *D* or *F*. The degree of self-pacing may be substantial in area *F* and insignificant in area *D*. A specific contract may be *drawn up* between the student and the teacher in area *D*, but *imposed* by the teacher in area *B*. By "nature of student/teacher interaction" we have in mind particularly two scales: (i) teacher as authority figure vs. teacher as tutor or facilitator and, (ii) high vs. low empathic understanding between student and teacher (see Barrett-Lennard, 1962).

Step 3. Get together with the students and discuss these alternatives with them, noting whatever additional suggestions they may have.

Step 4. Make a list of possible changes within each of the 28 boxes and arrange them in a rank order of extent of departure from current practices such that the change in rank position 1 would be minimal and that in position 10 (say) would be fundamental, with 5 being "somewhat rocking the boat but not pulling down the roof over your head." You end up with a matrix list of 280 changes (10 changes within each of the 28 boxes). This grid of 280 change items constitutes the possible theoretical path of the EBTA-mobile. To determine the actual path that is possible for you, with your particular students and in your particular school at any particular time, figure out the path of least resistance as follows.

Step 5. Draw a line *above* the first change item in each of the 28 boxes which represents for you the point of psychological stress, that is a change that you cannot live with comfortably if you were to function under those conditions. In some boxes your stress point may be at rank 2, in others you may be courageous enough to go down to rank 6 or 7. You end up with 28 scores for yourself varying between 1 and 10 (if you used a ten-point scale). This is your psychological change profile. Now determine in a similar way the psychological change profile for your supervisor, and also for each of your students if you are committed to an advanced individualized instruction program, or, if you are working in a mass-oriented environment, use the average student psychological change profile for the class. Determine the path of least resistance by computing a geometric average for the three psychological change profiles. This will give you the context-specific instructional profile that is possible in your school at this time.

Step 6. Implement immediately all the change items in each of the 28 boxes that fall above the line of the path of least resistance.

And presto!—you are well on your way toward an individualized program. A cautionary note: it should be good practice to recompute the path of least resistance at the beginning of each semester.

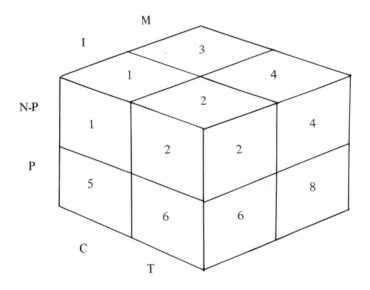

Fig. 1a

Nonprogrammed				Programmed			
Individualized		Mass		Individualized		Mass	
Comp.	Trad.	Comp.	Trad.	Comp.	Trad.	Comp.	Trad.
1	2	3	4	5	6	7	8

Fig. 1b

Eight Basic Approaches to Teaching: The EBTA Cube

TABLE 1

The Triadic Method of Least Resistance

Steps 1-4: The theoretically possible paths: 280 changes

	1	2	3	4
A. The shape of the overall curriculum 1 2 3 4 5 6 7 8 9 10				
B. Course content and materials				
C. Classroom activities and assignments				
D. Type of tests and their timing				
E. Nature of grading system				
F. Distribution of time and work modules				
G. Opportunity for diagnostic and remedial activity				

1 = Ratio of student/non-student initiated acts
2 = Specificity of student contract
3 = Degree of self-pacing
4 = Nature of student/teacher interaction (degree of
facilitation; empathic understanding)

Steps 5-6: Draw line above geometric average of stress points in each box between teacher/administrator/student, and implement.

REFERENCES

Altman, H.B. "Toward a Definition of Individualized Foreign Language Instruction." *American Foreign Language Teacher*, February 1971, No. 3.

Barrett-Lennard, G. T. "Dimensions of Therapist Response as Causal Factors in Therapeutic Change." *Psychological Monographs*, 1962, 76. (Whole Issue No. 562.)

Carroll, J.B. "The Prediction of Success in Intensive Foreign Language Training." In Robert Glazer (ed.), *Training Research and Education*. New York: Wiley, 1965.

———. "Foreign Language Proficiency Levels Attained by Language Majors Near Graduation from College." *Foreign Language Annals*, 1968, 1, 318-353.

Ervin-Tripp, Susan. "Sociolinguistics." Working paper no. 3, Language Behavior Research Laboratory, University of California, Berkeley, 1967.

Garfinkel, Harold. *Studies in Ethnomethodology*. Englewood Cliffs, N.J.: Prentice-Hall, 1968.

Gordon, B. "Individualized Instruction and Sub-cultural Differences." Paper presented at the Kentucky Foreign Language Conference, Lexington, Ky., April 1971.

Howatt, A.P.R. *Programmed Learning and the Language Teacher*. London: Longmans, 1969.

Jakobovits, L. A. *Foreign Language Learning: A Psycholinguistic Analysis of the Issues*. Rowley, Mass.: Newbury House Publishers, 1970a.

———. "Motivation and Foreign Language Learning: Part A. Motivation and Learner Factors." *Report to the 1970 Northeast Conference on the Teaching of Foreign Languages*. 1970b.

Lenneberg, E. H. *Biological Foundations of Language*. New York: Wiley, 1967.

Sacks, Harvey. *Aspects of the Sequential Organization of Conversation*. (Forthcoming Prentice-Hall).

Searle, J. B. *Speech Acts*. Cambridge, England: Cambridge University Press, 1969.

Smith, Frank and Miller, G. A. (eds.). *The Genesis of Language*. Cambridge, Mass.: M.I.T. Press, 1966.

3 New Directions in FL Education

There are two widespread views in the academic literature about the teaching-learning process. We shall refer to these as *the communication hypothesis* and *the natural growth hypothesis*.

The argument for the communication hypothesis can be developed as follows. At the outset, a distinction is created between internal to the individual and external to the individual. The *external* which has been separated from the individual, is now relinked to it by a channel. This channel is a mechanism that allows the transmission of messages. Messages are formal representations of the external. Representations that are free of error are true-to-fact, valid, real. This set of assumptive statements in the communication hypothesis is then used to account for such processes as learning and socialization. For instance, culture is defined as a large set of messages that exists outside the individual. The process of socialization is interpreted as involving the transmission of this set of messages to new human beings through the channels of communication. One special subset of messages is classed under the rubric of *education*. Society entrusts the transmission of this subset to institutions called "educational," such as the school. The school employs people who have been duly designated as "teachers." What teachers do in the school is called "teaching." Thus, according to the communication hypothesis, teaching is the transmission of messages from the teacher to the pupil via the instructional language. These messages are formally reposited in the *curriculum*.

Students are individuals, usually young, who have been designated by society as educationally ignorant, sometimes referred to as "uneducated" in the case of older individuals, and who therefore spend a number of years in schools learning the curriculum.

It is common practice in schools to employ a number of different methods to accomplish the transmission work. The effectiveness of a method is commonly viewed as a measure reflecting the number of messages successfully transmitted. Successful transmission is tested by "feedback," viz. the number of sent messages the student is able to send right back. Tests are held at various times, and when a predefined number in a predefined set is received back from the student, he is immediately graduated from school and designated "henceforth educated."

One more thing. From time to time changes are made to the curriculum which has the consequence that when "henceforth educated" people meet one another it often happens that their curriculum has very little overlap. In those situations they can be seen to engage each other in conflict.

That, then, is the argument for the communication hypothesis of the teaching-learning process. Presently, we find the communication hypothesis a funny argument, though we say this with respect and humility for its believers, having been ourselves proponents of it in our teachings for years, and remembering the sacred infallibility with which the hypothesis mesmerized us. Perhaps, too, it may be that the communication hypothesis is wrong only in the sense that Newtonian physics is considered wrong by today's relativists, which is to say that it is right for a restricted set of conditions, but wrong for the subsequent reality they have uncovered. The most prevalent current view of teaching may thus be right for education conceived as a transmission of messages, but wrong for education conceived in the manner of the natural growth hypothesis, to which we now turn.

The historical origins of the natural growth hypothesis reflect its philosophy and content. It was used throughout recorded history of society as the chief instructional strategy for training monks, priests, sorcerers, athletes, soldiers, performers, and political and religious leaders. Though this method of teaching lost visibility with the advent of mass educational institutions, it retained a pivotal role in the teaching activities of society and is still prospering throughout many small layers of the social hierarchy, though on the North American continent it is excluded from school-age people.

The natural growth hypothesis is essentially a *biological* theory. It is empirical and objective, rather than inferential and speculative. It takes the experiential here-and-now as the locus of the teaching focus, rather than the external and fixed curriculum. There is no predefined curriculum to be transmitted. There is no premise to graduate at a particular location. Each learner is handled separately and personally. There are no dropouts or failures. Success is defined as the point of quitting the apprenticeship. There are however individual variations in quality of performance. Quality of performance is defined by the elaborate opinions of other performers. A mutual judging society.

To the true believers of the communication hypothesis, which is to say to those to whom it is the model for *all* learning and teaching, the natural growth hypothesis makes no sense. How can one have the notion of "quality of performance" as a result of a teaching-learning transaction without having a curriculum? The paradox is insurmountable.

To the objective observer, however, the conceptual paradox does not present itself. What does he see? He sees an apprentice's performance improve over time. He sees the conditions of that improvement as the presence of the apprentice in the environment of the teacher. He sees that, as a rule, when the apprentice quits the relationship his performance is not as good as that of the teacher, but that with practice he approaches in quality his teacher's performance and sometimes surpasses it. All of this is clear, simple, experientially valid and direct. The problem begins when the observer attempts to build an explanatory model for these observations. He comes up with mechanisms, channels, messages, curricula, and sequential reinforcement. Pretty soon, he is either in a fantasy world discussing communication and reinforcement theory or, in the midst of jolting paradoxes whereby the concepts deny the senses.

Experiential and Cognitive Learning

The distinction we have drawn between the communication hypothesis and the natural growth hypothesis recalls a comparable distinction more familiarly discussed in the literature as *cognitive* versus *experiential* learning.

The content of cognitive knowledge is specified in terms of messages or verbal statements, spoken and written. The content of experiential knowledge is specified in terms of performances, physical or transactional. For example, cognitive knowledge about the structure of language is specified in terms of statements and formulas produced by linguists. Experiential knowledge about the structure of language is specified in terms of the successful performance in the production of sentences and discourse material. For the amateur, cognitive and experiential skills occur independently. For the professional, they may cooccur as when an ex-football player becomes a coach, or when a language teacher teaches facts about a language to others.

At this point, we want to discuss the relevance for the language teacher of the cognitive-experiential distinction. The communication hypothesis and the natural growth hypothesis offer two quite different solutions to the effective teaching of a language.

Two Approaches to Foreign Language Teaching

We begin by considering various possible intentions for setting up a foreign language curriculum in the school. One may be motivated by the intention to expose students to the study of a second language and culture. A second motivation may be the intention to teach students a set of facts about a language, like what is a sentence in that language, what kind of patterns sentences have, what meanings a dictionary would list for some of its words, etc., as well as a set of facts about the language users, like what they eat for breakfast, or what they say when they greet one another, and so on. A third intention in setting up a foreign language curriculum is to train students to perform as co-participants in transactional interactions with speakers of that second language. This third intention coincides *grosso modo* with what foreign language educators have discussed under the rubric of the ability to *use* the language, free or liberated expression, advanced foreign language training, and so on.

We want to discuss some instructional strategies that might be involved with each of these three intentions or goals.

First, exposure to the study of a foreign language. We understand that this used to be a legitimate and honorable goal for numerous generations of students in an age where traveling abroad was considered primarily an educational and intellectual experience rather than merely entertainment. Today, the context of foreign language learning has shifted for most young people on the North American continent away from seeing it as an intellectual experience to more utilitarian, practical, and transactional motivations. Surveys have shown that by far the two most frequent reasons for studying a foreign language today are either instrumental (needed for graduation or a job or travel) or transactional (wanting to interact with natives directly or through the mass media).

The instrumental motivation of studying a foreign language because it is a necessary part of the curriculum was created by the curriculum makers, in the first place, but in addition one can appreciate the fact that there is a vicious circularity to it whereby the content of the foreign language curriculum has been allowed to change in response to this motivation. Thus, the universal audiolingualization of the curriculum in the school over the past twenty years has gradually been specialized in the service of this purely educational motivation. Originally, the introduction of audiolingual methods was motivated by a desire to train students in the *use* of language, especially in oral interaction. Soon, however, it became streamlined for a different purpose, that of universalizing foreign language study, and so the foreign language course became a school subject in the curriculum, like history and science, thus fostering instructional methods geared to teach a foreign language as a school subject. Nowadays, given the wide use of standardized discrete-point paper-and-pencil achievement tests, the foreign language class has been very efficiently geared to maximizing the number of students who can graduate with a foreign language study background that enables them to pass these standardized tests. In that respect, it is fair to say that foreign language teachers have done a most efficient job. They have come to learn and apply techniques of foreign language teaching that have succeeded in establishing the foreign language course as a regular part of the curriculum in universal mass education. Having achieved that status, it is certain to remain as permanent a part of the school curriculum as any of the more traditional subjects.

Having achieved the primary goal, the goal of legitimate and permanent existence, foreign language educators can now afford to sit back and take a loving look at their outgrown and perhaps overgrown offspring, the foreign language part of the curriculum.

New Options Now

We now turn to a discussion of the instructional possibilities open to a well entrenched foreign language educational establishment.

An issue that has been on people's minds for a number of years relates to the possible diversification of the foreign language curriculum. One aspect of this problem has to do with student options concerning the choice of the language to be studied, when to start, and for how many years. Clearly it is the case that these sorts of options have been and continue to be rapidly expanding. Another aspect has to do with choice of method to be used, and this has had a long and turbulent history, as we're all aware, sometimes painfully so. A third aspect to the diversification issue relates to the specification of a package of behavioral objectives, and it is here that we wish to linger for a while in our discussion.

In the United States, the entire public educational establishment is gearing itself towards this conception, long in the making. Like standardized testing, accountability through behavioral objectives is an inevitable step in the historical evolution of the practice of mass education. It seems important, therefore, to examine the kinds of problems that this development is raising for the foreign language teacher.

We see two sorts of problems involved. The first is the choice of meaningful behavioral objectives for the foreign language course. The second is their effective instruction. Let us look at both of these.

First, the choice of meaningful behavioral objectives. No doubt it can be appreciated that this problem is another version of one raised earlier in connection with the diversification of the foreign language curriculum. If the goal is defined in terms of a predefined level of achievement on a standardized discrete-point test, the problem of selecting behavioral objectives becomes a routine problem of transforming the items or subtests of standard language tests into smaller steps defined in operational terms relative to them. But, now, if the goal is defined in terms of transactional performances, then it is clear the choice of appropriate behavioral objectives will depend on a suitable operational taxonomy of transactional performances.

Where does the teacher find such a taxonomic table? The answer is quite simple: he makes one up. Does this answer startle you? How does he make one up? Let's talk about that.

One thing is quite clear. Both the teacher and the pupil are expert transactional performers long before they walk into the language class on the first day. But now the problem becomes the transference of transactional skills displayed with participants in one's first language to a new context, that of the second language. Now, it makes a big difference whether the language teacher conceives of his objectives in terms of the teaching of facts about a second language as opposed to the teaching of transactional displays in the context of a second language. It is like the difference between teaching facts about driving in a classroom and teaching driving performances in traffic. The way you would measure achievement in the two cases will be quite different. If you teach facts about driving, a discrete-point paper-and-pencil test at the end of the course may be an adequate basis for specifying behavioral objectives. But, if you teach driving performances, you would need a field test in which you observe the student's quality of performance in various traffic conditions.

Simple as this distinction may sound in the case of a driving course, it has been greatly neglected and unrealized in the case of a foreign language course. One of the reasons has been undoubtedly the failure of language test makers to prepare tests of transactional performances, and until they catch on to this, the language teacher will labor under the oppression of present-day discrete-point achievement tests that measure the student's knowledge of facts about the language.

We shall discuss this problem more fully in a moment, but now let us mention the second problem that confronts the language teacher after the selection of meaningful behavioral objectives: how to teach them effectively. It will be appreciated that a solution to this problem must be considered jointly with the nature of the behavioral objectives selected. Let us look at an example.

Testing for Transactional Competence

Suppose that you have decided to draw up a graded series of exercises for the purpose of teaching a section of a foreign language course dealing with the use of conversation for transactional performances. Your first step might be to draw up a taxonomic table of commonly occurring transactions. You might come up with something like this:

1. Exchanging greetings
2. Making an apology
3. Expressing thanks
4. Taking leave

These are your four major instructional units. Each of these will now be subdivided into subunits, possibly as follows:

1. Exchanging greetings
    1. (a) displaying visual acknowledgment
       (b) approaching
       (c) extending hands
       (d) saying *"Bonjour"*
       (e) smiling
       (f) squeezing hand firmly
       (g) releasing handshake

You notice that the style of this example is given in terms analogous to the stage directions one might give to a beginner actor.

To continue with subunit 2. Making an apology:

2. (a) while shaking hands, bending forward and gently bumping coparticipant's head
   (b) immediately assuming concerned-face look
   (c) raising arms up in a gesture of alarm and holding for two seconds
   (d) saying: *"Oh, je suis désolé! "* with a sorrowful or constrained or concerned or dejected or casual or hysterical, etc., intonation
   (e) waiting solicitously, etc., for the co-participant's next response

Note that the format of this program unit leaves personality style pretty much up to the pupil-performer. One can express an apology in many different individual ways, with many different overtones and undertones. If the teacher wishes to program separately for these various sorts of eventualities, she may write a subroutine for a subunit. For instance, some alternatives to subunit 2 (*b*):

(i) immediately assuming *I've-just-made-a-heel-of-myself* look
(ii) maintaining poker face
(iii) slowly and deliberately glaring at co-participant for two seconds

Needless to say, the stage instructions and directions will be given in the second language *only*. One of us has attempted this instructional technique on the first lesson of the first day to level 1 students in French with amazing success. You can imagine that this type of language class looks and feels more like rehearsing for a staged production than a course in French 100. The teacher must be a director and a performer, continually enacting the content of his verbalized instructions in French, most of which is of course incomprehensible to the beginner pupil. The latter will understand the target performance not so much from the teacher's verbalizations in French, but because he will come to recognize what the performance stands for, i.e., its transactional significance, from the enactment of the whole scene. So, while the pupils are busy having fun making transactional fun, the teacher bombards them with a perpetual stream of relevant verbalizations in the target language which the pupils soon begin to mimick, little child fashion. Do you get the point?

Let us give another informative illustration. Let us consider subunit 4, Taking Leave, or rather, an interesting alternative to it, namely, postponing taking leave. This subunit might look something like this:

4.B. Postponing Taking Leave

   4.B. (a) watching out for the proper beginning of the strategy

   4.B. (a) i. noticing when other participant makes an announcement to propose closing the conversation (as in: *"Ecoutez, il faut que je m'en aille maintenant."*)

   4.B. (b) immediately finding a pretext for inserting into the conversation one last topic before the end

   4.B. (b) i. using a transactional idiom to preface the delaying statement (as in: *"Un instant, s.v.p. J'ai oblié de vous dire que ... "*)

   4.B. (c) waiting till new topic is exhausted and other participant renews his proposal to close the conversation, then, repeating step 4.B. (b) i., but using a variant form of the transactional idiom (e.g., *"Non, ne vous en allez pas encore. J'ai des nouvelles intéressantes à vous conter,"* or: *"Oh, la, la! Je ne me sens pas très bien tout d'un coup".)*

Techniques of this kind can be used quite readily in large classes, even up to 60 to 80 pupils per teacher. At first, the teacher goes around the classroom enacting several different versions of the transactional performance under study, while the other pupils look on. Then the class is broken up into groups of two or three pupils, each subgroup going through several enactments. It is advisable to practice subgrouping and un-subgrouping as in a fire drill so as to minimize the waste of time and general noise. The enterprising teacher may even bring along a whistle, with which she can signal the subgrouping and un-subgrouping.

We cannot overemphasize the fact that the teacher's attitude toward this technique of teaching a foreign language must be different from the usual in one particularly essential feature. She must not attempt to teach the language directly. This means that she may not be seen to display an interest in the "correct" use of language, as would be the case were she to correct a pupil's utterance in the usual manner. Instead, the claim she must continuously maintain is that she is interested in transactional performances, not in "correct" communication, pronunciation, or syntax. Let us forewarn you that this will be even more difficult than it sounds, for some students, being reactionary as they are, will attempt to distract the teacher by asking her for the "correct version of . . . , " and it will take determination of purpose and courage to stick to her goal. Soon, however, all of the common problems of the foreign language classroom will disappear, as students and teacher exchange transactional performances in a delightful fashion.

Now, what about the French? What will their French sound like to your supervisor? If he takes a reasonable position, he will come to your class and listen to the fluent prattle of your students after a mere semester's work and, in all justice, promise you a raise for distinguished accomplishment. If he takes an unreasonable position, he will hand you 60 copies of the French Cooperative Test, one version or another, and ask you to prove that you have not been wasting school time on creative experimentalism. At that point, you're in deep trouble. Because, your French-prattling students will surely do badly where their silent counterparts next door will shine with high percentiles. What can you do to save your career while also saving your soul?

It's at this point that you dig up your arsenal of behavioral objectives and hand your supervisor, with or without the results of the Cooperative Test, a set of results on a transactional competence test, which you have devised and succeeded in persuading the next-door teacher to administer to her students. The shining superiority of *your* students will undoubtedly sufficiently counterbalance their low showing on the syntax and vocabulary test—unless your supervisor is extraordinarily unreasonable, in which case we will all send you a birthday cake to cheer you up.

Now, what does your transactional competence test look like? It must have two important features. First, it must have a clear *face validity*, which means that the items on the test must visibly reflect intuitively important uses of language. Such things, for instance, as:

Subtest 1: The Ability to Describe Ongoing Events

For example, you have a cooperative assistant enact a series of predetermined behaviors, and the pupil gives a running commentary of what he sees (e.g., "She is walking over to the blackboard and writes something. Now she is turning around and looking at me. Now she walks over to the door, opens it, looks around, comes back in, and sits on the chair over there.")

Subtest 2: The Ability to Interview Someone

For example, you can pretend to be a famous movie actress and the pupil is covering your visit in town for the local radio station.

Subtest 3: The Ability to Be Funny in French

For example, you can ask the pupil to talk about his family life in such a way as to be humorous and funny, though truthfully informative.

Subtest 4: The Ability to Relate a Conversation

For example, you may play a tape recording of a spontaneous conversation in French between two speakers and ask the student to relate the conversation.

All right. So much for the nature of the behavioral objectives to be covered by the transactional performance test. We are not trying to be exhaustive in our examples.

Now, the second important feature of your test is its _reliability_. Here we will pass on to you an open secret in the arsenal of the experimental psychologist. It is a principle that can be phrased as follows: In almost any testing situation one can devise, you can make the test as reliable as you wish merely by increasing the number of observations that have been operationally defined. In this case, what you have to do is to provide a number of rating scales for each subtest and subsequently average them into one score. With two or three scales, the average will be quite unstable with small classes, though it may be adequate with very large classes. A rule of thumb for this type of test materials might be to use between 8 to 12 rating scales for class sizes up to 35, thereafter half the number of scales each time you double class size.

Let us present an example. Suppose you have a class of 30 students, and wish to provide 8 scales for subtest 4, The Ability to Relate a Conversation. You might pick a 10-point bipolar scale for each of the following 8 judgments:

1. **Accuracy of Information**
   very poor 0_____10 fully accurate

2. **Amount of Information Related**
   very little 0_____10 all of it

3. **Fluency of Speech**
   very hesitant 0 _____10 ordinary fluency

4. **Naturalness of Discourse Organization**
   abnormal 0 _____ 10 normal

5. **Style of Expression**
   foreign 0_____10 native

6. **Clarity of Expression**
   unclear 0 _____ 10 clear

7. **Gestural Fluency or Conversational Naturalness**
   odd 0_____ 10 normal

8. **Complexity of Transactional Performance**
   (e.g., Student contributed commentary on reported
   conversation in his reporting of it)
   Straight 0 _____ 10 skillfully intricate

An Action Plan

Now let us give you a few tricks of the trade which we are certain will alleviate the worst of your fears when contemplating the magnitude of this enterprise to be fitted in on your daily schedule.

1. You can begin on a small scale in an experimental fashion until you know what you're doing. Don't try to do it overnight. It might take you several semesters on a modest basis taking your schedule duly into account.

2. Perhaps your first step might be to reserve a few minutes of each class for the Game of Transactional Performances, along the lines we have suggested for Exchanging Greetings, Changing Topics, and Postponing Leave Taking.

3. After doing this for a while, and gaining confidence in yourself as one who enacts transactional performances in the classroom, and perhaps even beginning to like it and enjoy it, then you might pick a few rating scales along the lines we have suggested and practice rating

the performances of your students. Allow your intuitive understanding to guide you in all respects. Pretty soon you'll be using a set of rating scales that you feel comfortable with, as well as confident on an intuitive basis that it measures what you want to measure.

4. Now invite a colleague to join you in your project. If you get along together, she'll see and understand your goals and methods. Very quickly, she will be able to learn to use the rating scales in the same way as you do. Calculate the average interjudge agreement between the two of you. You'll find high agreement and good reliability.

5. Now, armed with knowledge, confidence, and a reliable test, you are ready to confront your supervisor. You make him inspect your test of transactional performance and you say to him: "Now, look. I have a very reasonable proposal to make. I want you to look at the title and descriptions of my subtests. Do they seem to you the sorts of skills you would want our students to be able to have? Yes? Fine. Now, I am asking you to let me teach one class on an experimental basis. I will define my goals in terms of behavioral objectives specified by reference to my test of transactional performance. I will agree to have the results assessed independently and objectively in cooperation with a colleague. At the end of the semester we will jointly reassess the situation. If we're happy with what's happening, we'll extend the project and modify it as needed. If we're not happy, we'll go back to the old way, giving the experimental class special attention in the subsequent semester so as to bring the students back up to date on phonology, vocabulary, and patterns. O.K. What do you say?" We ask you: How can he refuse . . . and still successfully maintain the claim that he is a reasonable person?

6. In some cases it might be advisable and/or necessary to undertake your project for the new program in cooperation with several colleagues having responsibility for various aspects and levels of the existing program. In this case, the effort becomes a departmental one, and you'll need the direct and active involvement of the chairman.

We wish you courage and good luck.

Summary

We would now like to summarize the position we have outlined. We began by arguing that the current prevalent conception of foreign language teaching as a school subject is a necessary outgrowth of the great effort exerted in the past twenty years to place foreign language study on the record in the regular curriculum of the mass educational system. We have argued that the continuation of this conception is being maintained by the wide use of standardized paper-and-pencil achievement tests which force teachers to continue spending a major portion of the available instructional time in teaching facts about a language and its people rather than teaching transactional performances using the foreign language as a medium of display. We have suggested that it would be advisable to diversify the foreign language curriculum by offering students the opportunity of choosing a package of mini-courses each of which is designed to give the student the opportunity of concentrating on a highly specific transactional use of the language. Some examples of these might be as follows: French 109: How to Read Newspapers and Magazines; French 115: Conversations in Public Places; French 122: Writing Letters and Other Correspondence; French 149: Conversations Among Friends; French 161: Telephone Conversations. And so on. If judicious use is made of individualized programmed packages, a large number of such mini-courses can be offered even by a small language department. These program units would be prepared by the teacher on principles analogous to what she now calls "lesson plans."

We have also made some suggestions concerning the need for evaluating such a new program in reasonable rather than unreasonable terms. A reasonable approach is one in which the supervisor assesses the program by cooperating with the teacher in the preparation and administration of local tests of transactional performances the pupil succeeds in accomplishing under test conditions, these being reliable and having face validity.

We have also talked about the attitude and goals of the teacher in teaching a foreign language. If her orientation is in terms of the significance foreign language study has for the pupil, and she conceives of the learning-teaching process as a meaningful transactional exchange in the natural growth of both parties, then her teaching in the classroom becomes a staged transactional performance of a personal nature, learning while she teaches, continually improving the efficiency with which she engineers the instructional transactions, thus actualizing her creative needs.

4 Pattern Practice: A New Rationale for an Old Habit

The Old Linguistic Rationale

The traditional rationale for pattern practice in language teaching contains the following three assumptions:

1. Language learning is a cumulative process, proceeding from the initial acquisition of syntactically simple constructions to progressively more complex sentential structures;
2. Linguistic analysis of syntactic structures yields a hierarchy of sentential materials from simple to the more complex, and this hierarchy can then be used to grade practice exercises;
3. Practice by pattern exercises, chiefly through repetition of restricted dialogue frames, will produce inductive insights about the underlying structure of sentences and, consequently, practice on a restricted set will generalize to related sets not actually practiced.

It is not our intention to review here the literature on the instructional effectiveness of pattern practice for language teaching. This literature is now well known, and we have presented some of our objections to this technique elsewhere (e.g., Jakobovits, 1970). Despite the controversy, the habit of pattern teaching continues as an important instructional strategy, both on the North American continent and elsewhere. Though we feel that the original objections still hold, nevertheless, because the habit continues, we wish to present a new rationale for its use, which we believe is theoretically more sound and leads to different and better selectional strategies for the graded exercises.

We can accept the first assumption presented above as a working hypothesis without insisting on empirical "proof," but also, without insisting that it is the only possible approach, or even that it is the best available. It seems intuitively reasonable to define the language acquisition process as cumulative, and progressing from simple skills to more complex ones. The problem begins when we attempt to specify the dimensions of simplicity and complexity of language skills. Assumption (2) provides one possible rationale, one that reflects the close relationship that has developed historically between linguistics and language teaching. The specific assumption made in this connection is that the simplicity-complexity dimension that linguistic analysis yields is directly relevant to the simplicity-complexity dimension of language acquisition and use. This represents one possible rationale and is the one traditionally presented. Our position on this shall be that though linguistics may be a relevant source of information for planning instructional strategies in the language course, it should not be the only major source, and consequently, we shall present an additional rationale for selecting pattern practice materials.

In connection with the third assemption, though we subscribe to the notion that practice is essential in the development of skills, including language skills, we shall suggest a rationale for selecting authentic conversational contexts for pattern practice as a preferable alternative to the current use of artificial dialogue.

Transactional Engineering Analysis
(T. E.) and Language Teaching

Typically, language teachers see their task in two progressive steps: first, elementary language training to familiarize the student with the "basics"—the sounds, the articulations, the vocabulary, and the "basic" sentential patterns; second, advanced language training designed to liberate the student from speaking sentences to partaking in a conversational exchange on a more or less ordinary fluency basis. Rather than reject this widespread belief, as we have done in the past (e.g. Jakobovits, 1970), we shall make some suggestions for ways in which these two steps can be more harmoniously integrated.

Advanced language training programs tend to be much less structured and standardized than elementary programs. One reason that no doubt contributes to this difference is the fact that linguistics and applied linguistics have not to date seriously undertaken the task of formulating a methodology for the analysis of conversational exchanges and written discourse, and, therefore, there is no shared instructional technology for teaching conversation and discourse.

Recent work by a group of sociologists, among them Garfinkel, Schegloff and Sacks (see references), has shown that conversational interaction can be analyzed in ways which exhibit its organizational structure. They refer to this approach as an "ethnomethodological" enterprise. For instance, they show that there are rules for opening and closing conversations, rules of interruption and taking turns in talking, rules for appropriately switching topics at particular places in the conversation, rules for storytelling and reporting, and the like, all of which leads one to conclude that conversation has underlying syntactical structure whose adequate description represents a theoretical challenge no more nor less than what linguistics has already achieved for the description of grammar.

The sociologist Erving Goffman has written over the past decade a series of books concerned with the adequate description of the transactional code that governs proper and ordinary social interactions. The principal notion elaborated in his work is that a large proportion of people's conversational energy is expended in what he calls "face work," which has to do with making and repairing face claims of the self and of others. For instance, friends can be seen to relate events about themselves in such a way as to give the impression that they are clever, composed, humorous, cool, charitable, understanding, patient, polite, and the like. They are making face claims and justifying them in various appropriate ways through what they say in the conversation. Similarly, participants in a conversation can be seen to say things which are designed to protect the face claims of others. For instance, should someone by his carelessness or by unavoidable circumstance come to offend the face of another participant, as in the case of a physical collision while passing each other in a crowded space, or in the case of a verbal insult or other transactional offense, the person can be seen to say things that constitute the making of an apology. Goffman has described many organizational features of what he calls the "ritual idiom" which refers to the conventionalized set of rules that govern conversational exchanges in public places.

We label the approach introduced in this book "transactional engineering analysis," or T.E., for short. It is not related to Eric Berne's method of psychotherapy known as Transactional Analysis or T.A. This method is in the ethnomethodological tradition and is closely associated with the work of Goffman on the ritual idiom. In content and motivation, though not perhaps in method and style, T.E. has some affinity with Firth's classic interest in "the context of situation" (see Halliday in Wilkinson, 1971), and some current ongoing work in Britain (see Sinclair, *et al*, 1972). Less similar in content, but still overlapping in motivation, is some recent work in sociolinguistics on situational context for speech, especially the formulations advanced by Dell Hymes on communicative competence.

That language is a structured system is, to the contemporary mind, a commonplace notion. But this was not always the case. The burden of structural linguistics was, during its beginnings, the satisfactory demonstration of this notion. It succeeded in establishing this thesis by inventing a so-called "objective" method of analyzing language data, though it fell short of attaining descriptive adequacy. It is with a parallel motivation that we are introducing an "objective" method for the analysis of conversational data, though we recognize that the task of arriving at an adequate description of these data remains to be pursued and is a task we expect to share with others (see Jakobovits and Gordon, in preparation).

We begin by specifying and defining the components of our system. The basic unit of our analysis is the *transaction*. We use the term to refer to social interactions with somewhat similar meaning to the ordinary expression, as in a "business" transaction. The psychological reality of transactions, as an interactional unit, is evidenced sufficiently by the existence of common terms people use to refer to social ongoings. Thus, if you show someone a description, in transactional terms, of a witnessed episode, the description should be found readily understandable, meaningful, and representative of the witnessed events. For example, the following is a sequential description of what happened when *A* and *B* met in the elevator on their way up to the office:

1. *A*, standing in the elevator, sees *B* rushing toward the door. He displays recognizing *B* by a smile and a nod and holds down the "Door Open" button.
2. *B* enters the elevator, displays recognizing *A* by a smile and a nod.
3. *B* acknowledges *A*'s help and courteousness by saying, "Thanks."
4. *A* greets *B* by saying, "Good morning."
5. *B* greets *A* by saying, "Good morning."

6. *B* extends an invitation to *A* by using several steps, as follows:

6(a). He announces to *A* that he has something to say to him, ("Say, I'm glad I ran into you. I tried to reach you yesterday afternoon, but you had already left.")

6(b). He then extends the invitation, ("Anyway, we are giving George a send-off party tomorrow night at my place. Can you make it around eightish?")

6(c). He then elaborates upon the invitation, ("Margie was supposed to give the party, but she is down with the flu. So, it was decided to move it to my place.")

6(d). He then reiterates the invitation, ("Can you come?")

7. *A* turns down the invitation in two steps, as follows:

7(a). He expresses an apology, ("Gee, I'm very sorry, but I can't make it.")

7(b). He justifies the refusal, ("We made plans to have the Johnsons over for dinner tomorrow night.")

7(c). He makes a request ("Gee, please tell George we are sorry to miss his party.")

8. *A* acknowledges the accounted refusal and the request, ("Well, that's too bad. I'll transmit your regrets to George.")

9. *B* expresses thanks and takes leave, ("Thanks, buddy. I'll see you later.")

10. *A* takes leave, ("I'll see you.")

Transactions are accomplished by participants through an exchange of *transactional moves* properly executed. A transactional move is made by a participant through a *display*. The *transactional code*, in force in a particular speech community, defines the format of proper displays in somewhat the sense that a dictionary defines words as the building blocks of sentences. Transactional displays may be made in a number of different ways; a nod of the head and saying, "O.K." or "All right," all constitute separate displays available to give assent to a request. To display greeting, participants have a number of alternatives to select from. "Yes, but . . . " is a verbal display that has been conventionalized in the use of expressing disagreement, though there are numerous other ways also available (e.g., "Well . . . , not quite . . . " or "I don't agree with you," and so on).

Conventionalized displays for particular transactions belong to the ritual idiom, and we refer to them as *transactional idioms*. Some examples of gestural idioms include smiling, waving the hand, and shaking hands for greeting; scratching the head for indicating doubt, confusion, or hesitancy; averting the eyes to indicate unavailability for contact, and so on. Some examples of verbal displays in ordinary conversations that stand as transactional idioms include such expressions as, "Well, I don't think so,"—for indirectly refusing a request, "Yes, of course,"—for emphatically accepting a request, "Gee, I'm very sorry,"—for justifying a refusal or for apologizing, "That's a good boy!"—for expressing approval, "Do it, or else,"—to express a threat, "Incidentally . . . "—to introduce a topic switch, "Finally . . . "—to announce the end of a series in a report, "Surely . . . " and "Isn't"—to request agreement and so on, to a very large class of displays that participants have available in their *transactional repertoire of performances*. Some examples of transactional idioms used in written academic discourse include "Nevertheless . . . ," "If . . . then . . . ," "Because . . . ," "Parenthetically speaking, . . . ," "As indicated above . . . , " "To continue the argument . . . , " and so on.

Transactional idioms are displays whose transactional significance is recognizable through surface content. Because of this, they represent a class of special interest for selecting pattern practice exercises, as we shall see in a moment. But, when we examine the stream of conversational exchanges, it becomes readily obvious that, for the most part, the significance of a transactional move is not derivable solely from its surface content, but instead is given by the *locus of the display* within the transactional exchange. Consider, for instance, an instructional unit designed to teach learners various display forms available in English for Asking Permission as a transactional move. Part 1 of the unit might deal with transactional idioms for asking permission, as follows:

LESSON UNIT: MAKING REQUESTS

 Part 1: Transactional Idioms for *Asking Permission*

  Token displays:

    May I, please . . . .
    May I . . . .
    Could I . . . .
    Could I, please . . . .
    I wonder if it would be possible for me to . . . .

Do you think I could . . . .
Do you think I could possibly . . . .
I would like to ask you if I could . . . .
Perhaps I might . . . .
It would be nice if I could . . . .
I'm sorry for disturbing you, but can I . . . .
Do you mind if I ask you whether I could . . . .
etc., etc.

Completions Appropriate completions may be provided by the teacher, depending on the instructional sequence she is following. For example:

A. elementary level:

. . . . join you?
. . . . go now?
. . . . leave?
. . . . use your telephone?
. . . . leave it here?
. . . . borrow your umbrella?

B. intermediary level:

. . . . call upon you in case of an emergency?
. . . . use your name as a reference?
. . . . involve you in this matter?
. . . . discuss this matter with you?
. . . . change my mind about going along?

C. advanced level:

. . . . discuss with you the ramifications of my decision to go along with the project?
. . . . explore the possibility of using your name as a reference should circumstances warrant it?
. . . . borrow your car to pick up the pizza Mother ordered?

LESSON UNIT: MAKING REQUESTS

Part 2: Transactional exchanges

Token Exchanges:

(1) A: How are you coming along?
   B: Fine, but I need additional space.
   (= May I have some additional space?)
(2) A: Is there anything else you need?
   B: Yes. More thread.
   (= May I have some more thread, please?)

(3) A: It looks like everything is here.
    B: Yes, except the thermos bottle.
    (= Could you please get the thermos bottle?)
(4) A: Time is up!
    B: Five more minutes!
    (= May I have five more minutes, please?)
(5) A: Well, it looks like it's in the bag!
    B: If only I could have Steve's blessing!
    (= Could you possibly intercede with him on my behalf?)
(6) A: You're wanted on the telephone.
    B: Who is it?
    A: Your friend, George.
    B: Well, I'm in the bathtub!
    (= Could you tell him I can't come to the phone right now?)
(7) A: It looks very nice on you.
    B: It's gorgeous, but I can't afford it.
    A: It's a very good buy.
    B: How about a discount?
    (= Can you discount the price for me?)

The most prevalent conception of language teaching takes the sentence as the unit of instructional discourse. This is because language teachers are themselves taught the so-called linguistic approach. They may be aware that natural speech does not proceed by an exchange of sentences, as is to be found in the lesson dialogues, but they assume that teaching sentences is a necessary step before teaching the natural and grammatically incomplete flow of utterances in a conversational interaction. We do not subscribe to this sequential hypothesis and note that, under natural conditions of language acquisition, child or adult, the learners are exposed to the natural flow of conversational speech, yet they still learn the notion of a grammatically complete sentence. It is evident, therefore, that teaching sentences is not a prerequisite activity for the eventual skill of recognizing and using grammatically complete sentences. On the other hand, it may be that pattern practice may be useful for certain purposes, and since current practice of it continues unabated, we are offering a transactional rationale for the selection of specific pattern practice exercises.

We suggest the following convenient method the teacher may use to make up pattern practice exercises:

Step 1: Define the transactional skills to be covered in a course or, within a course, in a block of lessons.

Suppose, for instance, you are making up lesson plans for the first ten hours of instruction in an intermediate level course. The following is an illustration:

Lesson   1: Greeting and Leave Taking
Lesson   2: Making Requests: Part 1.
Lesson   3: Making Requests: Part 2.
Lesson   4: Extending Invitations
Lesson   5: Making Apologies
Lesson   6: Describing Events: Part 1
Lesson   7: Describing Events: Part 2
Lesson   8: Reporting Events: Part 1
Lesson   9: Reporting Events: Part 2
Lesson 10:Reporting Events: Part 3

Step 2: Define the structural components for the transactional type listed in each lesson.

As an illustration, let us present an elaboration of Lessons 2 and 3:

Lesson 2: Making Requests: Part 1
A. Asking Informational Questions
    A. 1. That take Yes/No answers;
    A. 2. Other.
B. Requesting Agreement
    B. 1. For personal opinion or feeling;
    B. 2. For proposed action.
C. Asking for Permission

Lesson 3: Making Requests: Part 2
D. Demanding Justification
    D. 1. For expressed claim or belief;
    D. 2. For behavior.
E. Requesting Help

Step 3: Provide frame sentences that exemplify some transactional idioms available for each transactional type specified in Step 2.

We have already given an illustration of this at three different levels earlier in the case of 2C: Asking Permission. Here, now, is another illustration:

2B. Requesting Agreement
    B1. For personal opinion or feeling:
        (i) S + don't you think so?
        (e.g., It's a beautiful day, don't you think so?
        It's better than the other one, don't you think so?)
        (ii) S + isn't?
        (e.g., ditto)

    (iii) S + wouldn't you agree?
    (e.g., We're much better off here, wouldn't you agree?)
    etc. etc.
  B2. For proposed action:
    (i) How would you like to + VP
    (e.g., How would you like to take a walk?)
    (ii) How about + NP
    (e.g., How about a coffee break?)
    (iii) I'm proposing that we + S
    (e.g., I'm proposing that we break it up and go for dinner.)
    (iv) Let's + VP
    (e.g., Let's give it a try.)
    etc. etc.

Step 4: Provide conversational exchanges that exemplify the transaction but without the use of transactional idioms. Here are some illustrations:

B1. Requesting Agreement for personal opinion or feeling:
    (i) A: Children are nice.
       B: They're a lot of trouble though.
       A: Yes, that's true.
    (ii) A: How are you coming along?
     B B: It's very difficult.
       A: Yes, it is, at first.
    (iii) A: Are you coming over?
       B: I'm tired. Can we make it another time?
       A: Sure.
       etc., etc.

B2. Requesting Agreement for Proposed Action:
    (i) A: Shall we do it again?
       B: Do you know it's almost five?
       A: Oh, in that case, we'll do it first thing in the morning.
    (ii) A: Shall we quit now?
       B: Not yet.
       A: O.K.
    (iii) A: What do you propose?
       B: I'll check the basement, and you go upstairs.
       A: Right.
       etc., etc.

Pattern Practice: A New (Transactional) Rationale

There are many problems left to be worked out in this proposal as of this time, but the essential nature of the argument is clear right now and can be implemented in many ways within the current practice of pattern practice.

Let us recapitulate our argument.

1. The language teacher ordinarily assumes a two-step instructional progression from teaching sentences in "controlled" environments (e.g., pattern practice and restricted dialogues), to teaching the "liberated" use of utterances in ordinary conversational exchanges and in written discourse.

2. Though we do not subscribe to the advisability of such a radical separation in instructional strategy, we believe that a partial integration of the two strategies is preferable to their current virtual separation, and therefore, we are offering a new rationale for the selection of sequenced pattern practice materials.

3. The new rationale does not conflict with the old. The selectional features we are proposing are those that are transactionally relevant and, in principle, are independent of specific syntactic patterns. As we have shown in several illustrations, the syntactic complexity of the pattern practice sentences may be independently varied within the same transactional lesson plan.

4. The transactional approach to pattern practice thus involves selectional choices at two independent levels. The first concerns itself with sequencing transactional types. The second, concerns itself with sequencing syntactic types. The two are then integrated in a particular exercise.

5. An example of a sequencing choice at the first level (transactional) was given for the transaction Asking for Permission. Syntactic types of various complexity were then chosen as particular display tokens of this transactional type. A schematic representation of the two selectional levels can be given as follows:

A Transactional Rationale
for Pattern Practice

First Selection	Second Selection
Sequencing of Transaction Types	Sequencing of Syntactic Types

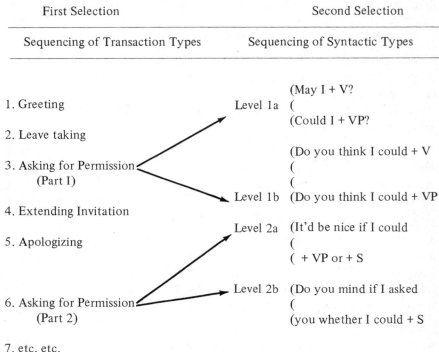

1. Greeting

2. Leave taking

3. Asking for Permission
   (Part I)

4. Extending Invitation

5. Apologizing

6. Asking for Permission
   (Part 2)

7. etc. etc.

Level 1a (May I + V?
          (
          (Could I + VP?

          (Do you think I could + V
          (
          (
Level 1b (Do you think I could + VP

Level 2a (It'd be nice if I could
          (
          (+ VP or + S

Level 2b (Do you mind if I asked
          (
          (you whether I could + S

6. The preceding illustration involves selection of transactional idioms available for initiating a move in Asking for Permission. A second necessary focus for selecting displays involves conversational exchanges that succeed in initiating a transaction without the use of a conventionalized idiom. Examples previously given include, among others:

(1)   A: How are you coming along?
      B: Fine, but I need additional space.
           (=May I have some additional space?)
(4)   A: Time is up!
      B: Five more minutes!
           (=May I have five more minutes, please?

Here again, a syntactic sequencing rationale may be superimposed on the choice of token exchanges of various grammatical complexity.

7. Strategies for sequencing syntactic patterns have been developed according to the linguistic complexity rationale and are currently in wide use. Similarly, there is a pressing need for developing strategies for sequencing transaction types. A rationale for this purpose will have to be based on a formal analysis of the transactional code, and that endeavor is now being pursued, as suggested earlier. In the meantime, the teacher's intuitive understanding of the problems involved can serve as an interim solution.

Authentic Conversational Context for Pattern Practice

In this final section, we wish to discuss alternative contexts for pattern practice exchanges, i.e., alternatives to the current practice of pupil responses to teacher cues and simulated dialogues in a restricted environment.

The simulated dialogue of the standard language lesson plan as is to be found in current widespread use is artificial in at least two respects which we would like to point out. In the first place, the register of the dialogue is different from that used in ordinary everyday situations. It is easy for the teacher to satisfy herself of this fact merely by making a transcript of some recorded conversations in everyday situational contexts and comparing a "natural" dialogue with the "faked" dialogue in the language text. The latter appears quite clearly faked, stilted, artificial, etc., compared to the former. This means that the conversational register practiced in the simulated dialogue using the text as a model is different from the target conversational register; the skills to be learned in the two cases are quite different.

In the second place, the simulated dialogue assigns inauthentic or unnatural roles to the practicing pupils. In the classic example of two pupils enacting the policeman-tourist dialogue exchange, it is clear that neither of them is then and there a policeman or a tourist, nor, for that matter, are they on the street in Paris or New York. Since neither pupil, in the usual case, knows much about the real role expectations of the parties they enact, nor for that matter does the textbook writer, what is actually being practiced is a particular stereotyped and unnatural dialogue routine. The expectation that this restricted routine will somehow mysteriously generalize to free, expressive speech enactments is gratuitous in the extreme.

What constitutes, then, *authentic conversational practice* in the language classroom?

The necessary and sufficient condition for authentic conversational practice *is that the pupil enact himself in the conversation.* That's all. By enacting himself in the dialogue exchanges, he is in fact practicing the target skills he will come to be using should the training be successful.

Why must the pupil *enact* himself, as opposed to, say, just *being* himself?

We provide the following rationale. In the first place, the pupil cannot be his ordinary self in the language classroom. Given the current usual definition of the second or foreign language class, the experience of the pupil is pictured as containing a double handicap, we might even be justified in calling it "the foreign language learner's double bind." On the one hand, he is given the task of acquiring a great deal of discrete knowledge about the target language, along with a type of practice that sets up automated habits in the display of restricted verbal frames within a restricted, artificial, contextual environment.

On the other hand, the target skills are not of a discrete type, and furthermore, they must be free from contextual restrictions. The picture is quite different under conditions of natural language acquisition, either of the child or the adult. There are no artificial roles to enact. The individual is being himself all the time. But in the school, particularly in the language class, the pupil cannot be himself. In comparison to the outside social context, the classroom constitutes a highly restricted environment. There are only two conditions for authentic interactions in the classroom. One of these consists of the set of instructional transactions that the school code assigns as proper to pupils and teachers. The other consists of the projected roles that are possible and proper for the pupil outside the school. Let us specify what's involved in these two conditions.

First, authentic instructional transactions. This category includes teacher-pupil exchanges whose topic and function are motivated to further the particular instructional goals seen by both parties as proper and relevant to learning and teaching, respectively. Thus, depending on the curriculum and the approach used in a particular case, authentic instructional exchanges will include such things as teacher directives, explanations, assignments and queries, as well as pupil requests, replies, justifications, explanations, and directed performances.

Second, pupil enactments of his relevant projected roles in the classroom and outside. There is no demonstrated need or advantage to simulated dialogues of a hypothetical and artificial nature. Instead of asking pupils to be a policeman, Mr. Jones, or the postman, etc., a more relevant assignment would require them to engage their classmates in a conversation on various relevant topics, and/or, in addition, the teacher and various other persons the teacher may invite to the classroom for that purpose. These will be seen by the pupils as enactments of themselves, rather than properly themselves, inasmuch as these interactions are performed in the second language, and therefore there will be a continuously evolving pattern in their complexity as the weeks go by and the pupil sees his enacted performances approximating gradually the expression of his own self, a change that will display itself as an increase in freedom of expression.

Authenticity in the language classroom needs to be fostered by the teacher through deliberate and persistent effort. To encourage authentic instructional transactions, it is necessary to spend classroom time and effort in learning the school register in the second language. Early selections for pattern practice should include the transactional idioms proper and frequent in the classroom: e.g., "Repeat after me," "Ask Mary a question," "Complete the exercise on p. x," "Write a paragraph about school," "Paraphrase the answer," "Work together as a team," etc., etc. Later selections should be topically relevant to the instructional process: e.g., "Do you understand what he meant?," "Can you ask him to help you with the exercise?," "Which part didn't you understand?," "How do you say x in French?," etc., etc. These standard instructional transactions are authentic to the language learning process, and they provide real, rather than artificial, opportunities for the authentic use of the target language.

Similarly, authentic role enactments require a favorable climate of interaction that is largely under the control of the teacher. Under authentic conditions of interaction, e.g., in the school yard and the streets or at home, children and adolescents proceed by means of natural and smooth switches in the topic of conversation. It is most unnatural and cramping to be required to restrict the interaction to one particular topic as assigned by someone else. The teacher's role should be, instead, that of a resource person who is present during the interaction and who can be called upon by the transactants to facilitate the unfolding conversation, wherever it seems to be headed, by itself, in its natural evolution of the moment.

Summary

Our purpose here has been to provide a new (transactional) rationale for the selection of appropriate materials for pattern practice in language teaching. The old (linguistic) rationale provides a grading hypothesis based on syntactic complexity. The two rationales, transactional and linguistic, are not exclusionary, and we have proposed their integration into a two-step selectional procedure: grading based on syntactic complexity is to be made within previously selected transactional types.

In addition to introducing a transactional rationale for grading pattern practice materials, we have specified two conditions for avoiding the artificiality of the restricted simulated dialogue and encouraging instead an authentic conversational context that approximates more nearly the target register. One condition involves the selection of pattern practice materials relevant to the authentic instructional register in the language classroom. The other condition involves the enactment of the self in conversational practice rather than the unnatural enactment of others.

REFERENCES

Garfinkel, H. *Studies in Ethnomethodology*. Englewood Cliffs, N. J.: Prentice-Hall, 1968.

Goffman, E. *Relations in Public*. New York: Basic Books, 1971.

Halliday, M. A. K. "Language in a Social Perspective." In A. Wilkinson, (ed.), "The Context of Language" (Special Issue), *Educational Review, 23* (3), 1971. (School of Education, University of Birmingham).

Jakobovits, L. A. *Foreign Language Learning*. Rowley, Mass: Newbury House Publishers, 1970.

Jakobovits, L. A. and Gordon, B. I. *Introduction to Ethnomethodological Psycholinguistics*. (In preparation, 1974).

———. (in collaboration with Gaston Renaud and Johanna Vander Beek). *Transactional Engineering and Language Teaching. Verbatim*. (in press, 1974).

———. *Performative Teaching*. (In preparation, 1974).

Sacks, H. *Aspects of the Sequential Organization of Conversation*. (Forth-coming, Prentice-Hall).

———. "An Initial Investigation of the Usability of Conversational Data for Doing Sociology." In David Sudnow (ed.), *Studies in Social Interaction*. New York: The Free Press, 1972.

Schegloff, E. A. "Notes on a conversational Practice: Formulating Place." In David Sudnow (ed.), *Studies in Social Interaction*. New York: The Free Press, 1972.

Sinclair, J. McH., Forsyth, I.J., Coulthard, R. M., and Ashby, M. *The English Used by Teachers and Pupils*. Final Report to SSRC, August, 1972. (Department of English Language and Literature, The University of Birming-ham.)

Part Two: The Personal Context

5 Freedom to Teach and Freedom to Learn

Today, many FL teachers suffer from a dis-ease of the spirit that we would like to refer to as the BALT syndrome (for: the "*Ba*ttered *L*anguage *T*eacher" syndrome). This is a neurosis that is characterized by the chronic and constant alternation between two irrational states of the mind: from self-elevation to instructional omnipotence and omniscience all the way down to self-denigration to infantile helplessness. The belief in instructional omnipotence and omniscience is founded on the implausible hypothesis that it is routinely possible to teach conversational fluency in a FL in the classrooms of our mass educational system, in spite of convincing evidence to the contrary. Infantile helplessness is symptomatized by an exaggerated dependence on methodological strategies that, like number painting and do-it-yourself kits, leave nothing but trivialities to be decided upon. The recent emphasis in education on accountability and the related requirement to develop behavioral objectives have so aggravated the BALT syndrome that language teachers are suffering from neurotic symptoms of confusion, anxiety, and uncertainty in connection with their work. What follows is an attempt to analyze the BALT syndrome, to expose the fallacies that underlie it, and thereby, hopefully, to ease the language teacher's burden by providing him with rationalizations that might serve for some of them to bring about a conversion to a new consciousness, a new reality about their teaching, one that is based on the premises of freedom rather than intellectual servitude.

Ordinary and Specialized Communicative Skills

The fact that people acquire languages is a commonplace event that needs no documentation. What needs to be discussed are the conditions under which languages can be acquired and the nature of the communicative skills thus acquired. We'd like to discuss two types of conditions of acquisition, natural and artificial, and two types of communicative skills, *ordinary* and *specialized*. We shall call "natural" conditions of acquisition those situations in which the individual is exposed to social interactional settings that exclude the learning of language as one of its recognized and legitimate functions. All other conditions of acquisition will then be "artificial." Some specific instances of natural conditions would include the regular use of a second language in the home, living in a community in which the second language is spoken, and working in a setting in which the use of a second language is regular and frequent. The classroom, the laboratory, FL conversation hours, and the like, are artificial conditions. There are settings which combine these two aspects. For instance, language camps, some summer school programs, and some group travel programs provide opportunities for social interactions that pertain to everyday, natural communicative acts, even though the overall intent of the experience relates specifically to the learning of a second language.

By "ordinary" communicative skills we mean to refer to the normal, everyday range of conversational interactions in which a member of a social community is expected to participate. For instance, an adult middle-class American living in an urban community would be expected to be able to engage in conversational interactions that include a neighbor, an acquaintance, an intimate friend, a family member, a teacher, a civil servant, service people, and the like. In addition he would be expected to be able to read newspapers, and popular books, write personal letters, and watch and listen to television and radio broadcasts. All other *types* of communicative skills are to be considered "specialized." An individual who is incapable of functioning in a particular setting that is ordinary will be considered abnormal or deviant by other individuals, but not so for specialized settings. For instance, a person who turns down a request for acting as an M.C. at a social affair (a specialized skill) may, without being considered deviant, turn down the request on the basis of a claim that he does not know how to do that, but he may not use the same justification for turning down an invitation to a party, for in that case he will be accused either of insincerity or abnormality.[1]

Thus, the distinctions between natural and artificial conditions of acquisition, on the one hand, and ordinary and specialized communicative skills, on the other, are founded in the expectations of members of a community with respect to the normal capabilities of the average person under ordinary everyday conditions. Natural conditions of language acquisition will promote the development of ordinary communicative skills. Specialized skills, on the other hand, usually but not always presume exposure to artificial conditions. This interaction—between type of conditions exposed to and nature of the skills acquired—is not coincidental but, rather, conditional or implicative. The totality of an individual's ordinary communicative skills is related in highly significant ways to the nature of his previous conversational interactions in day-to-day living.[2] Specialized communicative skills will be dependent upon previous exposure to nonordinary, artificial, specially contrived settings. We would like, now, to elaborate upon what we think is involved in the relationship between "being exposed to" and "acquisition of communicative skills." Here lies the central problem of language education, the "teaching-learning" interaction.

The Teaching-Learning Interaction

In the old paradigm of language teaching, it was asserted that language is made up of a set of specifiable unitary skills each of which can be taught consecutively by practice and conditioning. This belief is the foundation of the theory and practice of audiolingualism and is still, by far, the major approach today in second language education. It is based on the S-R learning paradigm and has a long and powerful tradition in American psychology. The new paradigm does not conceive of this kind of elementarism, and further, does not assume a specific causative relationship between communicative skills and teaching practices.

It is clear that the two paradigms differ in crucial ways in, first, the nature of the taxonomic elements that constitute settings and skills, and second, in the nature of the relationship between the two. To avoid the continued malpractice of language teaching made possible by the apparently attractive but false tenets of the sequential hypothesis it is necessary to show that the new paradigm denies both the sequential hypothesis and the elementarism of the old paradigm in any form. Let us briefly review the argument.

In the reality of the new paradigm, it is an unquestionable, manifestly evident fact that ordinary communicative skills need not be taught under natural conditions of acquisition. All but a few so-called abnormal children develop ordinary communicative skills during the first three years of life. The acquisition of these behavioral manifestations cannot be properly qualified as the result of any kind of "teaching" on the part of the parents, except in a meaningless extention of the concept of teaching, whereby everything we know has been taught to us, and everybody is a teacher. Similarly, adults will develop ordinary as well as more restricted, specialized communicative skills in a second or subsequent language whenever they are regularly and frequently exposed to social settings that have requirements for functional interaction (e.g., immigrants, foreign country residents, individuals living in bilingual work settings, those engaging in trading exchanges, military occupation personnel, etc.). It is sad, but we think essentially correct, to say that the development of communicative skills in a nonnative language is, and has always been, a nonproblematic, natural, and ordinary phenomenon until the attempt is made to teach it: at that point, we have invented a "learning problem," one that our "teaching" has been frustratingly incapable of solving. The point is that language learning is indeed a problem, but who needs it? Like the young, impetuous Alexander of an earlier, less problematic era, let us have the fortitude to cut out the abscess of the language learning problem so that we may proceed to the larger conquest of the development of multilingual communicative interaction. Two things seem outstanding about our current traditional mass education: the fact that it is of such general poor quality, and the fact that it is based, like much of our technological society, on unreality, or a false reality. These two facts are undoubtedly related. The profound alienation experienced by the youth of today is a costly symptom of the unreality of the schools they are forced to attend. The ideals of equality and justice are blatantly trampled upon by the intellectual imperialism of "the school achiever profile," the ethnocentric purism of "standard educated English." The ideals of individuality and creativity are countermanded by the despotism of standardization, percentiles, and levels. Even the hitherto magically powerful American cultural belief in practicality and functionalism is swept away by the more powerful device of the use of euphemisms in educational slogans that treat with such *lèse majestés* the requirements of "accountability" and make possible the continuation of educational malpractice.

Much of what is wrong with FL teaching is also wrong with education generally. But this should not absolve FL education from the necessities for change within the curriculum they are specifically responsible for. We shall suggest ways in which needed basic changes can be brought about, but first, we must understand, in a more profound sense, why we are failing, why indeed, it is impossible to attain our stated goals in FL teaching, given the current practices, in the classrooms of our educational system.

The classroom is a special social setting. By "special" we do not mean that it is less "real" than other settings such as the home or the school yard, but only that the communicative patterns that typically exist there are different from, and not normally included in other, ordinary social settings that form the background of everyday human interaction. Another way of seeing this is to realize that if a child were to spend most of his waking life during the first three or four years in a classroom atmosphere, he would grow up with almost none of the ordinary communicative skills that make him acceptable as "normal" to the people he interacts with. This holds true whether we are dealing with communicative skills in a first or a second language. A classroom-produced bilingual would exhibit as improbable and socially abnormal patterns of communicative skills in his second language as the unfortunate hypothetical child who was brought up altogether in a classroom. To both would be denied the most ordinary of conversational competencies: how to make small talk, how to enjoy verbal and intellectual squirmishes, how to express deep felt emotions, how to waste time by talking, how to argue, and flatter, and say whatever is on one's mind, how to congratulate sincerely, and pray meaningfully, how to convince and persuade emphatically, not rationally, how to laugh, and have fun, and feel the emotional, irrational power of words to move, to convince, to hurt, and to make love. Instead, the classroom produced bilingual will exhibit at his very best a number of specialized language skills such as talking in full sentences about a previously rehearsed topic, conjugating verbs, reciting translation, pseudo-equivalent terms and utterances, engage in question-answer interchanges that resemble reluctant interviews, use stereotyped verbal routines that stifle expressive creativity, read by duty or necessity, and write coherently and functionally but insipidly.

Our Current Educational Slogans in the Light of a New Consciousness and Their Consequences

According to the author of *The Greening of America* (Reich, 1971), two elements are necessary to bring about a change in consciousness, from II, the servile consciousness of the Corporate State, to III, the new consciousness of the youth generation, of freedom, of the self. These two elements are the realization of betrayal and the positive affirmation of an alternative, the denial of the inevitability of the status quo. The battered language teacher who exhibits the classic BALT syndrome suffers the pains of the double bind characteristic of the liberal intellectual at the level of consciousness II: he is honest and searching enough to feel and be aware of a sense of betrayal but his sheepishness makes him buckle under the system, and he robs himself of the imaginative, freedom-giving leap into the unknown. He accepts, condones, does not want to rock the boat, feels helpless against the mindless system, hesitates, falters, suffers, remains ineffectual, denigrates his creative potentialities for choice, never recovers his self. Like Reich, we do not believe in the necessity, or even desirability, of violent revolution, civil disobedience, strike action, resignations, or any other of the classic tactics of political and bureaucratic dissent. Radical and effective change in education is possible only through a personal change of consciousness on the part of individual teachers, a reaffirmation at the personal, individual level of the traditional ideals of education for equal opportunity, justice, intellectual growth, individual creativity, and the pursuit of life goals based on individual choice. Educational bureaucracy, like the Corporate State of which it is a product, has developed such mindless inertia, that mere humans cannot radically alter its course. There are no all-powerful educator-villains to shoot or to axe. Nobody knows how to do it better, even if all of us are dedicated. There is only the possibility of individual choice, in one's limited setting, in the little classrooms of Miss Jones and Mr. Hendrix. If enough such individual choices are exercised, in a significant number of classrooms, the educational bureaucracy will turn into an irrelevant superstructure that ultimately will collapse because nobody will care. The educational *process* will be saved, the teachers, and the students.

What do we mean by the exercise of individual choice in the context of a change of consciousness? To a large extent, we mean freedom to teach, freedom from the shackles of educational slogans, freedom from the tyranny of irrelevant expertise, freedom to feel the responsibility that goes with professional integrity. The FL teacher (no matter how much this is also true of other teachers) has given up all of these freedoms. His lesson planning sessions are devoted to rehearsing exercises invented by some authority or expert who knows nothing about his individual qualities and those of his students. His classroom and laboratory activities are dictated by the anonymous author of a commercially promoted package of goodies, usually chosen by a FL supervisor who is very conscious of "accountability" and insists on the administration of standardized cooperative tests, neither the teacher nor he understanding the frightfully complex and elusive problems of validity and meaningful comparability across heterogeneous populations. The "expert" and his research have been elevated to totally unrealistic levels of respect and adoration. We ourselves, considered "experts" on FL teaching, have been continually embarrassed by the nature of the questions we are asked, questions which presuppose a degree of knowledge and practical knowhow in applied matters that is all together out of proportion with reality. Being a prolific writer and talker, one of us has contributed his share in expert pronouncements, analyses, suggestions, and yes, even tests. *We accept the responsibility for making them* and this book represents more of the same. *The educator and teacher must accept the responsibility for taking them.* The teacher's *instructional activities* in the classroom are the responsibility of the teacher, not the supervisor, not the student, not the school system, not the academic expert.

In one sense, the one just discussed, the teacher has given up responsibility which is rightly his. In another sense, he has assumed a responsibility that isn't realistically his, the responsibility for what the students learn or don't learn. This pernicious form of instructional omnipotence has been thrust upon the teacher by the educational system. It has become part of his consciousness, part of his reality, part of his servitude. It stands in the way of freedom to teach, it blocks any possibility for free choice, for creative innovation.

It is possible, of course, to provide rationalizations that justify the attribution of responsibility to the teacher for what his students learn, such as, for instance, the rationale of "accountability." Similarly, it is possible to provide rationalizations that free the teacher from that responsibility, such as, for instance, the argument that student motivation, attitude toward school work, subcultural background, parental influence, etc., which together far outweigh the variance contribution of the instructional process. Either argument can be pursued rationally, neither would win out over the other. To pursue this matter further is to engage in never-ending controversy. It does not change anything. The only solution is a simple one: to simply stop arguing about it by making up one's mind, one way or the other. Those who feel the current betrayal of our ideal educational objectives and, at the same time, can bring themselves to a positive reaffirmation of them, will choose the way of freedom of choice and responsibility for the self, not for the other.

The FL teacher who still waivers can consider the following arguments, as a help in making up his mind. We are going to discuss a few widespread slogans in FL education and point out some of their weaknesses.

"We need more research": whenever there is confusion about some problematic aspect of the curriculum, whenever obvious symptoms of failure are perceived, the cry for more research goes up, the cry of frustration and helplessness. At this level of consciousness, the teacher sees himself at the mercy of others, the expert, the supervisor, the evaluator, the mandarins of teacher training programs. This deference to an all-powerful research divinity is entirely misplaced. It stems from a total lack of understanding of the nature of research in the social disciplines. It confuses academic research with the application of its findings to particular, concrete situations. It confuses the application of academic research with applied research. Much of the success of our technology is didrectly

attributable to applied research, and only indirectly to basic research. But we have no counterpart in the social and humanistic spheres to the applied research techniques of engineering.[3] Just because basic research techniques are being focused on educationally relevant issues does not mean that it constitutes applied educational research. An examination of the success of research in solving certain persistent problems in FL teaching would show the futility and gratuitousness of this exercise. Let us look at some of these.

(A) The relationships between age of learner and success in second language learning: there isn't a single piece of research in the known literature that contributes meaningfully to this problem. Nor can there be, given the nature of this problem and the presently available research techniques. To understand this, you must consider the three basic elements involved in the problem: first, the learner and his characteristics, which include not only age but, equally, style of learning and motivational structure both in their surface manifestations (attitudinal responses on questionnaires, observable study habits) and underlying aspects (subcultural value structure, need achievement, personality disposition); second, the instructional activities, which include not merely the easily identifiable elements related to materials and techniques of presentation, but also, equally, the nature of the teacher-student interaction, about which we know very little in specific terms, so-called interactional analysis being but a currently crude attempt to assess some of its features; and third, the assessment of "success" or the "amount" that is learned, a serious problem that research has not been able to solve, current standardized discrete-point tests being merely crude attempts at approximating certain superficial aspects of communicative competence.

In view of these fundamental difficulties in assessing the basic parameters of the problem of the relationship between age and FL teaching, research cannot contribute any definitive or conclusive answers. At best, it can only be "suggestive." But "suggestiveness" is not a part of research. When we say that "research suggests that . . . " we are merely engaging in nonscientific, selective reporting, guided by prior intuitive biases or preferences for the purpose of persuasion. In connection with the present problem, for instance, we can point to claims made by Wilder Penfield, the Canadian world famous neurophysiologist who had a personal predilection for bilingualism. Penfield claimed that the human brain undergoes a natural, maturational change such that by the age of puberty its ability to acquire languages has greatly decreased. This was not a scientific claim about the specific issue as to the best time to begin the study of a FL. Penfield never engaged in this type of research. He was merely making a highly tentative inference on the basis of his neurophysiological researches, yet his guesses about this became transformed by proponents of FLES programs into the slogan "research shows that . . . " or "research suggests that . . . ." Persuasive exploitation, ignorance, facile reliance on secondary sources, and sheer time (Penfield's remarks at a graduation ceremony were made twenty years ago), were all recklessly combined and gratuitously transformed into "scientific evidence."

We, too, are personally in favor of the early study of a FL. Experience suggests that children have a remarkable ability to develop communicative competence in a second language under natural conditions of acquisition. They seem to be able to learn a second language effortlessly (but who knows?) and sound more like native speakers than adults in comparable situations. But is this a result of neurophysiology? Why, then, do we have such little success in teaching Black children the effective use of standard English? And children on Indian reservations? And the children of Mexican Americans? And Latin Americans? And why have so many FLES programs for middle-class white American children been so unsuccessful? We can come up with many hypotheses: subcultural background, inadequate facilities, untrained teachers, and so on, but so what? Where does all this leave the neurophysiological claim about the brain's declining plasticity with age? Nowhere. So much idle controversy about what research "shows" or doesn't show.

(B) The relationship between bilingualism and intellectual development: for many years, investigators have attempted to "research" this problem, have contributed several hundred articles, reports, and books on the subject and ended up with the original problem as obscure as it had been before the heavy investment in research effort. Those who believe otherwise no doubt feel that the empirical data that have accumulated on this subject will eventually help us see "the pattern." Faith is a good thing; it is the basis of hope and optimism.

But it must not be confused with scientific evidence upon which educational practice is claimed to be based. It is important to understand why the problem we are considering has not been solved by hundreds of experiments. It is not because of "bad research" and the ineptitude of investigators. It is because the currently known research technology in the social disciplines is not of the sort that is suitable for applied research in education. Another five hundred experiments will not solve the basic problems involved in understanding the relationship between bilingualism and intellectual functioning on the one hand, and on the other, how that relationship should guide educational practice in second language teaching. Current research technology is operative only when the problem elements can be meaningfully and relevantly defined operationally, through the use of some measurement or observation technique. When this is currently done for vague, diffuse but intuitively meaningful notions such as "bilingualism," "intellectual functioning," "cognitive flexibility," "language skills," and so on, the resultant operational transformation yields tests, questionnaires, experimental tasks that are supposed to be related in significant ways to the underlying intuitive notions, but they are not. This crucial transformation procedure suffers from reductionism, and contemporary psychological research has not been able to routinely solve this problem. Furthermore, there are no indications, at present, that this problem is going to be solved in the near future. Thus, while basic academic research will continue to flourish and search for relationships in human behavior in reductionist terms, it is not likely to be of crucial service to the applied needs of society.

(C) What is the best method of teaching a second language?: here, the amount of empirical data that research has generated is even more formidable than in the previously discussed areas, but we are nowhere near an adequate solution to the problem. The student who must review this literature actually becomes more confused rather than more knowledgeable. Comparisons across studies is a gratuitous task inasmuch as the conditions that are known to be of relevance are not the same, and their variance contribution is unknown: the relationship between the investigator's theoretical description of a condition or method of instruction and the instructor's actual classroom activities is not controllable or even measurable to any

significant extent; what the investigator can control in terms of exposure conditions, he loses because what really matters is what the student does with it, and that is something the investigator has no control over; what the investigator can measure does not represent what the student has learned, and vice versa; and so on.

We have been discussing, over the last few pages, the inherent shortcomings of academic research as an approach to the problems of applied research in education. We hope we have succeeded in pointing out the gratuitousness of the ever present cry for more research in FL teaching. There are many other slogans in this field that, in our opinion, are just as gratuitous and shaky. We have already discussed the sequential hypothesis of basic versus advanced language training, the notion of early language training ("the earlier, the better"), and the very idea of a "method of teaching" (e.g., traditional versus audiolingual) in the absence of meaningful control of learner factors. There are others: "We need to teach language *use*, not facts about language"; "We need a native model for a language teacher"; "Practice makes perfect"; "We need to teach culture"; "We need more qualified, better trained teachers"; "Mistakes should be immediately corrected to prevent stamping in of errors"; "We need better materials"; "We need more and better standardized tests"; and so on. These slogans, offered as explanations for past failures and directions for the future, serve to maintain the current malpractice in FL education. The teacher who wants freedom to teach must divest himself of these insidious battle cries. The form in which they are posed appears harmless enough: who can quarrel with policies that call for "better things"—better teachers, better methods, better materials, better tests? To be against these is like being against motherhood and apple pie. But, in actuality, they serve to obscure the real problems involved in "better FL education." By "misposing" the problems, they effectively block needed creative solutions of an entirely different sort. It is essential to understand that what is wrong with FL teaching today is precisely what is wrong with our educational system generally: the total lack of freedom to learn and freedom to teach. To gain these freedoms, the student and the teacher must regain their selfhood from the school system and the established social institutions of which it is an expression. Already, the "new" student in school, and the youth generation everywhere, have begun this reaffirmation process towards a new consciousness, a new reality that will master technology for human benefit rather than buckle under its mindless tyranny. It's now up to each individual teacher to embark upon the new road, the new vision of our earlier ideals finally made possible by a technology whose real capacity to help man's dreams come true has not yet been realized. What is this new reality, and how do we work towards it?

The Greening of the FL Classroom

FL education in this country has gone through three historical periods: the period up to the Second World War, the period between 1940 and the late 1960's, and the current renewed vision of the new consciousness of freedom to learn and freedom to teach. Each period is aptly characterized by the slogans of their day. The period up to 1940 is the period of Consciousness I; it is the period of pedantic belletrism, of educational elitism: "No person is truly educated unless he has a knowledge of one or more FL's." It is the period of the dull study of vocabulary lists, verb tenses, sentence parsing, and of translation. Neither the instructor nor the student ever felt the realness of the living language, nor did they ever seriously entertain the possibility of communicative competence, for, as everyone knew in those days, "Americans lack the ability of learning a FL." Beginning with the war effort in the early 1940's, Americans discovered, under the necessity of the moment, that lo and behold, it was possible for them to acquire a speaking ability of a FL in a matter of weeks or months. With characteristic ingenuity and organizational ability that are the hallmark of the Consciousness II mind, this new found freedom was efficiently exploited for the purposes of mass education. The Golden Age of FL education in America was ushered in with the tape recorder, the language laboratory, and the pattern practice choir. "FL's for everyone" was the universal slogan of the audiolingual period. More languages were taught to more students more and more. We began to keep track of number of enrollments and viewed with deep satisfaction the geometrically accelerated shape of the curves. Standardized tests and percentile norms became ever present. FLES curricula were initiated. NDEA institutes for language teachers became the thing to do during the summers. The Bilingual Education Act began to pour millions of dollars into the FL and second language teaching enterprises. Everything became big, big, big, an accelerated bigness that, like the golem of Prague, was mindless and unstoppable.

A few little disturbing signs began, by their chronic persistence, to worry the production managers: the fact that students everywhere developed an intense dislike to FL study: the fact that most of them dropped out of the FL curriculum before the advanced stage of "liberated expression"; the fact that colleges and graduate schools began to give up the traditional FL requirements; and so on. These glaring failures were finally acknowledged publicly, and this resulted in renewed vigor for witch hunting activities: we need more research; we need better teacher training programs; we need better materials. . . . Suddenly, the cure was found: accountability, behavioral objectives, individualized instruction. Currently, the profession is gearing itself feverishly for these new slogans. The great wheel has been stopped, cleaned, and now it's taking off again. Shall we see once more its mindless momentum imprison two or three generations of teachers before it too grinds to a halt, to then repeat once more what it has always done? How much more of this can we afford? And why should we?

This picture would be funny were it not so sad. It is ironic because there is little doubt that many of the technological and instructional innovations that have been developed since 1940 have been real breakthroughs. Our own biased list of exciting innovations include the universal availability of audiovisual aids, self-instructional programmed packages of courses, computer-assisted instruction, summer language camps, language games, year-abroad programs, and individualized instruction. These instructional innovations in mass FL education made possible by ingenious technology have the potential of use and misuse. Thus far they have been mostly misused because their thoughtless application has been allowed to erode the basic freedom of the teacher. They have created the BALT syndrome.

We are going to outline our conception of the new consciousness that is needed to turn these technological innovations in FL education into a tool that is subservient to our educational aspirations. This new reality of freedom will cure the BALT syndrome. Nothing new is needed. Not even money. Only individual initiative, a positive affirmation toward the path of liberation.

The relevance of research

A clear distinction is to be made between "basic research" and "applied research." Basic research is esoteric, specialized, and inaccessible to the teacher. To be a consumer of it, to be dependent upon it means to be subjugated to the authority and expertise of others. It means giving up the freedom of choice in favor of faith and trust in the technocrat who very often is far removed from the realities and needs of the classroom, and in any event, is not the person who is held "accountable." Basic research is a method of arriving at general theories about basic human behavior. It deals with laws and principles in the abstract; its observations are made under "controlled" conditions which involve the creation of artificial, nonnatural settings. When basic research is carried out in naturalistic settings, its artificiality is not thereby reduced. Only some of the relevant factors are investigated at any point, and these are reduced to operational definitions by observation techniques that must meet certain restrictive standards (e.g., observability, objectivity, elementarism). The problems that are researched are dictated by these standards not by the real needs for greater practical knowhow. Their claimed relevance to teaching problems turns out to be false.

Applied research refers to the systematic investigation of a particular social setting. It is a tool used for gaining additional knowledge about the total configuration of interacting factors in the setting. The setting and the problem are defined independently of the techniques available through applied research. They are given by personal judgment, folk theory, ordinary experience, intuitive understanding. The systematic techniques made available by applied research are plugged in wherever possible or desirable. The overall integrity of the social setting, as given in the ordinary understanding of it, is never compromised, altered, or reduced to the demands of "scientific" standards. In a sense, it is the scientific standards that are being compromised for the sake of maintaining the full meaning of the problem being investigated. An example will illustrate this point.

Suppose a school in Miami decides to implement a new bilingual program in English and Spanish. This decision is a sociopolitical one and is independent of scientific considerations that pertain to choice of timing, location, availability of manpower and instructional materials. Various types of programs are possible and presumably known to the school administrators. Academic and educational consultants may be called upon to give their advice. When the basic research literature is consulted, whether laboratory-type or naturalistic, the information obtained is either inadequate or befuddling in its contradictions. For instance, program x at place y has been found "effective" and "successful," but careful examination of these claims reveals their inadequacy: "success" refers to mean scores on achievement tests whose relation to bilingualism and biculturalism, as ordinarily understood, is marginal or irrelevant. For instance, a graduating class of the program achieves higher mean scores on a set of standardized tests in Spanish proficiency than a comparison group, but very few of these students use their Spanish outside the classroom, even though opportunities are available, and they fail to enroll in a bilingual program in high school, even though it is available to them. In addition, it turns out that the same program tried subsequently in place z does not meet with equal success. When the problem is examined, further, it becomes evident that the description of the program on paper and a description of how in fact it is administered have but the remotest connection. Special training hastily imposed on the teachers involved only succeeds in reinforcing their confusion, their fears, their feelings of uncertainty. The materials adopted or designed for the program turn out to be too difficult and culturally irrelevant for the students in the teacher's class. The program is no longer what it was designed to be, and evaluation reports are either frankly disastrous or a whitewash of might-have-beens. The students that were the guinea pigs are forgotten: out of sight after graduation, out of mind.

This description is not an alarmist fantasy to prove a point. It is the norm as far as we can best determine, whether the new program deals with bilingual education, or FLES, or individualized instruction, or teacher training. Are there more desirable alternatives possible?

The first point to make is that the procedure typically followed in the implementation of a new educational program is one that may be suitable for the construction of a chemical plant but is totally unrealistic for a school. A blueprint program imposed externally, from the top, is an act of violence upon the individuality of the teacher and the student. It destroys, alienates, and cannot succeed. An educational program, in fact rather than delusion, is not a blueprint plan but a descriptive statement of ongoing activity. A program cannot realistically be planned and followed; it can only emerge after the fact, within the total configuration of a setting. A program cannot objectively be evaluated as to its overall "success"; evaluation can only consist of descriptive statements about isolated and separate aspects of the total educational setting. Many aspects that are intuitively meaningful cannot be directly and unambiguously assessed: the effects upon the teacher's morale and self-satisfaction, the long term effects upon student creativity and motivation, the quality of student-teacher interaction, the psychological climate in school, the support and involvement of the community. Just because these aspects cannot be scientifically and objectively described, assessed, or controlled is no justification for leaving them out of the overall picture and for making decisions without considering them in *equal* importance to those aspects that are measurable in more straightforward terms.

Applied research in education begins, not with a plan and its monitoring, but with the teacher. A beginning might be an encounter group experience in which the teacher is given the opportunity of taking a noncritical, loving look at himself: Where is his head at? What are his hopes and aspirations as an individual in his multiple social roles? What is the range and nature of his everyday interactions with friends, family, colleagues, students? Can he describe his philosophical views, his social attitudes, his political beliefs? What is his conception of the educational process, of human communication, of the foundations of his field of specialized knowledge? Does he identify with his profession, does he read, does he know how to obtain information on novel technological developments? Does he feel like a cog in a machine or has he retained an impression of freedom of choice? Does he view himself as an agent of assimilation, an authority, an enemy of the students or a friend?

Exploration of these broad, all-encompassing issues clears the way for more specific ones, those that are more directly related to the teacher's instructional activities in the classroom. He may find that he is dissatisfied with certain aspects of his teaching. He would like to explore with some new techniques but doesn't know where to start and what the consequences might be. He doesn't know how to get help, how to talk openly with his supervisor, how much freedom to allow his students. He may realize his understanding of the fundamentals of his field are inadequate, but how and to whom shall he make such an admission? He may have difficulty getting along with some young people in the class and needs opportunity to learn more effective interpersonal management techniques. And so on.

Finally, he may feel sufficiently involved and committed to do something concrete. He wants to be shown how he can use systematic observation techniques to monitor the process of change, how to prepare tests and questionnaires, how to change the participatory structure in his classroom, how to state behavioral objectives, how to use multiple evaluation criteria, and how to interpret them in the light of his own personal judgment which must always retain a primary status lest alienation and inhumanity destroy his effectiveness and sense of wellbeing. Out of these concrete activities, individually coherent and custom-tailored to his personality, interests, self-confidence, emerges the program, and with it the curriculum. There is no prodding from the school administrator, no externally imposed blueprint, no threat, no alienation, no loss of personal dignity. There is the recognition that the educational process is a complex configuration of fluid, changing, uncontrollable set of interacting factors. There is no personal responsibility for failure or success, no personal accountability, only that of the system as a whole.

The recent new emphasis on accountability in education has both positive and negative potentials. If used by school administrators to pressure teachers for improved student scores on standardized norms, it becomes a pernicious act of violence and injustice against the personhood of the individual teacher. If used as part of an assessment procedure for the overall educational process in a particular school setting along with other observation techniques, it may have some value as an information feedback system. However, the very concept of "accountability" contains the notion of individual responsibility within a complex system that is beyond significant individual control and choice. It is likely, therefore, to be more abused as an instrument of arbitrary punishment and scape goating than used constructively as an assessment instrument.

The issue of responsibility in education raises some extremely difficult questions that the profession as a whole must carefully consider and deliberate. Witch hunting must at all costs be avoided. Posing the problem in terms such as "Who is responsible for current educational failures?" and variously allocating parts of the blame to segments of the educational hierarchy is not going to be useful, helpful or just. Instead the creative potential of teachers and school administrators, of students, of legislators, and the larger community must be given a chance to unfold and flourish in an atmosphere that is free from the stifling restrictions of the philosophy of accountability. In the reality of the new consciousness, individual freedom alone can unleash man's creative energies, not coercion, not competition, not accountability, but faith, freedom, cooperation, permissiveness, trust, hope.

Freedom to teach is an essential component of the new educational process that is unfolding. It includes freedom from personal responsibility for students' percentile ranks on standardized, norm-referenced tests, freedom from administrative authority relating to decisions and policies governing the teacher's activities, freedom from the obligation of certification and specialized training. Freedom to learn is a necessary condition for the full development of the individual's creative potentials. It includes freedom from compulsory courses and curricula, freedom from authority, freedom from the requirement of tests, examinations, and grades.

To the person whose reality is at the level of the older consciousness, our description of the educational process under freedom to teach and learn must evoke a feeling of horror or derision, or both in turn. Visions of anarchy, chaos, abuse, waste, present themselves to his excited imagination. His reality of our technological society held in place by regimentation, bureaucratic order, certification, standardization, individual reward system, laws, regulations, guidelines, blueprints, etc., is threatened by the cataclysmic implications of an individual freedom that removes itself by one fell swoop of the sword of liberation. A world without systemic control and paternalistic rule is, for him, the worst imaginable hell. Man, who cannot transcend the reality of organization and technology, is fearful, restricted, restrictive, lacking hope and faith and trust. The only creative imagination that is left to him lies in the construction of visions of doom unless . . . . His blind faith in organizational structure robs him of any remaining faith in the goodness and capacities of free man. His restricted vision limits him to incapacitating slogans, the futile call for more and better of the same. Under the spell of these tired, old, worn-out, impotent notions he condones the current reality of mediocrity, injustice, inequality, intellectual poverty, dull regimentation, inhumanity, and dehumanization.

To the new consciousness of freedom, it is the current reality that is intolerable, and it is the future that holds the unfulfilled promises of democracy, of technology, of creativity. He is the true believer in free enterprise, not the socially organized injustices of a competitive economic bureaucracy, but the free enterprise of personal freedom to pursue the fulfillment of inner potentials and dreams. The more freedom to teach and learn is introduced in our current mass educational system, the clearer the distinction will become between the needs of society for trained manpower to support technology and the needs of the individual to explore his creativity and fulfill his true individual self. The recognition of this distinction is likely to be the most immediate and important consequence of the new freedom. Even in an atmosphere of less than total freedom, there is room for both types of educational enterprises to flourish. Industry will continue to demand training, certification, degrees, the mastery of a known body of knowledge, but it will have to do its own schooling and recruiting. Universal, state-supported education should not be allowed to be used exclusively for such a purpose. But, more importantly, as more individuals in our society become liberated, not just the young but those throughout the ranks of the establishment, we will see the emergence of creative and viable alternatives in individual lifestyles, not only the kind of alternative that isolates and removes the individual from the mainstream of society, but also a kind that allows recognition of the great potential of technology for human and humane use and allows coexistence with the machine, the organized system, mass production, and urbanization without spiritual enslavement. Industry, the Corporate State, and the technocrats will gradually come to respect the new freedom, and their internal organization will be realigned in the service of the new consciousness. Their changing character will make room for, and will be dependent upon people whose individuality and creativity will not be assassinated by the educational production mill. Economic opportunity need no longer depend on the successful adoption of the personality of "organization man" and the school achiever. The educational spectrum will thus be allowed to diversify, to destandardize, to individualize. Compared to the arid uniformity of our current schools, the classrooms of freedom will reflect the gorgeous colors of spring and autumn.

Freedom to teach will come to cure the BALT syndrome. With freedom from threat and retaliation, the liberated teacher will explore that vast range of possibilities that exists, in self-concept, between instructional omnipotence and childish helplessness, and in teaching, between the despotism of overstructuredness and the debilitating frustration of understructuredness. No doubt, some teachers will misuse this freedom, just as they now misuse the authority they are given by the system. This is no legitimate reason for witholding that freedom, but it may be instructive to consider how freedom to teach could be misused, so that those who do may come to gain more insight into their actions.

One of the greatest misuses of freedom of action is the arbitrary imposition of one's values upon others. An authoritarian, impersonal, and rigid teacher may become even more obnoxious in his disregard of students' freedom to learn when given "carte blanche" by the system than under the current restrictive conditions of routinized policies and guidelines. The imposition of directives and sanctions on the part of superiors in order to deal with this kind of misuse of freedom by some teachers is not an acceptable or workable solution to the problem. It would be itself an instance of the abuse of authority to curtail the teacher's freedom and lead back to the current vicious cycle of paternalism and helplessness. One does not cure the disease by killing the patient. Teachers who misuse their freedom are victims of mistraining and are in need of help. They should be given opportunities to reexamine their premises about teaching and their role as teachers without the threat of retaliation or sanction. They can participate in an encounter-communication workshop (see Chapter 6) with colleagues, with students, with supervisors. Their students can be encouraged to exercise their freedom to learn and to air their grievances. Bargaining sessions between them and the teacher may be held. Frequent individual consultation with the supervisor may be arranged, and so on, so long as none of these activities are used to restrict the teacher's freedom. These kinds of adaptive measures are more complex than the imposition of directives from above, and their outcome may appear less certain, but in the long run they offer much more than the simple solution; the teacher's individuality and creative capacity, the attainment of "the best he can offer," will be insured to the benefit and dignity of all concerned.

A second misuse of freedom of action is the abnegation of one's role, what in usual terms is currently referred to as "neglecting one's responsibilities" or, simply, "goofing off." Freedom to teach does not include the freedom not to teach, so long as the teacher retains his position as teacher. When a teacher retains a remunerative job he is claiming that he intends to honor a certain contract with his employers. This includes the agreement to uphold certain policies that are operational at the time the contract is entered into and for as long as it is mutually valid. For instance, if the contractual arrangements specify that every student must be given a grade, the teacher's refusal to do so is an act of violation of the contract. If the rules specifically state that all classroom sessions must be held indoors, he cannot choose to meet outdoors. If the rules state that he must use the text assigned by the supervisors, or engage in specific instructional activities prescribed by the supervisor, his refusal to do so is a contractual breach. It is clear that freedom to teach cannot take the form of open insubordination. The teacher can unilaterally exercise his freedom only vis-à-vis choices that are not specifically denied by the school's policies. The other decisions must be renegotiated. The freedom to renegotiate must be made part of the original contract. It should be a constitutional freedom. Given a constitutional right of renegotiation and given an attitude of cooperativeness and enlightenment on the part of school administrators, the teacher can proceed, limited only by his creative abilities, his curiosity, and his self-concept. In the absence of these preconditions, there is no freedom possible. As school administrators are themselves relieved from the debilitating restrictions and threat of a higher accountability, they will come to realize the ineffectiveness of an overloaded contract. They will hold specific policies, rules, and guidelines to the very minimum still necessary to protect their fear of anarchy and chaos. Eventually, as they themselves gain confidence and personal dignity, they will do away with all debilitating restrictions. Freedom to teach and learn will have become facts as natural as their absence now is.

For the School Administrator and the FL Supervisor

If you are an old-fashioned old-timer, you are no doubt ready to scoff at all that we have written in this chapter. O.K. Goodbye. It was nice knowing you. Don't call us, we'll call you. We are interested in talking to those of you whom the teacher considers "sensible, reasonable, often helpful and understanding, but unfortunately, overworked, not too aware of what goes in the hearts of the teachers, and constantly pressured by numbers, reports, accountability, failure rates, and an unreasonable principal or district administrator." To you we want to talk about freedom to teach and about the education of children, and let the teachers listen in on our conversation.

On the basis of our interactions with you in the immediate past, we get the feeling that you are operating at a level of thinking that we might describe as questioning pessimism with definite alarmist overtones. You are aware that there are many things wrong with the FL curriculum and the bilingual education program. You are not inordinately sanguine about the teacher's role in this and welcome such things as initiative, innovative ideas, in-service training programs. However, faced with confusion in the professional literature, shrinking budgets, an expanding student population, student radicalism, parental apathy, and serious drop-out rates, and a few other little things like that, you are a bound man sitting under the Sword of Damocles wistfully considering whether it wasn't better in those days when you had no other responsibility but your own classroom. We say to you: Beware! You're getting into a rut. You are suffering from an impairment in vision. Consider your reaction to my description of the greening of the FL classroom.

Oh, so much idealism! Sitting in our ivory tower, we don't have to cope with the realities of accountability, of drop-out rates, and inadequate budgets. Sure, greater teacher initiative and creativity is a good thing (that's why you put our book on the suggested reading list for your teachers), but if we did away with standardized achievement tests, gave freedom to the students, allowed the teachers to do what they please without holding them responsible for failures, removed certification procedures, then .... Then what? To what great lengths can your imagination go in spelling out visions of doom? You'll need a very active imagination to improve upon a mere description of the current mess we're in now, let alone what awaits us tomorrow if the present wheel continues to grind away as it has. One happy aspect of despair is that it is a precondition for conversion to the liberated path. The closed mind is willing to live with the "inevitable realities" of the situation. He confuses hopelessness with adaptability.

The despair that you might feel is a good thing (forgive us!). It contains the seeds of the dynamic energy for renewal and rebirth, not merely change. The despair comes from the realization that none of the solutions you can think of give you any degree of certainty that they will work. You echo the call for more research, better guidelines, better teacher training programs, more money and facilities, but deep down you are not reassured that any of these would work. So much new wine in old bottles: You need courage to face the beauty and the challenge of the unknown.

True, doing away with required tests would foul up your present neat divisions of levels; but are you certain that the concept of levels is a useful thing? Can you not entertain the hypothesis that the sequential teaching of language skills and lockstep instruction to a "homogeneous" class may, after all, be ineffective strategies based on false learning assemptions? Can you not accept the fact that standardized language tests do not represent adequate measures of what the students actually learn by way of communicative skills and hence, should not be inordinately relied upon in evaluation procedures?

True, giving freedom to the teacher may result in embarrassing statistics, but, then, *the opposite may also happen*, and after all, what have you got to lose under the present circumstances? Have you ever wondered why teachers do not show more initiative, more flexibility, more adaptability to changing circumstances even with your encouragement and prodding? Do you realize that bureaucratic, hierarchically organized institutions reward individuals for maintaining the status quo, and for demonstrated improvement, but punish exploratory activities whose success is questionable? A teacher, faced with such rules of operation, would need an unusual degree of self-confidence and economic independence to attempt truly novel solutions to old problems. Yet few are economically independent and secure, and few have had the kind of training that did not destroy their self-confidence and belief in freedom of choice. Your true contribution to improved FL education does not lie in the role of the "supervisor" whereby you impose policies and guidelines and maintain "standards of excellence" where there is no excellence in the definition of standards. Your true contribution lies in arranging for a climate of freedom in the school and the curriculum. How? Simply, and merely, by displacing where your head is at now to somewhere else, by changing your individual consciousness. Let's look at this possibility in greater detail.

On the subject of teaching approach, methodology, classroom participatory structure, levels, curriculum planning, you can keep in mind that each classroom represents a unique teaching configuration. Context-free, general statements of the type to be found in the basic research literature and in instructional guidelines are not directly applicable to your situation. If you're told that students learn better when the class has a homogeneous distribution for aptitude and attained performance, make sure you do not discourage, on that basis, a teacher's plan which disregards this dictum, for it may well be wrong in this particular case. Individualized FL instruction programs often capitalize on heterogeneous distribution of ability and achievement and use "buddy systems" of interaction between advanced and elementary students. If you're told that the use of the native language in class is to be avoided, that habit makes perfect in pattern practice exercises, that most of the classroom time should be spent in oral drills and simulated dialogues, that speaking and listening precede, in natural development, the acquisition of reading and writing skills, that immediate correction of mistakes is important, that one must learn to crawl before one can run, and on and on, if you're told all these things, beware! There are instances where these guidelines and principles simply do not hold, and you have no way of knowing in advance where these so-called exceptions will occur, because what you're not told, nobody knows. Nor can you afford to follow the shotgun principle whereby you hope to maximize your successes and minimize your failures by adhering to the best available guidelines of the moment. That policy is not only unjust and repressive, it is not efficient. Too many teachers and students get killed. In the long run it's too costly. It's unfair and self-defeating to take the position that it is the teacher's burden to convince you that the general guidelines do not hold in this case. They simply won't move.

On the subject of accountability, behavioral objectives, standardized tests, grading, promotion, keep in mind that what is measured on the surface in the contrived context of a short test may be far removed from what in fact the students have learned, and the latter may be far removed from what appears to have been taught when considered by such criteria as the amount of materials covered or the nature and frequency of classroom instructional activities. Do not dismiss or underestimate the importance of criteria that cannot be measured objectively or adequately: how the teacher feels about his teaching, whether the students are involved and enthusiastic or turned off by the educational process, whether they enroll voluntarily or only as a prerequisite to something else, whether they exhibit interest in biculturalism or just instrumental bilingualism, whether they attempt to use the second language on their own initiative or stay away from it outside the classroom, whether they improve even if the relative level of achievement remains low, whether they can *talk* with "mistakes" and gestures and impurities or merely *parrot* "correct" sentence routines, etc. It is simply not true that anything can be objectivized and measured, because one always adds . . . if you know what it is, and we don't.

The climate of freedom that you create, the extent of it, will be dependent on how you perceive your reality, the restrictions of the system that you feel you have no control over. How many of these restrictions you imagine are other-made rather than self-made? This is what you have to decide for yourself. In the final analysis, we are all in the same boat. The greening of the FL curriculum will depend on so many individual choices, not the overthrow of the system.

NOTES

[1] Of course, the individual concerned may have been previously categorized as a member of another subculture or culture. In that case, a different subsystem of rules of interaction comes into play to alter behavior and expectations.

[2] Not, of course, the particular utterances previously encountered, but rather, the nature of the underlying rules that account for the set of previously occurring utterances in his experience.

[3] Whatever the theoretical difficulties associated with functional behaviorism (see Part III), the applied research it has generated in special education and in clinical psychology is much to be admired.

REFERENCES

Reich, Charles A. *The Greening of America.* New York: Bantam Books, 1970.

6 An Encounter Workshop for Language Teachers in a Bicultural Setting

This chapter outlines a program of in-service training for teachers and administrative school personnel, which is designed to foster a better understanding of the problems involved in the education of children from minority groups within an educational system that is defined and administered by the cultural interests of the dominant social or national community. Most parts of the world are faced with this situation, to a lesser or major extent, inasmuch as linguistic and cultural pluralism is a more usual pattern of nationhood than uniculturalism. In the United States, the region which constitutes the sociocultural focus of this proposed training program, major viable and dynamic linguistic/cultural minorities exist, the most notable being the Black ghetto of the inner city in large metropolitan areas, the Mexican Americans in the Southwest, the Puerto Rican population in New York, the Cuban immigrants in Miami City, and the various Amerindian groups throughout the North American continent.

In the last decade or so, we have witnessed a major upsurge of militant expression on the part of linguistic/cultural minority Americans, Afro-, Mexican-, Puerto Rican-, and Indian, giving us such slogans as Black Power, Chicano Power, and Red Power. While there are many obvious differences that distinguish the history and context of these various movements, they all share the common characteristic of being attempts at cultural revival and assertion in the face of a long history of repression and assimilation on the part of the dominant middle-class, white Anglo-Saxon culture.

One of the most important social devices used by a dominant culture in its attempt to acculturate and assimilate minority groups is, of course, the formal educational system represented by the schools. Teachers thus constitute primary agents, not only of socialization in the *en*culturation process of the children of the culturally dominant group, but also of the *ac*culturation process of the children of the cultural minority groups. Teachers, therefore, given the role that society relegates them to, as the transmitters of the dominant cultural values, tend to be conservative, and in the face of challenge by militants of minority groups, they become in effect reactionary agents, standing in the way of liberation from perceived cultural repression.

In the context of cultural conflict, the school becomes a battlefield reflecting the social reality of the community, and the teacher becomes the focus of opposing forces. To members of minority groups, the teacher has become a symbol of repression, an enemy to be feared and mistrusted, and the school an alien place to be left as soon as the law permits. Small wonder, then, that up to 80% of minority group children are high school dropouts. The vicious cycle of the economically underprivileged is thus perpetuated generation after generation, continuing to undermine the stability of society as a whole. The very institution that is supposed to establish and maintain stability and order in society thus becomes a barrier to them.

It is only recently that some awareness of the process just described has become widespread in American society, but it has already resulted in some very important changes in policy on the part of government and the educational establishment. The Bilingual Education Act under Title VII has fostered, in the past few years, the development of dozens of experimental programs throughout the country, representing a new recognition of the necessity of legitimatizing the aspirations of minority groups for the maintenance of their cultural heritage. The psychological climate in many schools in the Southwest that have large groups of Spanish-speaking children has changed from linguistic repression on the playground to, at least, linguistic tolerance, if not yet wholehearted approval.

Despite these visible signs of change, however, it cannot be said that the problems have been solved, or even that the wheels have been set in motion for their eventual solution. For instance, graduates of the largest and oldest bilingual elementary school in the country, Coral Way School in Dade County, Miami, overwhelmingly choose not to continue bilingual education in junior high school, despite the availability of such a program (Beebe, 1970). Furthermore, despite a burgeoning of research in a new vein on the part of linguists—sociolinguists—which shows how simplistic and uninformed teachers' conception is of Black English, there remains an apparently unshakeable conviction that it is an inferior mode of communication, unsuitable for the expression of ideas involved in school subjects (Bereiter and Engelmann, 1966; Kochman, 1969). There is taking place in educational circles a subtle but insidious shift from racial to ethnic prejudice, away from the Black man's biological entity, to his social entity, his language and culture. Prejudicial shifts of no less virulent form are to be expected in the case of the Mexican Americans and the Puerto Ricans, away from an outright linguistic repression, to cultural aspects of the individual's integrity, (cf., "They are a good and simple people; they like flowers and dancing; they are not ambitious to make money.", etc.)

We are dealing here with nothing less than outright ethnic prejudice in the traditional forms of American ethnocentrism. There is no evidence that a fundamental change has taken place in the melting pot policy of promoting The American Way of Life. There is no evidence that the educational establishment is ready to abdicate its role as an agent of assimilation for the dominant middle-class, white Anglo-Saxon culture. The American ideal of "equal opportunity for all" still presupposes the unstated condition, "for all who are willing and capable of becoming good Americans first." The recent Bilingual Education Act, the very symbol of a new attitude of tolerance toward cultural minorities, may, within the context of the old climate of ethnocentrism, become one more tool in the arsenal of an assimilatory agency. The Title VII program explicitly affirms the primary importance of *English*, and its main justification is the hope that it might help to prevent retardation in school performance. The current objectives of the American school system remain the same. Nowhere is the possibility raised that the various cultural minorities in the United States may have different objectives for an educational system. The possibility of allowing these cultural groups to define and evolve their own educational objectives is nowhere raised. And yet, it is doubtful that anything short of this can sustain a viable, dynamic culture and restore dignity to millions of "aliens" and alienated people in this country. For, just as the survival and evolution of the dominant American culture depends in large measure on its educational institutions, so does the survival of the Afro-American, Mexican American, and Amerindian cultures depend on educational institutions designed by them and for them within their cultural premises.

Until such time as the minority cultures gain sufficient political freedom to implement and evolve their own educational objectives, the concept of the bilingual school remains the least destructive alternative within the present sociopolitical reality. The problem that faces us in this endeavor is, *How can we evolve the bilingual school into a bicultural school*? Whatever Congress and educational administrators might say or do about this problem, its solution ultimately lies with the teacher and what he does in the classroom. A bicultural *policy* is a set of directives on pieces of paper, or something one makes speeches about, but it isn't a bicultural school. A bicultural school that is so in fact, rather than in policy, is a place where certain forms of transactions take place between teacher and pupil. The characteristics of these bicultural forms of interaction are different from those in a unilingual school or a unicultural bilingual school. To bring about the reality of a bicultural school, the teacher must know what these particular characteristics are, understand them in a personal and intimate way, and must, furthermore, consider them intrinsically valuable for himself, as well as for his pupils. To know them intellectually is not sufficient; he must want them, desire them, as a personal goal in life, as an enrichment of his self. To achieve bicultural transactional competence an individual must become a bicultural person. This goes for both the teacher and the pupil.

It should be noted at this point, that bilingualism is not the issue here. Our conception of the ideal bilingual overlaps with biculturalism, true, but, which comes first, bilingualism or biculturalism? It isn't useful to phrase the problem in these divisive terms, for the two processes are interrelated in their etiology. Research in this area, (e.g., Lambert, 1967), suggests that a *precondition* for the development of ideal bilingualism is an "integrative" orientation toward the second culture on the part of the learner. Similarly, for bicultural interaction to develop, there must exist on the part of the interactants a prior attitude of mutual acceptance, respect, and a feeling that the other's culture is worthwhile to acquire as one's own.

As is the case with bilingual performance, the ideal end product, that of achieving fully bicultural status, is not the issue, but rather the psychological climate that is favorable for its development and occurrence, for bicultural interaction can take place in the absence of either "perfect bilingualism" or "perfect biculturalism." For instance, as the unilingual, unicultural, Spanish-speaking child enters first grade, taught by a bilingual or semibilingual American teacher, a cultural confrontation takes place in the classroom. For meaningful transactions to occur, that confrontation must be transformed into an encounter. The pupil must want to become more "like the teacher," and the teacher must want to become more "like the pupil." As the weeks and months go by, they learn from each other and they grow together, each of them becoming more than what he was before. They now belong, in greater or lesser extent, to two cultures, even though neither of them may ever be perfectly bilingual or perfectly bicultural. This is the context of bicultural interaction we must strive for in the bilingual school.

Cultural Confrontation vs. Encounter

Cultures in contact may be in a state of confrontation as in Canada, Belgium, or India, or they may be in a state of encounter, as was the case in ancient Rome after the conquest of Greece, or is today the case in Finland, in Switzerland, in Israel, or in Japan. What is the difference?

Confrontation implies competition; encounter implies cooperation. In a competitive relationship, what one wins, the other loses; in a cooperative relationship, both are winners, and there are no losers. When two people interact, each of them must take certain personal risks: to address someone may mean a rebuff through the other's silence; to ask a favor may mean refusal; to reveal an attitude may mean condemnation; and so on. When the interlocutor isn't trusted, as is the case in confrontation or competition, one doesn't like to take many or significant risks; one must remain shielded and guarded. When the other is trusted, one can afford to take risks, to open up, to communicate, to encounter, to cooperate.

What leads to mutual trust?

The "safest" atmosphere is that in which the one values and admires the other and proves it by wanting to become like the other, the *culturally integrative orientation*. There is no way of faking this process by paying lip service to the other's "right to be different"; the diplomatic subterfuge is quickly discovered; it can be felt like a brick wall. No significant risk-taking will be attempted; no encounter, and no personally meaningful interaction.

Most of us have experienced at some time or other in our lives, the process of encountering someone, although in a competitive society such as ours, that wonderful experience is rare and the instances few and far between. We must search our memories way back, into early childhood, to recapture that taste of trust, safety, and freedom. As socialized adults, we have learned to be discreet, polite, cautious, self-reliant, strong, ambitious, successful, mature, outer-directed, task-involved, autonomous, dutiful, and of course, repressed, guarded, secretive, isolated, and alienated from each other.

Though our memory of the encounter process be distant, our longing for it remains strong and immediate. People throughout the country, of all ages and walks of life, have begun to form small artificial groups, in an attempt to get back together again. What distinguishes these basic encounter or sensitivity groups from natural groups such as the family and the social party, neighborhood, or church group, is the recognition of why they are there, and the members' agreement to attempt to interrelate by means of *a new social contract*: cooperation instead of competition, at the personal feeling level. Differences in feeling and attitude are not just tolerated or politely "respected"—in fact, they are frequently challenged, sometimes vigorously rejected, but the members commit themselves to protect each other's selfhood, to feel for each other, to make the other person's pain one's own, so that, should one make the other suffer, he will be causing his own suffering, and should he give pleasure to the other, he will contribute to his own delight; in short, to encounter rather than confront.

To contemplate the encountering way of life can be quite threatening to most of us. Is it really possible? Isn't it dangerous? It may even be immoral! Isn't it subversive to our American ideals? Won't it destroy ambition, the will to conquer nature, individuality, the very strongholds of a free, enterprising and entrepreneuring, economic, technological society that has brought us the highest standard of living in the world? With all this free talk of "love," what should happen to the blood ties of the family, the sacred bond of marriage, the pride in one's nation, the right to maintain and preserve the "interesting and valuable" differences among "foreign peoples" of the world?

To most people who join encounter-sensitivity groups, these philosophical and moral issues seem irrelevant, and even distasteful, a smoke screen of "head tripping" to prevent one from getting "down to the feeling level." At present, the members of encounter groups are a very distinct, self-selected group of people; they form a counterculture to the mainstream of American society. They are "odd balls" culturally even though significant numerically. Yet the message they sound finds a nostalgic echo in the longing of most of us, in our pursuit of greater happiness, human fellowship, and personal integrity. Increasing numbers of thoughtful and concerned people have come to believe that we cannot afford, we do not wish to, reject outright the possibility of a better, more rewarding way of life. We must examine this possibility and explore it *on our own terms*. This is the purpose of the encounter-transaction workshop, and in the present context, it focuses on bicultural education.

The encounter-transaction workshop (henceforth, ETW) is the entry of the "squares" into an area of endeavor hitherto claimed as the exclusive property of the "with-it generation." It is "head tripping cum feeling" and begins where the others have left off. The members of an encounter group are psychologically committed to its goals before they join; the persons who join an ETW are only committed to examine and explore these goals. How does it work?

The Structure of ETW

An ETW program centers around two types of activities: (A) a transactional analysis of the setting, coupled with an action program that introduces corrective measures in interpersonal behavior; (B) basic encounter experiences that explore and monitor the subjective psychological concomitants of the action program. The first type of activity is objectively analytical and is oriented toward overt actions. The second type of activity is subjectively analytical (not necessarily in the psychoanalytical sense) and is oriented toward inner feelings and attitudes. It is not "psychotherapy" in that it is not specifically designed to bring about reprieve from anxiety and "psychological problems." Rather, it is "honest psychological talk among lay equals," the kind of interchange that may take place between intimate friends. It is both analytically explorative and mutually succoring.

Most of the interchange in an ETW program takes place in small group sessions (5-10 people) held periodically throughout the academic year, under the direction of the program leader. These special sessions, each of which may last for several hours of intensive interaction, are held in the context of the day-to-day routine of the teacher's work and the various ongoing action programs attempted in connection with the ETW program. We shall now examine in greater detail the nature of these two activities.

Consider an analysis of the following conversation.

Daughter: Jimmy is here!
Mother: You haven't cleaned up your room.
Daughter: We still have to pick up Donna.
Mother: Mother is coming. And I still have to shop for some groceries.
Daughter: She'll understand. Besides, she isn't that well organized herself.
Mother: But you promised!
Daughter: Oh, but you don't understand! Last time, he got very mad, because traffic is so heavy at this time of day.
Mother: Oh, he is such a finicky! What's wrong with Steve, anyway? He is so much nicer.
Daughter: He doesn't like Bernie.
Mother: I thought Donna was going with Archie?
Daughter: The Redmen are playing at Queen's this weekend.
Mother: Mother will never understand. I'll have to speak to Dad again.
Daughter: Oh, all right! I'll make my bed, but you do the rest.
Mother: All right. Hurry up!

Ordinary conversation is highly elliptical. To understand this interchange, we must supply a great deal of information that is *implicit*. Some of this information is culturally available, and some of it is situation specific. For instance, Mother's concern is understandable only if we know the critical attitude which a mother-in-law can have *vis-à-vis* her son's wife, and the anxiety on the latter's part about making a good impression. Furthermore, we must be aware that granddaughters do not share this concern, but they in turn are much more anxious about how their boyfriends feel, a concern not generally reciprocated by mothers. In addition, we could guess that cleaning up one's room has been a chronic problem in this family and that Mother has some leverage on Daughter by threatening to complain to Dad, the disciplinarian with whom Daughter would rather avoid another clash. Other aspects of this interchange need situation specific information to make them understandable. For instance, we must know that Steve is another boy with whom Daughter has gone out in the past; that Bernie is a substitute for Archie, the latter being Donna's regular boyfriend; that Archie is a football player with the Redmen, and so on. All this remains unstated and implicit, since Mother and Daughter share a common background experience and knowledge, and there is no need to state these facts. They are "understood."

In addition to sharing background knowledge, both cultural and situation specific, the transactants have in common certain background expectations and engage in certain specific sorts of inferential reasoning. For instance, Daughter knows that Mother expects her to help in house cleaning chores, especially at a time of crisis (e.g., when mother-in-law shows up). Mother knows that Daughter expects her to ease up on her house cleaning demands when Daughter finds herself in a crisis situation (e.g., grouchy Jimmy is waiting). These are unstated background expectations that regulate their interaction and without which each person's appeal wouldn't make sense: "Jimmy is here!" (therefore you can't expect me to keep my promise to clean up the room); "Mother is coming!" (therefore you are supposed to drop everything to help me straighten up the house). Both interactants must in addition engage in inferential reasoning that is peculiar and appropriate to the nature of the particular transaction in progress. For instance, someone who isn't organized herself can't be critical of others for being like they are . . . so, "She'll understand." Note that this kind of "can't" isn't a physical impossibility, or even a logical one, but more like an injunction that she "ought not." On the other hand, the fact that Donna is going with Bernie rather than Archie ("The Redmen are playing at Queen's this weekend.") is to be deduced on logical premises, given the knowledge that (a) Archie plays for the Redmen and (b) the Redmen are away at Queen's—*ergo* Archie can't take Donna out.

Thus, to understand the process of commonplace, everyday conversation, our analysis will have to deal with implicit, unstated information of a cultural and situation-specific sort, with shared background expectations, and with several types of inferential reasoning. But this is just the beginning. Why do Mother and Daughter have a disagreement in the first place? How is the disagreement resolved, and why is the halfway solution acceptable to both parties? What else goes on between Mother and Daughter, besides the overt argument about cleaning up the room? (cf., "But you promised!" and "What's wrong with Steve, anyway?").

To resolve these issues we must widen our circle of analysis to take in individual factors such as Mother's and Daughter's "personalities," their personal construct and reality, physical and subcultural factors such as the family's socioeconomic status and religious affiliation, their conception of the role of parent, boyfriend, mother-in-law, and their conception of social institutions such as the family and marriage, and of social practices such as dating; and, ultimately, moral and philosophical premises within which all the previous factors are embedded.

Put in this context, a full analysis of even the simplest verbal interchange is a quite formidable undertaking. And yet, it is difficult to escape the conclusion that some such analysis, of at least this complexity, is made by an individual in everyday life, in commonplace conversations. But, of course, the analysis is done "unconsciously," automatically, effortlessly, and it becomes prohibitive only when we attempt to make explicit all the steps that make up this complex human activity. A child of four has developed and internalized an extremely complex system of rules we call "grammar" that enables him to produce and understand an infinite number of grammatical sentences. This knowledge is almost totally unconscious and is arrived at seemingly effortlessly, naturally.

From a practical point of view, there is a great deal to be gained from explicit descriptions of implicit or unconscious processes, even though these descriptions remain partial and incomplete. Consider the technological achievements made possible by an incomplete, partial, and even internally contradictory description of the physical universe. We do not need to have a complete description of communication processes in order to be able to either improve their quality or control them in some ways. It is likely, however, that the better, more valid, and more complete our description is, the better our chances will be to affect them in ways we deem advantageous. This is the motivation and the anticipated payoff for doing the kind of analytic activity we are discussing.

The structure within which the analysis is to be made has already been presented in the previous discussion. Thus, we shall be concerned, among other things, with identifying differences in background expectations and in inferential reasoning between the participants.

Background expectations, particularly those that are culturally defined, tend to form clusters, such that given expectations r, s, t, it is more likely to find expectations u, v, w cooccurring in that cluster, than, say, a, b, c. For instance, given that the receiver is an adult male, he is likely to respond favorably to a request such as, "Pardon me, do you have a match?", when accosted by a stranger on the street. Similarly, a pupil in the lower grades may make of the teacher a request that he be allowed to go to the toilet, which he would not make of his parent at home or a stranger on the street. Or again, a school principal's comment on the teacher's behavior in the classroom has different import for her than a similar comment addressed to her by a pupil, fellow teacher, or assistant teacher. These clusters of expectations form what we call *role behavior*, and this is to an extent culturally defined. Transactions are conditioned to a greater or lesser degree by these socially defined role behaviors. Differences in role expectations often lead to disagreements in conversations. Unrecognized differences in expectations are the many sources of so-called "misunderstandings" in communication between people. Consider the following interchange:

> Teacher: Johnny doesn't seem to respond to any form of punishment I administer in the classroom.
> Father: I can't understand that. At home, he doesn't dare disobey me.

Johnny happens to respond extremely well to physical punishment. Father's puzzlement comes about through the fact that ·he misunderstands the teacher's reference to "any form of punishment I administer," failing to realize that physical punishment is implicitly excluded from "any form" due to her own (or the school's) definition of her role behavior.

Similarly, differences in inferential reasoning may bring about exasperated misunderstanding. Consider this familiar situation:

Teacher: Blake, I told you there is to be *no talking* during the examination. Please, hand in your paper.
Pupil: But, Sir, I only asked him for an eraser!
Teacher: I said there is going to be *no talking.*

A dramatization of Blake's reasoning may go something like this: the teacher said "no talking" because it is forbidden to exchange information during the test; but asking for an eraser is not cheating on the exam, hence that is permissible. The teacher's reasoning was, of course, something different: I don't want verbal interchange of any kind, since I won't know whether they are asking for an eraser or exchanging information about the test. The older pupil who understands the teacher's reasoning would instead raise his hand and make the request of the teacher.

In the following example, two simultaneous conversations are recorded, the overt interchange and the very different internal verbalizations that accompany it:

Principal: Please sit down, John. I received a phone call this morning from Lester Wardaugh's father. (He must think my office is an awful mess. I know how particular he is about neatness.)
Teacher: Oh? What about? (Wardaugh is on the school board. He must have complained about something. I'm gonna get the treatment. Old Joe (the principal) is getting soft in his old age.)
Principal: It's about our summer travel program. He thinks he can get the money for us, but there's a hitch. (Wardaugh has always taken a lot of interest in our school. I hope he can convince the Washington people that our school could do a better job than Uni High. Too bad they decided to compete against us for the funds.)
Teacher: Actually, I've decided not to lead the group this summer. I'm going to enroll in summer school at the University.(A hitch indeed! Wardaugh is furious at me for flunking his lazy son. I won't give good old Joe the pleasure of forcing me out.)
Principal: Gee, that's too bad, John. I understand your motives, but it puts me in kind of a pickle. (What's eating him, anyway? He hates my guts for not being a pedantic S.O.B. like himself.)
Teacher: I'm sorry. Joe, but that degree is important to me. You know how

it is. (Actually, it would've been real nice to go to Europe. Mabel would've enjoyed it too. But I'm not gonna prostitute myself for Wardaugh. Lester wouldn't do a stitch of work all year.)

Principal: I understand, John. I'll think of something. (With John out, Wardaugh will never get the money now! He had to conk out on me at the last moment!)

This may seem like an extreme example, but actually we have no data to assess the relative frequency with which "misunderstandings" of this sort occur in everyday life. The example shows how, within the context of a particular set, one may be led to formulate expectations and inferences leading to interpretations of the other's utterances that are totally different from those intended. In this case, the expectations and the drawn inferences are both role conditioned and personal (individual): Wardaugh, *the school board member*, has certain powers that he can use to induce Joe, *the principal*, to act unfavorably against John, *the teacher*.

It would appear, then, that one strategy which might prove useful in an attempt to improve the transactional climate in a particular setting is to isolate the important role dyadic interactions that occur in that setting and to proceed with a detailed specification of the expectations and inferential behavior that are typical for them. One way of doing this is through analysis of real or hypothetical interchanges. For instance, a teacher and a principal can tape-record some of their daily verbal interchanges and participate in the analysis done by the group as a whole. An additional method is to tape-record a dyadic interchange produced by "role playing," in which one teacher, say, plays the role of a principal, and another that of a parent. "Role reversals" can sharply point up differences in background expectations such as, for instance, a teacher playing the role of a pupil and vice versa.

The number of role dyadic interactions in a school setting can be quite large: teacher-teacher, teacher-assistant teacher, teacher-principal, teacher-pupil, parent-teacher, etc., etc. It is not essential that every possible role dyad be analyzed as part of the ET workshop. Furthermore, much of this kind of analytic activity can be done by the expectations are primary sources of so-called "misunderstandings" in communication between people. Consider the it can be used by the individual *when he chooses to do so*. This may seem a very artificial, ponderous, and cumbersome way of engaging in conversations, but the intention is not to eliminate spontaneity, but to develop sensitivity and awareness. To achieve this goal, the individual must develop methods of obtaining feedback from the interlocutor that would give him information about the other's assumptions, presuppositions, expectations, and inferences. Consider, for example, another version of the interchange between the principal and the teacher presented above. The original parts of the conversation are italicized to set them apart from the new material:

Principal: *Please sit down, John.* Sorry about the mess; it's been a hectic day.
Teacher: Oh, I know how it is.
Principal: *I received a phone call this morning from Lester Wardaugh's father.*
Teacher: *Oh? What about?* Lester hasn't been doing any work in my class. I suppose Wardaugh is unhappy about my flunking him.
Principal: Oh, it was nothing personal at all. He didn't even mention it. Anyway, that is something between you and Lester. *It's about our summer travel program. He thinks he can get the money for us, but there's a hitch.*
Teacher: Oh, oh! Wardaugh is on the school board, isn't he? Is he trying to put some pressure on you?
Principal: Oh, no, not at all. I mean, Uni High has decided to compete with us for the money, but Wardaugh is trying to convince the Washington people that we have better supervisory personnel.
Teacher: Actually, I have been thinking . . . .

And so on. It is hard to believe that John would have persisted in his plans to withdraw from the program. What made the difference? Note that part of their previously internal and unreported verbalizations are now reported, so that *second guessing* diminishes in importance. Note also that the principal is careful to counteract the role expectations that the teacher may have had about a school board member exercising improper influence.

At this point, one may ask what one can do to improve the transactional climate when the problem is not one of "misunderstanding," but, rather, genuine disagreement about means, methods, and ends. While this question is also quite pertinent to an objective analysis, it touches more intimately on such psychological factors as attitudes, conflicts, perceived threat and insecurity, trust, ego strength, maturity, and the like, and it will be more conveniently handled in the next section, to which we now proceed.

The Encounter Process

An explanation of some event, process, phenomenon, etc., constitutes a set of statements or assertions arranged in some sequence whose structure follows certain rules. One important difference between "good" and "bad" explanations is that if we act upon the premises of the good one we are more likely to achieve some goal, such as change or control of other or similar events. To put it in reverse, an explanation that gives us that power of change and control is better than one that does not. There are numerous psychological explanations and theories about people, how and why they think and act in the way they do. We do not wish to get bogged down in polemics about which are the really "true" explanations. Let us simply agree that we shall accept as "working hypotheses" certain psychological accounts of interactions, as long as they seem to give us the capability of changing and affecting communicative acts in ways we deem desirable—their "truth" or ultimate validity is of no concern.

Here, then, are a series of statements of a psychological nature that purport to describe how people may think, feel, and act in a role dyadic interaction. (Remember that here, as in previous analyses, it is not claimed that these are conscious, explicitly recognized processes.)

The Private-Public Dichotomy

(a) As a person, I consist of two parts: a private self which I feel consciously as the subject or actor of my thoughts and actions, and a public self, "me," of which others are aware.

(b) In the eyes of others, my private self, the "I" or ego, is to be held responsible for the actions of my public self of which they are aware, the "me."

(c) Society (parents, friends, neighbors, colleagues, employers, "the law," etc.) has established certain rules to which people ought to conform. When my public self, the "me," conforms to these rules, the private self, the "I" which is responsible, is rewarded in various ways (money, praise, friendship, etc.). Similarly, when the "me" departs from these rules, the "I" is punished in various ways (imprisonment, social isolation, disapproval, etc.).

(d) If I am to maximize the rewards society has to offer and minimize its punishments, "I" must put the best "me" forward.

Now, if these are indeed some major premises upon which an individual acts in his mental and interpersonal behavior, there are certain consequences that will follow, which we ought to examine.

A. *The Danger of Discovery.* Any policy or strategy, which involves the "I" putting the best "me" forward confronts the "I" with the ever present danger of being exposed as a fraud, with dire consequences (loss of acceptance and friendship, ostracism, retribution, etc.). The "I," therefore, labors under this constant stress and fear. For instance, if "me" is presented for others' benefit as religious, law-abiding, honest, genuine, friendly, loving, pure, compassionate, charitable, etc., while "deep down," the "I" knows that it isn't like that, it must always be watchful, be continually on its guard, lest others "see through" the "me" and withold the rewards which the "I" craves. It follows from this that others become a source of threat; they are the "Inquisition." An impenetrable barrier is thus set up between oneself and others, whether the other be a stranger like the customs officer past whom one is trying to smuggle something, or an intimate like a spouse from whom one is trying to hide "selfish" thoughts and desires. Trust between two people cannot develop while one is trying, through subterfuge, to "con" the other. In addition to the stress due to the danger of discovery, there is added the no lesser stress of loneliness, the feeling of being "by oneself," rather than "with another."

B. *The Cancer of Guilt.* If one looks more closely at the "I," one discovers that it too contains an internal barrier and is divided against itself. Freud popularized the three-way division of the "ego," "super-ego," and "id," standing respectively for the self, the authority representative, and the biologically given urges. Religious spokesmen emphasize the "good" and the "evil" within us. Some psychologists speak of the "real ego" image versus the "ideal ego" image. However one chooses to conceptualize the divisiveness of the self, one is faced by the sad ravages wrought by the opposing forces within us: guilt, self-hatred, ambivalence, conflict, self-punishment, self-denial, etc.

It is important to realize that, so long as the individual is going to act consistently upon the premises outlined above (under statements *a* to *d*), *there is no solution to the impasse*: it is a classic instance of what psychologists have come to call "the double bind." The argument can be stated this way. Society sets up a distinction between the "I" and the "me." It furthermore sets up rules which govern how the "me" ought to be. The individual internalizes this division, and the system of differential rewards and punishment that is designed to insure its continuance. Now, the individual is caught in a double bind of, "damned if you're right and damned if you're wrong," since if he plays society's game of putting the best "me" forward, he is confronted with guilt and self-condemnation, even though he minimizes the danger of discovery by being a good con artist; on the other hand, if he tries to avoid the guilt of duplicity, by letting his true self show, society will punish him for not being as it prescribes one ought to be. The individual caught in this game trap can never win.

C. *The Ways of Liberation*. There are essentially three solutions to this double bind which men have offered over the ages. Let us examine each in turn.

(i) *The Way of the Straight Path*. Man is born with "animal" instincts which, if allowed free expression, would destroy him. Society establishes rules of behavior designed to supress, counteract, and keep in check these destructive tendencies. "Conscience" is the internal censor-watchdog (whether God-given or created by society) and punishes infractions not externally detected by society. Neuroses are symptoms of the internal conflict between the animal urges fighting for expression and the counteraction of conscience trying to keep them in check. Guilt feelings, unhappiness, and the extremes of depression are caused by wayward actions, feelings, and thoughts. Three methods are recognized for handling these negative consequences. One is atonement and restitution for wrongdoing which gives the individual a reprieve and a next chance; a second is the strengthening of the "voice of conscience," through discipline and dedication, which allows the individual to resist temptations; and the third, much more recent in history, is that proposed by Freud and the psychoanalytic movement, which consists of weakening the unreasonable demands of a stern conscience run wild with power, and the greater acceptance of the biological urges within us—a kind of midway solution, a practical compromise.

(ii) *The Way of Self-Actualization*. Man's instincts are not necessarily destructive and can be channeled into ways which would satisfy both the individual and society. Various lines of thought exist, concerning which channel or channels would lead to this mutually acceptable *modus vivendi*: finding and constructing "meaning" in life, actualizing our inner potentials, learning how to love oneself and others, etc. The various existential philosophies, and the motive-rationale behind the current "small group movement" (encounter, sensitivity, Gestalt therapy, etc.) concerned with ways of experiencing, can all be classified in this category. The emphasis has shifted from a medical view of neurosis and guilt to "alienation" (from oneself, from human fellowship) or loneliness, which is attributed to the artificial creation by the socialized individual of a separation between how one really is and how one ought to be. The solution proposed is, then, abandoning notions of how one ought to be, and finding out how one really is, substituting the latter for the former as a goal of life. At the same time, it is asserted that being "how one really is" is not merely the only sane solution, but also that it is not inimical to a well-functioning society.

(iii) *The Awakening from the Illusion of the Social Game*. This solution for the double bind is found in Eastern philosophies, especially in Zen Buddhism and Taoism. It is only recently that these ideas have come to be popularized in the West. There are many interpretations and versions of the "Eastern Ways of Liberation," and we shall discuss only one of these, as interpreted in the writings of Alan Watts.

The reality of the distinction between the "I" and the "me" is denied and is viewed as a social fiction, an illusion encouraged by society as a means of controlling the individual. The assertion of the existence of "I" as a cognizant, responsible subject-actor makes it possible for society to maintain a system of differential rewards and punishment, both externally through social sanctions and internally through the "voice of conscience." In fact, it is asserted, no such distinction exists, the "I" being an abstraction of the total "me," and indeed, of the environment and the world. The illusion of the "I" as an actor (and, hence, an agent to be held accountable and responsible for one's actions, feelings, and thoughts) is achieved by a deliberate repression of the total "me-environment," by ignoring it—an act of "ignore-ance" as well as ignorance. Loneliness and alienation are not caused by an *actual* separation—between the "I" and the "me," between the "me" and the "other," between life and death, but rather by the *illusion* of a separation, hence the way of liberation from this misery is to awaken to this subterfuge perpetrated by society, to realize it is illusory, not real. Unhappiness, the fear of death, the struggle between good and evil, the striving to be better, are paranoid constructions, and liberation from them comes about by realizing that they are illusions, not realities.

This philosophy, unlike the first two discussed, specifically denies the necessity of acting upon the major premises contained in statements *a* to *d* above. There is no solution to the double bind, so long as the "I"–"me" fiction is retained. Guilt is not possible, if there is no "I" to be held responsible for how the organism *is being* (does, thinks, feels, are terms which necessarily retain the actor-action dichotomy).

This solution to the double bind is not to be equated with the Western scientific premise of "determinism" or other Eastern philosophies of "fatalism." On the surface, there are points of similarity. Determinism views the organism as a machine (in the formal, mathematical sense) controlled ("programmed") by environmental contingencies interacting with biological structures and properties; it thus denies "free will," "consciousness," and the like, treating these as "mental" fictions. Fatalism is the mystical belief in a preordained order, which individual choice and decision making cannot affect or change. On the other hand, the Zen Buddhist and Taoist metaphysics denies the validity of such dichotomies as "determinism" versus "free will," "preordained order" versus "individual choice." The concept of determinism makes sense only in conjunction with or in contradistinction to the concept of "free will": in effect, one must first accept the *possibility* of the actor-action model of the "free will" hypothesis before one can reject it in favor of the deterministic hypothesis. But in Zen Buddhism and Taoism, the actor-agent model is not accepted as meaningful, relevant, hence possible; it is seen as a pseudoquestion, and consequently, the determinism-free will issue never arises.

It is for this reason that if everyone became "liberated," the world and society wouldn't suddenly and drastically change, since the world and society already are the way they are, not by anyone's "doing," but because they cannot be what they are not. Society is not an "artificial" system set up against nature; it is part of nature. Sanctions that men "set up" to "control" each other are not "artificial" rules to thwart "natural" urges, they are part of man's environment, and they will, of course, continue that way; otherwise, they wouldn't exist in the first place. The only essential difference between the "liberated one" and those who are not, is their *attitude*—toward the self/environment dichotomy, the paranoia "against" death, the illusion of alienation, the fiction of the "I" as the house divided against itself. This difference in attitude will certainly make a difference, since men who labor under the illusion that they are unhappy and alienated *have* neurotic symptoms and *are* at war with themselves, their fellow men and the world. Men who do not have this fiction *cannot have* neurotic symptoms and *cannot be* at war. It is, thus, not a question of choice, but a statement of what is.

This third interpretation of the ways of liberation from the double bind is more abstract and general than the first two, the latter being subsumed under it. For practical purposes, it would seem better for the individual to adopt one of them, or some version of it, as a working hypothesis upon which he can act consistently, than to wait for a theoretical resolution. Whichever interpretation is adopted, it will enable the individual to become more analytic about his interpersonal interactions. Furthermore, even if we wish to assume that if one interpretation is correct, the others must be wrong, it is still possible that acting consistently on any one of the interpretations may lead to improvement in one's relationships with others; and, in addition, it provides the individual with further evidence upon which to make future choices.

What does it mean "to act consistently and analytically" on some premise or interpretation? Another way of putting it is to say that the individual must be explicitly aware of his situation, psychical as well as interpersonal. For instance, what is the nature of the social game he is playing with others, or with a particular individual? What kind of a contractual arrangement does he have? What are the rules that govern his interactions? This kind of analysis can reveal the self-contradictory nature of many of our activities, and while such revelation does not necessarily enable a person to change, it would seem to be a precondition for change, and in addition, such a realization may reduce the distress that accompanies the feeling of being moved by blind forces.

Let us take a concrete illustration. A teacher may genuinely and firmly believe that bilingual education should be used as a means of acculturation, given the fact that her Spanish-speaking pupils are going to grow up to be in the American scene, and, hence, must adopt white, middle-class standards, if they are going to be successful in life. She is encountering a great deal of trouble in her task; the pupils show no real desire to learn English beyond certain rudiments of everyday commonplace communication; they show no real progress in reading and writing; their interest in history and arithmetic is slight; they do spotty homework; they are unenthusiastic and unfriendly; they show no real ambition to achieve and get ahead. She has tried being friendly and "understanding"; she learned to be fluent in Spanish, and even paid a few goodwill visits to the homes of some of her pupils. But, year after year, the fruits of her teaching remain very modest and unsatisfactory. She has reached a frustrating and incomprehensible impasse. What can she do?

The first step in an analytic approach is to examine objectively the premises upon which she is acting. She may begin with the background assumptions and presuppositions of three of her central concepts—the American scene, middle-class standards, being successful in life—and the inferential reasoning that links them into a proposition: (a) they are going to grow up in the American scene; (b) given the fact that one is going to grow up in the American scene, it follows, therefore, that he must adopt middle-class values; (c) to be successful in life, one must adopt middle-class values.

The next step is to get feedback from the pupils to see what their premises are about these issues. Two possibilities now arise: (a) pupils share the same premises, or (b) pupils do not share the same premises, and presumably, she can now identify the important differences.

If the case is (a), she now must examine whether her interactions with the pupils are interpreted by them in the same way as she interprets them, namely that what she does in the classroom and outside is designed to and does contribute to the objectives of their shared premises. If their interpretation is different, or if alternative (b) is the case, then she is going to realize in a more profound way than she has until then why it is that her teaching has remained unsuccessful. On the basis of this knowledge, she can introduce some changes into her activities, specifically designed as corrective measures.

Suppose, for instance, that José figures it this way: "I cannot become a true North American unless I think and act like one. If I do, my family and friends will consider me strange, and I am going to lose them. O.K. But, now, if I try to really become a North American, like my cousin, Pedro, and maybe even marry an American girl and live in an American neighborhood, they're not going to accept me, 'cause my name is Spanish, my skin is dark, my family lives in the slums, etc. So, where will I be? Nowhere! That's not for me! Teach is not going to make an American out of me. The hell with school! I'm gonna go work and have fun with the boys."

And suppose Ramirez figures it this way: "It would be a good idea to do well in school, graduate, and get a good job, and make more money than José, and live in a bigger house, and have a new car. But, why do I need to know all that stuff about American history and that poetry stuff, and write all those compositions in English. Ugh! And, Teach isn't interested in us anyway. She pretends to talk like us; her Spanish is pretty good, actually, but then she won't even give Rogelio a good strapping for coming late every day. She doesn't give a damn! If I could only graduate without having to do all that homework, and get a good job, and . . . . "

Writing hypothetical accounts such as these is itself a good exercise for showing up one's misunderstandings or ignorance of the other. In this case, my own misconceptions would be shown up by having "José" and "Ramirez" and "Rogelio" and "Pedro" comment on them.

Continuing in this vein, the teacher would now set up new and clarified contractual arrangements between herself and her pupils, or Spanish assistant teacher, or teacher colleague, or principal, or parents. The content of these new "contracts" would depend on her needs, values, wishes, as well as those of the other party. She may not wish or be able to become bicultural herself, in which case she cannot make her pupils bicultural and achieve bicultural communication with them, but as long as her relationship with the other is clarified and does not masquerade under false pretenses, the two parties can still perceive each other as being of mutual benefit, within the limits of the contract. People can tolerate differences for the sake of mutual interest, so long as the arrangement is clearly recognized and entered into *voluntarily*. In the absence of both explicitness and voluntary participation, such interaction is tainted by mistrust and perceived as manipulation or subversion.

The setting up of new, explicit, and voluntary contracts requires honesty and equality. The two are preconditions for building trust. Honesty involves analytic self-examination as well as risk-taking, for if one isn't honest with oneself, the other person, not knowing which of your actions and feelings are deliberate and which are "unconscious," will interpret contradictions as dishonest intent and dissimulation. Equality presupposes respect and acceptance, and the realization that most of the values we so dearly cherish are culturally given, not immutable truths of nature. This realization, in turn, presupposes an analytic understanding of our concept of the self, our knowledge of the nature of guilt, our definition of what constitutes responsibility, and the ultimate metaphysics to which we unconsciously subscribe.

In the past, two different approaches have been used in the study of human "communication." On the one hand, academic disciplines such as psychology, applied linguistics, and sociology have given us a tradition of "objective analyses" and a formalized language of theory, within which hypotheses are formulated and checked against certain empirical consequences, using the "scientific" or experimental method. On the other hand, sensitivity training laboratories and basic encounter groups also deal with the problem of communication, both with the self and the other, but from a very different perspective; emphasis is placed on the subjective aspects of experiencing the communication as an interpersonal transaction of feelings, agreements and disagreements, sympathy, support, hostility, threat, trust, and the like. Traditionally, these two approaches to communication have not only remained distinct and separate, but they were seen as mutually exclusive and incompatible. The "scientific" method did not admit concepts that had no objectively definable parameters, and excluded from its input evidence that was not observable under "controlled" conditions. Those concerned with feelings and experiencing, felt constrained and frustrated under the requirements imposed by the experimental method. "Two cultures" of discourse and activity have thus developed in recent years, each viewing the other with mistrust and suspicion. The encounter-transaction workshop represents a "third culture" activity, different from the other two, yet drawing upon both. The three words in this expression encapsulize its focus and method: "encounter" reflects the fact that a different social contract (see below) defines the interpersonal behavior of the group participants; "transaction" not only represents the main concern of the study program, its content and focus, but draws attention to the process itself, which includes a new way of being present to others, of encountering them; "workshop" is intended as a distinguishing feature from "course" or "seminar," and is a way of emphasizing the self-exploratory and participatory nature of the activity.

Some explanation is in order as to the meaning of social contract as used here. All transactions between people are governed by some set of rules or regulations, either recognized or implicit, that may be called *the social contract*. Everyday commonplace conversation takes place within the context of such participatory rules that specify such things as what one may talk about, in what way, and under which circumstances. For instance, the extent to which one overtly renders internal verbalizations depends on the formality level of the interaction (how intimately the conversants know each other, whether other listeners are present, etc.) and the degree of risk-taking they are ready to engage in (how much they trust each other, whether they are engaged in cooperation or competition, etc.). In sensitivity and encounter groups, a "cultural island" is established, in which the social contract governing interactions is made explicitly different from "the outside" of everyday life: honesty is mandatory, feelings must be expressed, self-disclosure is encouraged, growth-producing confrontations are attempted, nonverbal physical contact is deliberately engaged in, and so forth. The success of the group experience is defined in terms of the extent to which the individual develops the capacity to relate to others in the group, in the ways specified by the "artificial" social contract. In the encounter-transaction workshop, no specific social contract is set forth as the "desirable" way of interacting and toward which the individual is supposed to aspire for his interpersonal growth. Instead, the participants are encouraged to explore interpersonal transactions under various social contract obligations as defined by role dyads. To do so, they must first learn how to identify in explicit terms the sets of rules that define a particular role dyadic interaction as experienced in their daily lives. Once this is successfully accomplished, they can then experiment with changes in some of the specific rules. For instance, a teacher might wish at one time to decrease the formality level that characterizes his typical interaction with the principal and, at another time, he might wish to *increase* the formality level of his typical interaction with a teacher-aide. In the former case, greater expression of feelings will take place; in the latter case, less intimacy is wished. The success of the encounter-transaction workshop will be measured, not by the capacity to adhere to any specified social contract, but by the extent to which the individual comes to develop the ability to bring about desired changes in some specified aspect of an existing relationship outside the workshop. The special and artificial contract in the ETW derives from the fact that it makes possible such exploratory activity, without the usual social consequences that accompany such activities outside the group.

REFERENCES

Bereiter, Carl and Engelmann, Siegfried. *Teaching Disadvantaged Children in the Preschool*. Englewood Cliffs, N.J.: Prentice-Hall, 1966.

Bales, R. F. *Personality and Interpersonal Behavior*. New York: Holt, Rinehart, and Winston, 1970.

Egan, Gerald. *Encounter: Group Processes for Interpersonal Growth*. Belmont, Calif.: Brooks/Cole (Wadsworth), 1970.

Ellis, Albert and Harper, R. A. *A Guide to Rational Living*. Hollywood, Calif.: Wilshire Book Co., 1961 (8721 Sunset Blvd). (Also available from the Institute for Rational Living, 45 E. 65th St., N. Y. 10021).

Fromm, Erich. *The Art of Loving*. New York: Harper & Row (Harper Colophon), 1962.

Garfinkel, Harold. *Studies in Ethnomethodology*. Englewood Cliffs, N. J.: Prentice-Hall, 1968.

Goffman, Erving. *Interaction Ritual*. Garden City, N. Y.: Doubleday (Anchor Books), 1967.

Jakobovits, L. A. *Foreign Language Learning*. Rowley, Mass.: Newbury House Publishers, 1970a.

Kochman, Thomas. "Black English in the Classroom. Department of Linguistics, Northeastern Illinois State College, 1969 (Mimeo.).

Lambert, W. E. "A Social Psychology of Bilingualism." *The Journal of Social Issues, 23*, 1967, 91-109. (And other articles in that issue.)

Rogers, C. R. *Freedom to Learn*. Columbus, Ohio: Charles E. Merrill, 1969.

Schutz, W. C. *Joy*. New York: Grove Press, 1967.

Searle, J. R. *Speech Acts*. Cambridge, England and New York: Cambridge University Press, 1969.

Smith, A. G. (ed.). *Communication and Culture*. New York: Holt, Rinehart, and Winston, 1966.

Steinberg, D. and Jakobovits, L. A. (eds.). *Semantics: An Interdisciplinary Approach in Philosophy, Linguistics, and Psychology*. Cambridge and New York: Cambridge University Press, 1971.

Tyler, S. A. (ed.). *Cognitive Anthropology*. New York: Holt, Rinehart, and Winston, 1969.

Watts, A. W. *Psychotherapy East & West*. New York: Ballantine Books, 1969.

Part Three: The Theoretical Context

7 The Analysis of Transactional Engineering Competence

The medium in which formal education is transacted is the conversational mode: teacher talks to students and students talk to the teacher and to each other. Sure there are textbooks, instructional materials and machines, assignments, exams and tests, but these are tools the teacher uses in the school context in order to supplement and facilitate his teaching. It remains true, nevertheless, that the primary conception of teaching in mass educational systems is through teacher-student *talk*: the lecture, the demonstration, the explanation, the question-answer interchange, the inspiration, the admiration, the expression, the examination. *To teach is to tell; to learn is to listen.*

The concept of teaching as conversation is a truism, a platitude. We like to start from platitudes for two reasons. One is that, this way, we are sure that we are together when we start. How can you disagree about truisms? The second reason is that platitudes *are* truisms: they have been sufficiently validated by ordinary experience to serve as truisms. In practice, it is more accurate to say that platitudes are forgotten truisms. Think of some current platitudes that are being widely discussed today: God is Dead; Equal Opportunity and Justice For All; The Protection of Privacy and Individual Freedom; Know Thy Body, Know Thyself; To Love the Other, You Must Love Yourself; To Search Is Not to Find; The Whole is More Than the Sum of Its Parts; Particle is Wave, Wave is Particle; Good Implies Evil, and Evil Implies Good. We are certain you can extend this list or make up a new one. (Do it now, just for fun!)

The originator of a platitude (really: a truism, later to become a platitude) is a man of genius. He is a respected public figure, a well-known scientist, a much-read author. The observation his statement represents is so penetrating, the arguments he presents to support it are so convincing, its validity is so undeniable, that it comes to be accepted by others as, first, a marvelous discovery, and later, an unquestioned truism. At that point it becomes a fashionable topic of conversation and reaches the status of a platitude. When the original discovery has become a platitude, the truism which it embodies has been forgotten. No one remembers to read the original justifying account of the discovery. New initiates (e.g., students, perusers of textbooks and other critical, review, or summarizing books and articles) no longer have access to the primary validating justification. They never come to learn the truism, the marvelous truth; they can only report the platitude, rote fashion, without the validating experiential meaning that has made it worth learning in the first place.

What are the truisms embodied in the current platitudinous conceptions of teaching as conversation?

There are many aspects about *talk* (talking together, conversing) that we should remember in this analysis. Like the fact that *talk* (the use of language) is much more than communication. We once heard Paul Goodman make a statement of the following approximate form:

> When I talk I don't *think*, not usually. I don't plan, I don't try to communicate, I don't try to transmit messages. Right now, as I'm talking to you, I haven't got a single thought in my head. I just talk. Humans are chattering monkeys. That's all.

We felt, at the time, an immense relief. He echoed beautifully and simply what we had been refusing to admit, that our work in psycholinguistics (the *old* kind) had remained sterile under an antiquated and false conception, the communication model of language, and the very simplicity of his statement, the direct corroboration of the truism it contained, liberated us right then and there, in the auditorium with bad acoustics, of the intellectual tyranny and poverty of the communication model of language. We recalled Austin's (1962) remarkable little book, *How to Do Things with Words,* and we immediately formed the concept, *How to Do Things with Talk.*

Aha! Talking is doing things. It is to communicate. To greet. To flatter. To dissimulate. To attack. To caress. To stimulate. To inform. To express. To fill the time. To sniff out. To make ties. To break ties. To insult. To promise. To accuse. To deny. To defend. To gain status. To save face. To protect. We couldn't stop. Our minds were feverish. To cajole. To agree. To disagree. To manipulate. To convince. To reason. To report. To teach. Hey, wait a minute! TO TEACH! To teach is to talk! Teaching as conversation. We were off to a new start. A new psycholinguistics (later to be called "educational psycholinguistics"). And it had relevance to FL teaching. That part we worked out later, in the small hours of the morning.

The Transactional Model of Talk

Typical, ordinary, commonplace talk takes the form of face to face conversation. A conversation is not *merely* a verbal interchange (the behavioristic fallacy of reductionism) it is a transaction, it is doing something together. Berne, 1964; Goffman, 1972; Garfinkel, 1967; Sacks, 1971: these are people who have written about conversational transactions without reducing the concept to verbal interaction. A transaction has prerequisites, an initiating proposal, a receiving response, a successful completion, a legitimization. Searle: *Speech Acts* (1969) are transactions. In order for A to successfully promise something to B, both A and B must know, prior to the initiation of the act of promising, what the rules for promising are. The prerequisites: A claims that he intends to do something and that it is within his power to do it (You can't promise someone to give him title to the Brooklyn Bridge!); B must know what it means "to promise" and must be able to recognize it when A does it (e.g., it refers to a future action; other factors may prevent A from carrying it out—a prerequisite children often forget about)—it is to be distinguished from other acts like "I may do it, if," or "I can do it, but . . . , " etc.).

A transaction, thus, needs the following conditions: (a) contextual prerequisites (e.g., a "promise" under threat is not the same as a promise freely given); (b) an initiating proposal (e.g., "I promise that . . . " "I undertake to . . . "); (c) a validating confirmation (e.g., "O.K.," "Thanks").

Conversations consist of a set of transactions, sequentially performed in time and hierarchically organized. Let us give you an example of a short conversation to illustrate some of its organizational aspects.

1. A: (a) Oh, Hi, John. (b) What's up?
2. B: (a) Hi. (b) Mr. Hendrix hasn't come in today. We've got to make a decision on the Weatherweight proposal before the weekend. But I can't reach Hendrix. (c) Do you have any idea where he might be?
3. A: (a) Did you try the golf course?
4. B: (a) I tried *all* the reasonable places. (b) No one has seen him. (c) Could you do me a favor?
5. A: (a) Yeah, sure.
6. B: (a) Drive over to his weekend place. There is no phone there, and he just might have decided to start an early weekend.
7. A: (a) Well, I can't leave the office until 4:30. (b) Board meeting in half-an-hour. (c) But I'll ask Nancy to do it. (d) She's the dependable one in the office. (e) She can leave right away.
8. B: (a) Thanks, friend. I appreciate it. (b) If we see this thing through successfully, both of us are in for a promotion.
9. A: (a) You mean that? Really?
10. B: (a) I have it from the horse's mouth. B.J. has a personal stake in this. I can promise you that.
11. A: (a) O.K. I know you've got long fingers. (b) I did spend an awful lot of time on the case. Now it's out of my hands. (c) Say, (d) how about dinner out with the girls tomorrow? (e) I promised Jane, and . . .
12. B: (a) Uh . . . (b) Real sorry. (c) Sylvy's parents are descending upon us this weekend. (d) How about next week at our place?
13. A: (a) Sure. (b) I know Jane will love to. (c) I'll check with you later about Hendrix. (d) I'd better go tell Nancy to leave.
14. B: (a) Thanks again. (b) She can phone me at the office. (c) I'll be staying till 7.
15. A: (a) O.K. Will do. (b) Chow.
16. B: (a) See you later.

Nothing special. An ordinary conversation. What happened?

A series of transactions were performed between A and B (refer to numbered sequence in conversation):

1. (a) Greets. (b) Asks for explanation.
2. (a) Greets. (b) Gives explanation. (c) Asks for suggestion.
3. (a) Gives suggestion.
4. (a) Rejects suggestion. (b) Gives explanation. (c) Makes a request.
5. (a) Grants request.
6. (a) Gives elaboration (of request).
7. (a) Denies request. (b) Gives justification. (c) Makes a promise.
   (d) Gives justification. (e) Gives elaboration.

8. (a) Expresses thanks. (b) Makes a promise.
9. (a) Dramatizes.
10. (a) Gives explanation.
11. (a) Dramatizes. (b) Gives elaboration. (c) Changes topic.
    (d) Makes invitation. (e) Initiates elaboration.
12. (a) Interrupts. (b) Rejects invitation. (c) Gives explanation.
    (d) Makes invitation.
13. (a) Accepts invitation. (b) Gives elaboration. (c) Changes topic.
    (d) Gives explanation.
14. (a) Expresses thanks. (b) Gives instruction. (c) Gives elaboration.
15. (a) Dramatizes. (b) Takes leave.
16. (a) Takes leave.

Thus, this short conversational episode is actually made up of 39 transactional acts of various sorts. The identification of transactions is a fairly straightforward analytic task. You'll get the hang of it after doing a few of your own. The labeling problem is not crucial at this stage. Pick whatever name you like for a transaction, although later a labeling strategy and rationale will become a practical necessity.

Before going on to a discussion of the organizational structure of this sample conversational episode, we'd like to point to some features of a few of the transactions identified.

Gives Explanation: (e.g., 2.(b), 4.(b), 10.(a), 12.(c), 13.(d).) How does the talker know (i) when, at which point in the conversation, he should give an explanation, and (ii) what the explanation should be: what pieces of information to select, what their logical (discourse) structure should be? The "should" in both instances relates to the requirement "in order for the other participant to be satisfied." Note that in 2.(b) the explanation given is in response to the request in 1.(b). (Note in parenthesis that the explanation is delayed until after the greeting (2.(a))—a hierarchical requirement, see below). The content of the explanation is dictated by the *joint* and *prior* evaluation on the part of both participants of the problematic element in the setting. For instance, it is this joint, cooccurrent evaluation or definition of the situation that must account for how A knows that "Something is up" (2.(b)) and how B knows what A means, what kind of an explanation he is asking for, and what will satisfy him in terms of an answer. Without this concept of a prior joint cooccurrent evaluation of the problematic elements of the setting, A's question "What's up?" (1.(b)) would remain unanswerable, its meaning contextually indeterminate, obscure. The nontransactional communication model of information theory can only say that *A* encodes a question, that *B* decodes it, and leaves unanswered the central problem: how does *B* know what the message is, what *A* intended, since "What's up?" can have an indefinitely large number of meanings or situational referents. The transactional model, because it is transactional, (i.e., it takes *two* to tango), focuses on the need for accounting for how both participants know the same thing, so that they can successfully transact. This prior common knowledge pertains to the code book of the conversational ritual, the rules of talk in a particular speech community, the transactional dialect. The nature of these rules will be discussed later, but it might be helpful to see how they are generated. For instance, the explanation in 4.(b) is an explanation given by *B* for the rejection (made in 4.(a)) of *A*'s suggestion (in 3.(a)). These relationships imply that there might be a general conversational rule that is in some such form as the following: "If talker rejects a suggestion just given, he must give an explanation as to why he has not accepted it." In this case, *A* suggests that *B* call the golf course, just in case he hasn't yet. (The syntactic form of the question in 3.(a) is but one of many possible ways that *A* could make such a suggestion.) *B* rejects the suggestion in 4.(b) by implication (*A* needs to know this kind of a rule as well; otherwise he won't be aware that his suggestion was rejected). After rejecting *A*'s suggestion, *B* then explains the reasonable grounds; to dramatize: "Since no one has seen him, there is no use in your thinking of places for me to call, *especially* the golf course, since that's a reasonable place to have called right away.", etc.

We won't go into further details, but you may wish to pause here and work out similar solutions for the remaining transactions involving Gives explanation.

Gives Justification: (e.g., 7.(b), 7.(d)) How does a talker know when justification is necessary? In this particular case, *A* is justifying why it is that he can't leave the office until 4:30. Justification is called for inasmuch as *B* would expect *A* to cancel all his previous plans as an acknowledgment that *B* finds himself in an "emergency" situation and could count on *A*'s help. If *A* wishes to retain the claim that his relationship to *B* is of the sort that *B* can count on *A* for help in an emergency, then a justification for his rejection of *B*'s request (6.(a), 7.(a)) is needed. This kind of standing claim between conversationalists, and the expectations it implies, forms part of the background context, the setting of a conversational episode.

The problem of what constitutes the context, the setting of an utterance in a conversation has been discussed in the literature (e.g., Wilkinson, 1971) and is an area that needs immediate and intensive investigation. We can distinguish between the following kinds of transactional contextual features: *sociological* (i.e., the behavioral operative procedures that the transactional code specifies for conversational dyads in an institutional setting that assigns proper roles to participants—colleague, boss, secretary, stranger on the street, bartender, father, wife, older brother, son, etc.), *subcultural* (i.e., the culturally given definition of the physical setting, e.g., secretary talking to the boss in private in his office vs. secretary talking to the boss in the outer office during the annual Christmas Party), *emotional* (e.g., husband talking to wife at breakfast in a preoccupied mood on Monday morning vs. husband talking to wife during Sunday brunch), *informational* (the shared background knowledge of the conversational setting, the joint prior identification of the problematic elements in it, all that has gone on before, etc.), and *inferential* (the rational, logical, common-sensical—viz. practical—implications of what's going on, and the steps that need to be taken as attempted solutions).

Thus, in the particular example we are considering for the transaction Gives Justification (7.(b), 7.(d)), and the related question of when is justification needed, the account will have to consider the sociological features (A and B are executives, colleagues involved in a routine transaction), the subcultural features (it is early afternoon in the office on Friday and B is trying to get in touch with a colleague), the emotional features (B is in an emergency, A is rushing off to a Board meeting), the informational features (where Hendrix might be, who also can help locate him, what it would mean to the proposal if he couldn't be found, what A and B would ordinarily be doing at the time this particular conversation takes place, etc.), and inferential features (what it would mean for A to refuse to help B). The transactional code will specify how the conversationalist must behave within this lattice of features, and the participant's transactional competence will determine the level and quality of his actual performance within this code. We find it practical to elaborate the transactional code in terms of if-then rules. For instance, one rule related to Gives Justification can be stated as follows: If you claim *x*, then you must do *y*, or, if you did *p*, you must do *q*. A further elaboration of *x*, *y*, *p*, and *q* might be particularized as follows: If you claim you're a colleague executive in good standing, then you must justify why you're rejecting a request for help. If you failed to justify (when you should have), then you must, as some later appropriate time, engage in repairing activity (give an explanation appealing to attenuating circumstances, apologize, promise not to do it again, etc.). The force of the must-statements that appear in these if-then rules is that unless the rules are followed, the practical consequences will not be those that are desired by the conversationalist.

Gives Elaboration: (6.(a), 7.(e), 11.(b), 11.(e), 13.(b), 14.(c)) How does the talker know when giving an elaboration is appropriate or necessary and what the nature of it should be? Take 6.(a), for illustration: it is an elaboration of the request "Could you do me a favor?" (4.(c)). It consists of a subroutine of embedded transactions, as follows:

6.a.   (i) Drive over to his weekend place.—Gives Instruction.
     (ii) There is no phone there.—Gives Information.
     (iii) and he just might have decided to start an early weekend—Gives Opinion.

The sequence of this particular *Gives Elaboration* transaction is thus: *Gives Instruction* ⟶ *Gives Information* ⟶ *Gives Opinion.* This sequence is contextually appropriate, i.e., it takes into account the informational and inferential features of the conversational setting (e.g., In case you don't know, or don't remember, Hendrix does have a weekend place. I am instructing you to drive over there. I am also informing you that there is no phone there. That is the reason I am asking you to *drive* over there. It is my opinion that he might have gone there.)

Dramatizes: (9.(a), 11.(a), 15.(a)) Dramatization in conversations relates to a participant's style of modulation when he expresses emotion, tells an anecdote or a joke. It relates to his conversational style, the kind of feature ordinarily referred to by such expressions as, He is funny, amiable, relaxed, accessible, sociable, grouchy, clumsy, direct, tactful, clever, blunt, and so on. The transactional code allows for stylistic modulations, and because there are subcultural standards of propriety and excellence in being a "good" conversationalist, these personal characteristics will also form a part of what is to be included under the study of transactional competence (see Kochman (1969) and Mitchell-Kernan (1969) for interesting ethnographic descriptions of dramatization styles among Black ghetto residents).

The analysis of the sequence of transactions of this particular conversational episode has yielded the following list:

Greets

Takes Leave

Asks for ⎫
Gives   ⎬ Explanation

Asks for ⎫
Gives   ⎬ Suggestion
Rejects ⎭

Makes ⎫
Grants ⎬ Request
Denies ⎭

Gives Elaboration

Gives Justification

Makes Promise

Expresses Thanks

Interrupts

Changes Topic

Dramatizes

Makes   ⎫
Accepts ⎬ Invitation

Gives Instruction

It is clear, however, that these transactions are related to the conversational episode in a structural fashion, not linear. There is here the same nomothetic relationship between the overt sequence of transactions, as performed, and its underlying organizational structure as there is in linguistics between the surface phonetic shape of a sentence and its underlying syntactic and semantic structure. Deeper analysis will show that the aspects of the theory of transaction shares many of the organizational features of the *Aspects of the Theory of Syntax* (Chomsky, 1965). In particular, the grammar of a conversational episode has a surface level structural component (transaction) that can be expressed algebraically (or through a branching tree diagram), and a transformational component at the deep structure level that includes such processes as sequencing or ordering rules, and deletion and substitution rules. Some readily apparent features of these rules can be outlined as follows.

Sequencing Rules: Greeting and *Leavetaking* transactions must be placed at the beginning and the end of a conversational episode. Some transactions such as *Expresses Thanks, Accepts Invitation*, and *Denies Request* always appear *after* certain other transactions have occurred (here, respectively, *Makes Promise, Makes Invitation, Makes Request*). The transactions, *Interrupts* and *Changes Topic*, on the other hand, can occur anywhere. *Asks for Suggestion, Makes Request, Gives Elaboration, Dramatizes, Gives Explanation*, are transactions that can occur whenever a priority rule for some other transaction is not invoked. For instance, given the particular setting for our sample conversation, 12.(c), *Gives Explanation*, has a higher priority than 12.(d), *Makes Invitation*, immediately following 12.(b), *Rejects Invitation.* An example of an embedding rule has already been presented earlier in connection with the discussion of the subroutine in 6.(a), *Gives Elaboration* (viz. *Gives Instruction→Gives Information→Gives Opinion.*).

Deletion rules: These allow for the elliptical character of commonplace ordinary conversations (see Garfinkel, 1967) and concern the interstitial structure of utterances, viz. what isn't there to be said, as opposed to what's actually being said. The nature of deletion rules within subsystems of the transactional code pertain to the conversational register. Typically, the intimate face-to-face register contains a much higher usage of deletion rules than more formal registers, which is one reason why talk between intimates is often incomprehensible to observers. Contextual setting features, such as subcultural, informational, and inferential, determine the deletion rules that are allowable in a particular conversational episode. As an illustration of the operation of deletion rules, consider an elaborated version of the more restricted exchange that occurs in 1 and 2: (the restricted version is italicized, the elaborated version follows):

1. A. *Oh, Hi, John. What's up?*

   Oh, Hi, John. I see you're coming to see me. I was just on my way to somewhere else. I know you are very busy today with the Weatherweight proposal and so, would not expect you to just drop in and chat as you did yesterday afternoon when you told me about your current problems. I guess, therefore, that something urgent has come up, and you want me to get involved in some way. Speak. I am listening.

2. B. *Hi. Mr. Hendrix hasn't come in today. We've got to make a decision on the Weatherweight proposal before the weekend. But I can't reach Hendrix. Do you have any idea where he might be?*

   Hi. You no doubt guess that I didn't come to chat. You know the problem I've been having in getting the Weatherweight proposal ready before the weekend. I am terribly upset, and I came to ask for your help. Hendrix hasn't made a decision yet, and he didn't realize that B.J. wants the proposal ready to take with him to Washington Saturday morning, tomorrow. I'm trying to locate Hendrix to tell him. But I can't find him. You've got to help me. Have you any suggestions?

It should be clear that we are not making any claims about the actual form of the deleted utterances and the consequent substitutions that occurred. We are only claiming that the substance of the elaborated version, in some relevant sense equivalent to the dramatization we have given, must be represented at some point in the underlying structure of the interchange in 1 and 2. It is also clear to us that no amount of detail that can be included in the elaborated dramatization can be considered sufficient or complete since it would involve retracing all that is relevant to the two participants' knowledge about the setting and their inferential capacities for its practical implications (see Garfinkel, 1967). How ordinary conversations can proceed in such a rapid yet smooth pattern given this openness aspect, remains for us a mystifying marvel.

Engineering Authentic Transactions in the Classroom

A TE Workshop (Transactional Engineering Workshop) is a small group led by two co-leaders, "transactional engineers." Its purpose, its "behavioral objective," is to liberate the teacher, to get him to develop a personal pedagogic model which will allow him freedom in his teaching, will help him be an inspiring teacher, and will promote his personal growth and sense of fulfillment. In a TE Workshop, the members commit themselves to participate in self-analytic authentic transactions. We shall attempt to describe this process, but first, we need to introduce the concept of the authentic conversational dyad.

An authentic dyadic conversation consists of five "participants" or "social witnesses":

1. Participant A's public identity.
2. Participant B's public identity.
3. Participant A's private identity acting as an observer (his "metanoid" self).
4. Participant B's private identity acting as an observer (his "metanoid" self).
5. The dyadic "us" (*we*) (being a new creation larger, stronger, smarter than either A or B separately and existing as an entity cumulatively built upon and developed, retaining permanency over time).

We use "metanoid" in R. D. Laing's (1967) sense, a construction that is parallel to "paranoid" and means, literally, "to stand beside oneself," viz. to be a self-analytic observer. We borrow from Bales (1970) the concept of "self-analytic group" which refers to participant interactions whose topic is the ongoing interaction (hence, self-analytic). Here is a dramatized version of a sample authentic self-analytic transaction.

A_1 = Participant A's public identity.

A_2 = Participant A's metanoid self.

B_1 = Participant B's public identity.

B_2 = Participant B's metanoid self.

AB = The new "Us."

(Assume that every utterance is overtly verbalized.)

A_1:   I undertake to interact with you in an authentic fashion. I hope it will work. I hope you'll agree too.

A_2:   I am excited and scared.

B_1:   Me, too, I agree to interact with you in an authentic fashion. I accept your proposal. Don't be scared. I've done it before with someone, and it works.

B_2: I'm filled with anticipations. I've got butterflies in my stomach. I am wondering what it will be like with you.

AB: (said by spokesman B) We have taken the first step. We are departing together.

A_1: Can you teach me how to do it? I am willing to be the pupil. I'll follow your instructions not knowing where you lead me. I trust you not to hurt me. I trust you to put my feelings above the task, above all else. I trust you to relinquish your role as teacher when I want to tell you something about me.

A_2: I feel some hesitation, some ambivalence. It lessens when I think about and am able to feel the "Us."

B_1: I accept all your conditions. If by mistake, or lack of adequate competence, I violate any of these stipulations, I promise to repair it immediately, as soon as I become aware of it, or you point it out to me.

B_1: I feel some anxiety about this. I am not completely confident. I detect your ambivalence. Your hesitation causes me to tense up.

AB: (said by spokesman A) We are together now. We will watch out over A's and B's feelings.

A_1: I've seen you in the past attempt to manipulate people. How can I trust you completely?

B_1: First, I've got to tell you about "authentic objective reporting." There are three rules you must follow: do not disagree; be objective, report all relevant feelings.

A_1: How can I tell you what I think if I'm not allowed to disagree? Seems like that's not a very good rule.

B_1: Disagreeing doesn't lead anywhere. It won't help you learn. You must never disagree.

B_2: I'm getting uptight. I feel the tension in my body. I feel you are all tensed up. You act like you're ready to attack me.

A_2: Yes, I feel uptight. I feel frustrated. I am angry at you. I feel like hitting you.

AB: (said by spokesman B) We are disagreeing. We are far apart from each other. Let's get back together again. We are performing a disagreeing transaction. I suggest we both back off. I have failed to legitimize your earlier comment about how you could trust me when you have seen me manipulate people. I'm sorry. I was being defensive and felt like you were attacking me. I switched topics and went on instead to tell you about rules. I see my mistake.

A_1: I'm glad you see that I feel better.

A_2: I feel relief.

B_2: I feel relief.

AB: (said by spokesman A) We have just moved closer again. There is a warm glow around us.

B_1:   That's what authentic interactions do. They make you feel a glow.

A_1:   Ah! I see! I *see!* Yes, I feel the glow. Please, let's go on. Tell me about the rules. (Etc., etc.)

The dramatized conversation we have just presented represents one instructional unit in the SAOROGAT method of transactional engineering. SAOROGAT stands for "Self-Analytic Objective Reporting of OnGoing Authentic Transaction" and is the current approach used in TE Workshops. We shall now describe some of its features.

1. Each such instructional unit of interaction constitutes a learning step, a forward motion. A learning step is always accompanied by a feeling of relief, of a release of tension. It represents the attainment of an insight, a discovery. The teacher perceives this liberation reflex given off by the pupil and experiences a similar relief, a release from (instructional) tension. When it occurs, a feeling of warmth, a happy "glow" seems to encompass the two participants and prepares them for the next instructional unit, the next learning step in the forward motion, the next insight, the next relief, the next moment of liberation.

2. Successful completion of an increasing number of instructional units cumulatively facilitates the successful completion of the next instructional unit, so that the rate of authentic transactions increases in a geometric proportion. The rate of inauthentic transactions quickly decreases. At that point fast progress is made possible on the conceptual development of the problem, and the teacher can concentrate on the appropriate sequencing of the subject matter that is designed to bring about the specific behavioral objectives of the course (the DESOCS unit, see below). From time to time, and as needed, there is a reaffirmation of the authentic teaching contract (see below), viz, its voluntary and protective nature. The pupil never feels manipulated, alienated, dehumanized. He retains his freedom to learn.

3. The teaching-learning interaction—in the model that views teaching as conversation—is performed in the telling-listening transaction. Three types of learning are to be distinguished, these being related to ways of telling and ways of listening. First, we identify *conceptual learning*. This relates to a cognitive representa-

tion of the problem in the pupil's register (e.g., a geometric theorem to be demonstrated, a critical essay to be written, a research project to be assessed, an account of an historical event to be paraphrased, a pattern practice drill to be executed, etc.). Second, we identify *experiential learning* (Gendlin, 1967). This relates to an insight, a discovery, a reorganization of personal constructs, and is accompanied by a feeling of relief, release, liberation. Third, we identify *instructional learning*. This relates to a higher-order integration of conceptual and experiential learning and enables the individual to formulate a personal pedagogic model, a reporting competence, an ability to tell someone else what one knows, to teach by devising an instructional strategy individually tailored to the listener.

4. Ways of telling relate to the teacher's instructional strategy. Two aspects are to be considered in describing a particular teacher's pedagogic model: the nature of the *developmental sequence of the* conceptual *statement*—which we call *DESOCS*—and the personal reporting style—which we call *dramatizations*. DESOCS is task-oriented and includes selection of information to be presented, its sequencing and appropriate reporting register. Dramatizations are pupil-oriented and reflect the teacher's overall storage of information (his mental encyclopedia), what he can call upon in order to illustrate, give examples, recapitulate, summarize, paraphrase, put it in a story. The effectiveness of the teacher's pedagogic model (his instructional competence) will be a joint function of the validity of DESOCS (its authenticity) and the inspirational quality of his dramatizations (its inauthentic aspects—how mesmerizing and seductive he can be).

5. Ways of listening relate to the pupil's learning strategy. Two components are to be considered: attitudinal and performance factors. Listening attitude refers to the pupil's prior orientation toward the manner of his involvement in the listening process: *the flattened state* (a back-seat relaxed onlooker of the game; his emotional reactivity is low and he neither identifies nor empathizes with the players; it is a state of emotional asynchrony); *the reactive state* (a front-row excited observer of the game; he both identifies and empathizes with the players; he has emotional synchrony, but his reactions are private, not reported); *the participant state* (being

one of the players; in addition to emotional synchrony, he reports his reactions and his critical evaluations of the ongoing events). The successful performance of authentic transactions, i.e., transactional exchanges in which participants share awareness of what is going on, either publicly reported or tacitly understood, requires the participant state of listening attitude. Victimizing transactions occur in the flattened state. Manipulative transactions make use of the reactive state.

Performance style refers to the pupil's attempts to develop a cognitive model of the task. A number of activities are involved: *shooting style* (as in, shooting a film) which refers to the areas he chooses to focus on, to manipulate, to assimilate, and the rate, in time, at which this is done; *projecting style* (as in, projecting a film) which refers to the information he selects to report, to talk about, to ask questions about, to tell; *integrating style*, which refers to how shooting and projecting are related to each other by the pupil in listening, by the teacher in telling. Integrating styles are either balanced or imbalanced. A *balanced* integrating style synchronizes rate of shooting and rate of projecting (the talker says what he means and means what he says). An *imbalanced* integrating style either has a higher shooting than projecting rate (the talker doesn't say what he means) or the reverse (doesn't mean what he says).

6. Some important features of the teaching-learning process can now be stated. These will, at first, appear to be extremely involved. Part of the difficulty will be that you have not quite assimilated the meaning of the technical concepts. Don't give up after your first attempt. Go back a few pages and, as needed, re-read the elaborations we have given. Before proceeding further, be sure you understand the meaning we have given for the following expressions. These expressions are elements in a general pedagogic model, the model that we use to teach, to train teachers, to develop a personal pedagogic model that is appropriate for a particular teaching task, to conduct TE Workshops.

Language Teaching:
Elements in the General Pedagogic Model
of Conversational Transactions

Personal pedagogic model
Authentic conversational dyad

SAOROGAT method: self-analytic objective reporting of ongoing
    authentic transactions
Instructional unit
Learning step, forward motion
Liberation reflex, release of tension
Authentic teaching contract
Types of learning
    conceptual learning
    experiential learning
    instructional learning
Reporting competence
Ways of telling
    DESOCS: developmental sequence of the conceptual statement
        validity of DESOCS
    dramatizations
        inspirational quality
Ways of listening
    listening attitude
        the flattened state
        the reactive state
        the participant state
    performance style
        shooting style
        projecting style
        integrating style
            balanced
            imbalanced

If you're clear about what all the elements refer to, you'll be able to follow the descriptive statements that come next.

A teacher develops an effective personal pedagogic model through the SAOROGAT method. In the TE Workshop the authentic teaching contract insures that the participants will be engaged in authentic conversational dyads, that they will experience the liberation reflex, that they will move forward, step by step, through appropriate instructional units, that their reporting competence will be developed. In short, the TE Workshop experientially duplicates for the participant teachers precisely those processes that their pupils in their own classrooms experience. The SAOROGAT method insures that the participants of the TE Workshop engage in instructional learning about teaching and pedagogy. As they experience the learning process, the TE Workshop leaders continually point to, reflect, the ongoing events. Their teaching is deictic: Look! See?

Maintaining an authentic conversational dyad between teacher and pupil is essential for insuring the validity of a particular DESOCS strategy. Skill in dramatizations will promote inspirational quality. Jointly, they will promote the development of an effective pedagogic model that will permit the teacher to take into account learning styles: diagnosing blocks to forward motion due to ways of listening, making allowance for particular performance styles, promoting the participant state of listening attitude, promoting a balanced integrating performance style, in short, insuring effective instructional learning.

Educational Psycholinguistics:
Teaching as Telling—Learning as Listening

You now have a better picture of the transactional model of conversational interactions, and we can continue our analysis of "teaching as conversation." An interesting consequence of looking at this truism in a serious way is the reasonable and powerful hypothesis that the teaching-learning process can be investigated through a transactional analysis of the organization of ordinary talk. To our knowledge such a proposal has never been attempted (or, at any rate, is not generally known in the literature), and we label this enterprise "educational psycholinguistics."

Let us recapitulate some questions that came out of the previous analysis of an ordinary conversation—questions that are relevant to the teaching-learning process.

1. How does the talker know: (a) when, at which point in the conversation, is an explanation appropriate, and (b) what constitutes a satisfactory "explanation" (e.g., what pieces of information to select for reporting, what their logical (discourse) structure should be, when is it sufficient, etc.)?

2. How does the talker know when giving a "justification" is necessary, and what is its nature and sufficiency?

3. How does the talker know when making an "elaboration" is appropriate or necessary, and what the nature of it should be?

4. What are appropriate and effective styles of dramatization in talk?

In essence, we are dealing here with three types of very basic transactions in conversations (explaining, justifying, elaborating) and their style of execution (dramatization). In teaching as conversation, the teacher's personal pedagogic model specifies an initial formulation of the DESOCS that takes into account the conversational setting in the classroom and the logical organization of the topic (the subject matter). The SAOROGAT method of deictic telling (Look-See Method) insures adequate feedback for the continual reformulation of the DESOCS. Explaining, justifying, elaborating represent steps in time at which the DESOCS is being reformulated. The effectiveness of the teaching-learning process is jointly determined by the teacher's reporting competence, his style of telling, and the pupil's listening competence, his style of learning. To illustrate this interaction process, we are going to present a brief analysis of a passage in *Time Magazine*. Recall that "conversation" broadly defined, includes the writing-reading transactions, and because the previous illustrations we have given involved face-to-face conversations, we shall now use the written medium. In this analysis, ways of telling or reporting are to be identified with ways of writing (conversational style, writing style) and ways of listening with ways of reading.

What is to be learned from a written passage is a joint function of the writer-teacher's reporting competence (the validity of his DESOCS and his style of execution) and the pupil's reading effectiveness. The DESOCS in the written medium does not have the same power as that in the face-to-face medium since it is, by necessity, frozen. There is only the initial formulation to guide the execution. The following passage appeared in the March 20, 1972 issue of *Time*, a special issue devoted to "The American Woman Today." (pp. 26-27).

Second-Class. The New Feminism has touched off a debate that darkens the air with flying rolling pins and crockery. Even *Psychology Today*'s relatively liberated readers are not exempt. Male letter writer: "As far as Women's Lib is concerned, I think they are all a bunch of lesbians, and I am a male chauvinist and proud of it." Female: "It's better to let them think they're king of the castle, lean and depend on them, and continue to control and manipulate them as we always have."

Activist Kate Millett's scorching *Sexual Politics* (TIME, August 31, 1970) drew a frenetic reply in Norman Mailer's celebrated *Harper*'s article, "The Prisoner of Sex," which excoriated many of Millett's arguments but concluded in grudging capitulation: "Women must have their rights to a life which would allow them to look for a mate. And there would be no free search until they were liberated." Arthur Burns, chairman of the Federal Reserve Board, complained last month: "Now we have women marching in the streets! If only things would quiet down!" Washington Post Co. President Kay Graham left a recent party at the house of an old friend, Columnist Joseph Alsop, because her host insisted upon keeping to the custom of segregating the ladies after dinner. Other social habits are in doubt. A card circulating in one Manhattan singles bar reads: IF YOU'RE GONNA SAY NO, SAY IT NOW BEFORE I SPEND ALL OF MY GODDAM MONEY ON YOU.

Many currents of social change have converged to make the New Feminism an idea whose time has come. Mechanization and automation have made brawn less important in the marketplace. Better education has broadened women's view beyond home and hearth, heightening their awareness of possibilities—and their sense of frustration when those possibilities are not realized. As Toynbee had noted earlier, middle-class woman acquired education and a chance at a career at the very time she lost her domestic servants and the unpaid household help of relatives living in the old, large family; she had to become either a "household drudge" or "carry the intolerably heavy load of two simultaneous full-time jobs."

A declining birth rate and the fact that women are living increasingly longer—and also longer than men—has meant that a smaller part of women's lives is devoted to bearing and rearing children. The Pill has relieved women of anxiety about unwanted pregnancies.

All of this helped ensure a profound impact for Betty Friedan's *The Feminine Mystique*, published in 1963. In it, she argued that women lose their identities by submerging themselves in a world of house, spouse and children. The book came just at the height of the civil rights movement in the South; the pressures to give blacks a full place in society inevitably produced a new preoccupation with other second-class citizens. The Viet Nam War also led to far-reaching questions about traditional American assumptions and institutions, to a new awareness of injustice.

Readers of *Time* will recognize the characteristic reporting style in this passage. It embodies a straightforward DESOCS: the claim to an overall impersonal, impartial "objectivity"; the juxtaposition of quoted personal opinions and systematic facts and behavioral trends; the cumulative, "rational" development of the topic in terms of three steps: What are the relevant questions? What are the attempted answers and known facts? What are the proper conclusions to be drawn?; the stylistically sober expression of the claimed strategy: "Let the facts speak for themselves; Let the obviousness of the implied conclusion remain unstated."

Note how the heading of the passage (*Second-Class*) anticipates the theme of the last paragraph: American women today are preoccupied with and conscious of their status as second-class citizens. Nowhere is a conclusion directly stated. That is the "point of the passage," the instructional goal, and it is left up to the reader to induce it on the basis of the development of the passage.

The first two paragraphs represent the writer's attempt to "justify" the topic introduced by the first sentence: "The New Feminism has touched off a debate that darkens the air with flying rolling pins and crockery." The style of dramatization with which the problem is introduced is characteristic of *Time* writers: personalizing a large social issue by giving a metaphor for it that brings it down to earth, to the commonplace happenings of a Hadassa Women's Luncheon Meeting. The Girls are at it again, and, Well, Girls will be Girls. *Time*'s dramatizations are at once folksy and paternalistic, the perspective of the Johnsonian Ideal American Leader, Cautious yet Progressive, Steeped in Practical Experience, Dependable and Predictable, Aware yet with a Knowing Diffidence for Fads and New Trends.

The first two paragraphs thus represent the first instructional step in the DESOCS: the girls are out fighting for their rights. The justification of this conclusion is elaborated through the presentation of opinions by appropriate "spokesmen" (an appeal to our respect for the views of Responsible Leadership) who echo the anonymous statements of "the little guy" presented first. Following the "public statements" an anecdote involving Respected Figures is given whose force is to show (a) that social habits of a discriminatory nature against women are commonplace, and (b) that a Respected Leader has taken a stand against this discrimination, i.e., that the revolution has spread to high places. By way of extension, this one episode points to "Other social habits" that are in doubt. Finally, by way of clinching the bet, an example that has just the right amount of humor and spice, is presented. "A card circulating in one Manhattan singles bar reads: IF YOU'RE GONNA SAY NO, SAY IT NOW BEFORE I SPEND ALL OF MY GODDAM MONEY ON YOU."

The presentation of this last anecdote within the structure of the second paragraph is a masterpiece of implicative, indirect talk. It is presented as an illustration of doubtful social habits that are discriminatory against women. The underlying reasoning can be dramatized in the following terms:

BOY: Be fair, Girl. I don't mind buying you drinks; after all, it *is* a Man's World, but don't make me waste my money. That's unfair. If you don't feel like going to bed with me, tell me right away, so I don't spend my money for nothing. After all, this is a Singles Bar, and you're supposed to be a Liberated Female with none of those old sex hang ups. Play your part, Be Equal, you wanna ball or don't you?" Just the right appeal to the old respected American Fair Deal ethic: We'll let you have your freedom if you play your part right.

There are basically three levels of listening-reading. The first level represents textual behavior, what many educators refer to as "reading with meaning" or "reading with the proper intonation pattern that shows understanding." At this level, the "good" student will be able to repeat sections of the passage, paraphrase the topic, remember the "supporting" arguments and will answer correctly "objective" multiple-choice items based on the passage. In this case, he will be able to state that there are numerous commonplace social habits of a discriminatory nature against women and that various particular famous and establishment people are both practicing them and fighting them.

At the second level, the "excellent" discriminating reader-pupil will be able, in addition, to capture, report, and talk about the way in which the writer presents his thesis. This has been called "critical reading," and in this case, the pupil can make evaluative statements about *Time*'s DESOCS strategy, in some such terms as we have presented thus far.

There is a third level of reading which goes beyond these two, which I shall call "instructional reading," a concept that relates to instructional learning and the SAOROGAT method (see above). In this case, "instructional reading" refers to a strategy of learning from the *Time* passage that goes beyond the writer's instructional strategy and focuses on his particular DESOCS strategy as an object of study in order to further our understanding of the topic of the DESOCS, here, discrimination against women today.

The reader-observer at this third level has two sorts of data to analyze: (a) the arguments for the existence of male chauvinism marshalled by the writer, and (b) the writer's own potential prejudices, the sociocultural values he or she has internalized. A talker talking about male chauvinism, irrespective of the overt content of his arguments, represents one more situation where evidence for male chauvinism can be observed. Just as the writer can present observations, in the form of quoted statements, to argue for the existence of male chauvinism, in the same manner, the reader at the third level can make observations about the writer who quotes other's statements. In this case, the dramatization we have offered for the underlying meaning of the note on the alleged card circulating in the Manhattan singles bar clearly shows the insidious form that entrenched male chauvinism can take: the sexual form of dehumanization of women whereby the superior male (who buys the drinks) expects the girls to commit themselves to going to bed with the man, *prior* to a validating interaction which would leave her freedom to decide on the basis of that interaction. This form of male chauvinism is particularly pernicious because it puts the girl in a double bind: either she has to say No right away, in which case she doesn't get a chance to meet a prospective sexual partner, or she has to say Yes right away, in which case she might have to go to bed with someone she doesn't find sexually attractive. The writer of the *Time* passage shows no awareness of the double bind and erroneously presents the anecdote as an argument for a doubtful social habit that is intended to show that women themselves continue to conspire in male chauvinistic practices, viz. by refusing to play the equality game, hence the necessity of circulating the alleged card. Rather than being the underdogs supporting women's equality rights, the men who circulate the card (and the *Time* writer who relates the anecdote) are instead perpetrating upon women a newer and more virulent form of male chauvinism. Having made this observation, the instructional reader knows more about male chauvinism than the "expert" *Time* writer himself.

A similar and additional observation can be made vis-à-vis the statement at the end of the third paragraph in the writer's evaluation of Toynbee's comments: "she had to become either a 'household drudge' or 'carry the intolerably heavy load of two simultaneous full-time jobs.'" The writer's presentation of Toynbee's phrases as a juxtaposed either-or statement shows the underlying logic of his conception of women's roles or, at least, the conception expressed by Toynbee that he allows to stand unchallenged: once women have gained the *right* to choose between a career and remaining home, to exercise this right and remain at home amounts to being a "household drudge." The subtlety of the male chauvinism that underlies this logic is so fine that many women themselves fall prey to it: they are no longer free to act upon a preference and feel guilty to be "*just* a housewife" when they have been "lucky enough" to get a college education. The identification of the neutral "housewife role" with the loaded "household drudge" excludes the possibility of a free and equal choice for creativity and self-fulfillment as a "housewife" on the part of women with a college education. Both Toynbee and the *Time* writer offer evidence of deep felt male chauvinistic attitudes.

We shall mention one final point in this analysis. The last sentence of the fourth paragraph is a step in support of the argument that social, medical, and technological developments have come to liberate women from their earlier inferior status. "The Pill has relieved women of anxiety about unwanted pregnancies." At the first level of "textual" reading, the pupil will have stored this piece of information so that he could quote it as "one of the factors contributing to Women's Liberation." At the second level of "critical" reading, the pupil will have "assimilated" this fact to his prior knowledge of the topic, and he would be able to elaborate that "the Pill" was a liberating development inasmuch as it gave women sexual freedom to choose when and with whom they wished to go to bed. At the third level of "instructional" reading, the pupil-observer will recall that, in point of fact, the history of "the Pill" was anything but a medical success. The negative side effects for many women are so severe that it has placed women in another double bind: either they eliminate anxiety of unwanted pregnancies by taking the Pill, in which case they suffer debilitating and anxiety-provoking side effects, these new plagues representing a newer form of women's anxiety about sex, or they refuse to suffer this new form of anxiety about women and sex by refusing to take the Pill, in which case they are faced with the old anxiety of unwanted pregnancies. The writer's failure to note this new form of anxiety created by the Pill (Doctor, should I take it or not?) shows once again the error in his conceptual statement (the lack of validity in his DESOCS; his inauthenticity).

Written materials are particularly amenable to this kind of analysis, which is why we encourage TE Workshop members to tape-record and transcribe verbal exchanges in the classroom. By doing an instructional reading of the transcribed conversations they are involved with, they gain a deeper, fuller understanding of their reporting style and competence. But the classroom is by no means the only observation place for the teacher. Every conversation represents valid data for the teaching-learning process, because in every conversation the teacher-pupil roles continually alternate between participants, who take turns in telling (reporting, teaching) and listening (understanding, learning). The individual who sharpens his observational competence of ongoing transactions in the conversations in which he is a participant-observer is learning all the time. *The ideal teacher is the perpetual student.* Topical specializations (*what* is being observed; the subject matter being taught) are mere dramatizations, an esthetic expression of preference for certain practical consequences in the conduct of human affairs. Fundamentally, there is only one kind of learning, only one kind of teaching: the self-analytic accurate observation of our own selves.

Pedagogic Ambiguities and Levels of Insight in the Instructional Register

Recall that we are viewing teaching as that aspect of conversation, of talk, that has to do with ways of telling something, and learning, as that aspect of talk that has to do with ways of listening. Recall, further, that the rules involving successfully *telling* something apply to both the face-to-face as well as the written modes of discourse. We wish to go into an elaboration of the factors that contribute to successfully telling something as well as the characteristics of listening that facilitate learning. The former relates to teaching strategies and pedagogic effectiveness, the latter to learning sets, modes, styles that facilitate or hinder learning. We shall proceed by presenting an analysis of the conceptual structure of an illustrative case of telling something.

The pedagogic problem in this example involves a talker's attempt to tell someone about a learning strategy that is designed to improve the listener's ability to study. Imagine that you are a teacher talking to a group of students on the topic of "Study habits and how to improve them," and you make the following statement:

> *Level 1.* You have to learn to *focus* on the problem at hand, to concentrate on it, to eliminate extraneous distractions.

A transactional analysis of this statement indicates the following:

1. The theme being initiated is the transaction, *Gives Instruction:* You have to learn to X." This is a typical teaching-learning transaction.

2. The main topic of the transaction is "the acquisition of some skill."

3. The statement, as formulated, involves an embedded transaction, *Gives Elaboration* (of the main topic), which includes three subtopics:

  (i) to focus on the problem at hand;
  (ii) to concentrate on it;
  (iii) to eliminate extraneous distractions.

Note that each of these involves an additional *Gives Instruction* transaction: you are to focus, you are to concentrate, you are to eliminate distractions. The DESOCS plan of the statement thus has the following structure:

Theme of Transaction	*Topic*
Gives Instruction	You have to learn x
Gives Elaboration	x consists of to focus, to concentrate, to eliminate.
Gives Instruction	Focus. Concentrate. Eliminate.

The legitimizing rationale of the DESOCS plan is that, if you complete the transactions as proposed, you'll find that you can study more efficiently. The effectiveness of the pedagogic strategy involved in this DESOCS is related to the ease with which the student can successfully perform the proposed transactions. To the extent that the proposed transactions are not clear to the student, i.e., contain ambiguities, the difficulty of complying will be enhanced. We shall refer to these as "pedagogic ambiguities of the instructional transactions proposed by the DESOCS." We shall investigate the number of such ambiguities as well as their generiticity (i.e., the abstractness level at which they occur). In general, the quality of the DESOCS will be a negative function of the number and generiticity of the pedagogic ambiguities that are allowed to remain in the particular formulation of the teacher's statement. We shall list these from the point of view of the listener (student) using the Method of Dramatization, already illustrated earlier:

Pedagogic Ambiguities:

1. In order for me to comply with your main instruction, viz., to learn this skill that is going to improve my study habits, I've got to know how to learn it, not just the fact that I must learn it. But you haven't told me that.

2. Not only do I not know how to learn that, but I don't even have a clear picture of what "that" is supposed to be. For instance, what exactly does it mean "to focus," "to concentrate," "to eliminate"? *How* do I do these things?

3. Assuming I've been able to work out for myself your intended meaning of "to focus, etc.," and further, assuming that I've found strategies that allow me to practice "focusing, etc.," I still would like to know how such a skill will be to my advantage as I attempt to pursue my goals in life, to fulfill my potentialities. In other words, is my problem really that of improving my study habits, or is it something else, too, or something else altogether?

These pedagogic ambiguities are extremely severe. They occur at three levels of abstractness or depth: *What* do I have to learn? *How* do I learn it? How is it personally relevant to me? The quality of the controlling DESOCS is thus low. The level of learning it insures is the lowest, i.e., rote learning (see above). The student can memorize the statement and possibly could paraphrase it at a level that retains the ambiguities.

Let us attempt a reformulation of the original statement in such a way as to eliminate the ambiguities it contains:

Level 2. You have to get personally involved in the topic so that distractions won't occur. "Personal involvement" refers to getting into the problem and evidencing interest and perseverance.

At this second level, some of the ambiguities left over at the first level are eliminated. For instance, instead of the obscure instruction,

"eliminate distractions" (and "focus on the problem, " "concentrate"), the statement asserts that distractions won't occur if you get
personally involved in the topic. Furthermore, what it means to "get
personally involved" is specified in terms likely to be meaningful at
the ordinary experiential level: "getting into the problem."
Conceptually, "getting into the problem" is at the same level as
"focus, concentrate on the problem," but experientially, it is more
familiar, more authentic. The specific instruction is more likely to be
effective because even students who have faulty study habits and are
distractible are likely to have experienced in the past a feeling they
would label as "I'm really getting into it," more so than "I can focus,
concentrate on it"—these being conceptual labels specified in a
conversational style (register) characteristic of the "good student,"
the "school achiever," the teacher, the psychologist, the counselor.
Furthermore, although an important pedagogic ambiguity remains in
this second formulation of the statement—*How to* do it, enough
information is given the learner to at least be able to watch out for
performance factors that will indicate to him whether or not he is on
the right track as he goes about practicing the instruction as best he
can.

To summarize, the statement at level 2 fails to adequately specify
the strategy to be followed by the student in his attempt to comply
with the specific instruction, but it is superior to the statement at
level 1 in that (a) it steers the student into a direction at the
experiential level ("getting into it") and (b) it provides criteria for
recognizing when performance is successful (feeling interest,
persevering).

Let us try a third formulation.

Level 3. When you get involved in the topic in an appropriate way, your
performance improves. "Appropriate" has the sense of "that which is
effective for your goal." "Goal" relates to the nature of your
personal structure, your own conception of reality, what you want
out of life. "Personal structures" vary in terms of specificity,
efficiency, and esthetic quality. An "efficient person" has practical
methods for obtaining goals specified by an individual's personal
structure. These "practical methods" include such things as "getting
into the problem," "focusing or concentrating on the problem,"
"getting personally involved in the problem," and the like. Distractions do not occur frequently when these practical methods are
successfully applied.

This formulation is superior to the other two because it is pedagogically responsive to all three levels of ambiguities left unspecified in the first formulation: What do I have to do? How do I do it? What is its personal relevance to me? To wit:

1. I have to learn practical methods for obtaining goals specified by my personal structure, my conception of reality, what I want out of life.

2. These practical methods will allow me to be more efficient in attaining the goals that I want.

3. Examples of such practical methods include "getting into the problem," "focusing," "concentrating," "getting personally involved," and possibly others. Of these, I recognize from my past experience "getting into it" and "being personally involved," and I infer that when I have these feelings, I am "focusing" or "concentrating" successfully, at which point distractions won't occur.

4. I also realize that the idea of "personal construct" is important, that it has something to do with life-goals, although you haven't told me what you mean by "specificity" and "esthetic quality."

At this point further formulations of the statement are possible at still higher levels, but we won't go into them here. Note that the length of the statement in the illustrative case given here is correlated with its pedagogic effectiveness, but it is the character of its structure (the nature of its elaboration) rather than length per se that is related to effectiveness. To illustrate this point, consider a more lengthy statement at level 1:

Level 1. You have to learn to focus on the problem at hand, to concentrate, to eliminate distractions. "To focus" means to keep your mind free from irrelevant topics. "To concentrate" is to restrict your attention to a single aspect of the problem. "To eliminate distractions" is to keep topics that are extraneous to the problem at hand from interfering with your attention. The more you can focus on the problem, the better you're able to concentrate, the more you'll learn.

Though this statement is several times longer than the original formulation at level 1, it adds nothing to it, leaving the same pedagogic ambiguities at all three levels.

The concept of "level," as used here, refers to genericity or centrality of the conceptual structure that controls a particular DESOCS formulation. In other terms, it refers to the level of the node in a linguistic tree hierarchy: the higher one goes in levels, the more abstract, the more generic, the more central is the conceptual element or component. Errors committed at more generic levels are more serious than lower level, surface components. Another way of looking at this is the level of insight afforded by an experiential learning step, a forward motion in a successful DESOCS. To illustrate this notion, consider the following dramatization of a meditation experience during which successive forward motion steps are attained, each step leading the learner to a higher level of insight.

Prelude: I am lying on the bed and am overhearing my wife in the kitchen coaxing my three-year-old son to come to the dinner table. I am thinking that that's not a very good thing to do. I am annoyed. I feel like jumping up, running to the kitchen and telling her to stop doing that, since it will aggravate the "eating problem" we have been having with my son.

Level 1 Insight: Hold it! You'd better not do that. If you interfere with her now, she'll just get angry. Besides, the damage is already accomplished. He got the attention he wanted. Better wait for later, when she isn't busy, and discuss it with her then.

Prelude: I feel a relief. The tension I felt a moment ago is gone. I can relax now.

Level 2 Insight: Look what happens when you relax the reins! Your uptightness disappears when you give up the attempt to control a situation. You must remember that next time. Hang loose. You won't assume responsibility for what others do. Stop fighting with people all the time!

Prelude: I wonder why I do that? Why do I fight all the time? Why do I put my sail up in the winds created by other people? Why?

Level 3 Insight. Oh! Look! You're putting yourself down! It hurts. I feel the pain. I am knocking myself over the head for something that I do frequently. Maybe I shouldn't be so hard on myself. There. That feels better. It's not fair to be so self-critical. I'm only human.

Prelude: Yeah, that's true. O.K. But still, I should try to stop doing that because, even if it's not a "crime," I really don't like that sort of thing. I don't enjoy it. So, therefore, I should try to stop doing it. I should stop doing something I don't like.

Level 4 Insight: Reverse the problem! I should stop doing something I don't like versus I should stop disliking something I do. I haven't thought of that before. I don't usually think of the reverse possibility. Why do I dislike something that I do all the time? Maybe what's wrong is not what I'm doing, but rather the way I'm evaluating what I'm doing. Ah, that's relieving. It may be easier for me to stop disliking it than to stop doing it. Yeah.

Prelude: I'll have to think about this some more. Maybe I don't really dislike being controlling and fighting. Maybe that's my natural style. It suits me well. Maybe I'm just telling myself that I dislike it, when actually I like it, but I am operating on a value system that puts a negative connotation on fighting with people, controlling the situation, interfering. That's something I've been taught. It's a foreign system to me. It's alienating. Self-dehumanizing. I'll have to work on this later. Right now I'm so relaxed. I feel sleepy.

This kind of self-engineered experiential bootstrap operation can go on to still higher levels of insight, of self-discovery, of forward motion, of growth. In principle, there is no limit to the operation. We cannot develop here the notion of the controlling DESOCS that is responsible for producing the successive learning steps in such self-analysis, the nature of the pedagogic model for personal constructs, how they are formulated, how they are acquired. You will note however that, in this illustrative case, the strategy used by the underlying controlling DESOCS is fairly straightforward:

1. *Check up:* Where are you at now? What are you feeling? What are you thinking? How are you evaluating these?

2. *Process behavioral implications:* What would happen if you responded in this particular way? Will it bring about a desirable goal? Have you considered all the alternatives?

3. *Check up:* How do you feel about the various possible outcomes?

4. *Choose the alternative that produces a feeling of relief.* Elaborate its rationale. Examine the new implications about yourself.

5. *Check up:* How do you feel about the reformulation, the elaborated statement?

And so on.

We have considered thus far the characteristics of the DESOCS that generates an instructional statement of how to tell something to someone. The account is incomplete until this is related to how to listen to someone who is trying to tell you something. Just as there are DESOCS strategies for telling, there are DESOCS strategies for listening. An analysis of ways people listen reveals a number of such strategies. Consider, for instance, a member of an audience listening to a lecture. We can distinguish the following listening set or learning strategies:

1. I am listening in such a way as to be able to find out something of interest to me related to: (a) the topic; (b) the speaker; (c) the audience and their reactions to the speaker and his comments.

2. I am listening in such a way as to be able to find out information of type x about the announced topic.

3. I am listening in such a way as to be able to find out anything of interest.

4. I am listening in such a way as to be able to give the impression to others that I am the sort of person who: (a) is a member of the audience in that setting; or (b) understands that sort of topic; or (c) can perform certain types of transactions in that setting.

5. I am listening in such a way as to be able to evidence my previous conclusion that I am usually right and you're wrong now about (a) the validity or coherence of statements you are making, or (b) the appropriateness of the transactions you are attempting.

6. I am listening in such a way as to be able to accomplish each of these:

   (a) to legitimize your statements;

   (b) to comply with as many of your transactional requests (see below) as I can;

   (c) to store the content of your statements in their original form;

   (d) to observe and be aware of all my feelings in this situation;

   (e) to reformulate your statements within my own conceptual system;

   (f) to report my opinions and feelings, when appropriate.

The DESOCS that controls the last of these listening sets (6, a-f) is more powerful than the others and represents the minimal as well as adequate conditions for instructional learning to take place. Let us elaborate each of the subconditions involved.

6a: Legitimizing Transaction: for the listener to successfully legitimize a statement he must indicate to the talker that he heard and understood the statement. In ordinary conversational settings, listeners use a number of stylistically modulated variants to perform a legitimizing transaction: periodic but brief eye contacts; nods; expressions of assent, encouragement, reassurance: "Mmm Hmm . . . ," "Yes," "I see," "I'm hearing you," "Right on," "Yeah, Go Baby," "Go ahead," and so on. Legitimizing transactions can be minimal, adequate, or enthusiastic; these may further be either direct or indirect. Here is an example of an indirect enthusiastic legitimizing transaction given by B to A's statement:

A: Yes, I just finished reading his (Castaneda's) second book (*A Separate Reality*). I found it extremely stimulating.

B: It's a mind blower!

B shows that he understood A's statement, but in addition indicates that he shares A's enthusiasm for the book. Though B's response does not directly state that he heard what A said (cf., "Oh, yes, you did? I see. I think so too"—which would be an example of a direct adequate legitimizing transaction), nevertheless the indirectness of it does not leave any doubt whatsoever about the fact that he heard and understood A's statement. Minimal legitimizing transactions (nodding, assenting verbally) are often ambiguous (Did you really hear me or are you merely being polite?) in which case they are inadequate and introduce elements of doubt in the smooth flow of the conversation.

6b. Complying Transactions: in ordinary conversations, a speaker may make several transactional requests simultaneously. Consider the following example:

A: Yes, I just finished reading his second book. Isn't it an extremely stimulating book?

B_1: Ah, did you? I read it too.

B_2: Oh, did you? I thought it was terrific, too.

A makes two transactional requests: (a) can you legitimize my statement by indicating whether you heard and understood me, and (b) can you share my feeling that it was very stimulating. B_1 complies with request (a) but fails to comply with request (b). B_2 complies with both requests. In principle, there is no limit to the number of such simultaneous requests that a talker may make in a single utterance.

Consider:

1. A:(a) I don't know what'sa matter with me, (b) you know . . . (c) My parents are on my back all the time, (d) you know what I mean, (e) like I'm scared I won't make it through the day, (f) you know, like, uh, (g) I'm fed up!

2. B:(a) Hey, man, you're doin' okay. (b) Wheeew. (c) They're so freaky. (d) They're all like that, see. (e) I've been through this hell, like you, like the rest of us. (f) Bang. It freaks you out. (g) Like you wanna blow the whole deal. Keep cool. You'll make it.

This is an example of a smooth, synchronized transactional exchange, the kind that is characteristic of good friends and close intimates. Note that *B* is responsive to every one of the seven transactional requests *A* makes during his "single talking turn":

a. A. Requests sympathy.   B. Gives encouragement.
b. A. Requests empathy.   B. Expresses pain.
c. A. Requests legitimization.   B. Gives indirect enthusiastic
                                        legitimization.
d. A. Requests empathy.   B. Justifies his claim to being
                                        able to empathize.
e. A. Requests support.   B. Reassures by justifying his
                                        competence to help.
f. A. Requests empathy.   B. Dramatizes shared feeling.
g. A. Requests legitimization,   B. Expresses shared feeling, acts
        empathy, and support.   reassuring, encourages.

We cannot go into additional details, but just in case you want to, here is a tip: notice how the levels of transactions are intermingled; for instance, in (e), *A*'s statement is made up, at the surface level, of a *Reports feeling* transaction. When you consider its transactional context (*Requests sympathy, empathy*), and the contextual setting (compliance takes the form of giving reassurance by implication: to have lived through the same stressful situation and survived proves not only that *A* can survive it too (a potentially reassuring realization), but further, that *B* is competent; given that he is a Friend and Eager-to-help, such demonstrated competence is reassuring. Notice, too, that the nature of one's responsiveness to transactional requests (what the listener chooses to respond to) is a common strategy conversationalists use to attempt to engineer certain special kinds of transactions that the participant favors: in this case, *B* complies with every one of *A*'s requests. He plays the Being-a-Good-Friend-Game by the book, observing all the rules. He could have, instead, attempted Bluffing, Controlling, and Victimizing transactions by complying to legitimization and empathy requests but withholding compliance to sympathy and support requests.

6c., 6d., and 6e.: Learning Transactions: Practically effective listening strategies cover all three levels of learning: the ability to codify for reporting what the speaker said (rote learning; 6c.), what he himself feels about it (experiential learning; 6d.), and his worked-out integrated reformulations of the topic (instructional learning; 6e.).

6f. Reporting Transactions: Choice and timing of reports are crucially important decisions a conversationalist has to continually make. His competence within the three types of listening/learning, sets upper limits for the quality of the DESOCS that controls these decisions. The appropriateness of particular reporting transactions is a joint function of the transactional register that applies to a particular conversational setting (as selected by the transactional dialect in force) and the degree of practical transactional skill possessed by the participant in that setting (cf., How to Win Friends and Influence People).

To summarize this discussion on ways of listening, we can recapitulate by listing the three levels of listening sets:

1. *Rote learning level*: Listen to every word spoken. Do not stop to process implications at this time. Memorize as many as you can in their original form.

2. *Experiential learning level*: Listen to the meaning of the statements. Relate it to what you already know about this topic. Process its implications. Do not worry about what you're missing while you're doing this. Come back to the talker whenever you feel like it, or when and if you get stuck.

3. *Instructional level*: Listen to as many as you can of the facts and statements presented. Memorize as many as you can in their original form. Listen to the meaning of the statements and relate it to what you already know about this topic. Process its implications and evaluate their internal consistency. Reformulate the original statement taking into account the results of their previous processing and contextualize it. Rehearse the original formulation. Rehearse the reformulation.

4. *Transactional level*: Determine the point of the statement (Why is he saying this particular thing in this setting at this particular time?) and label the theme (*Bluffing*: he is trying to put one over on me; *Making a Request*: he is asking me to pay attention to him; he is asking me to agree with him; he is asking me to slap him down; *Challenging*: he is daring me to prove my point; etc.). Decide what you want to do about it (complying, legitimizing, invalidating, withholding, etc.). Initiate your response by whatever means the

moment allows as specified by the transactional code. Observe his repartee.

Do you notice the close relationship between types of learning, discussed earlier, and ways of listening? Our model requires this in view of the identification of the learner as the listener in a conversational interaction. Let us present a dramatization that illustrates the contemporaneous multilevel processing necessary in an ordinary conversation.

1. A: (a) I think perhaps he deserves another chance. (b) He's had that job for 15 years. (c) I don't know if you're aware . . .
2. B: (a) Of course, I am. (b) It's happened too often. (c) He's fired, (d) and that's all there is to it.
3. A: (a) I don't think it's fair; (b) he couldn't help it.
4. B: (a) What do you mean?
5. A: (a) Well . . . (b) you know about his nervous breakdown last month, (c) right after his mother died . . .
6. B: (a) What?
7. A: (a) Uh, uh . . . (b) I thought you knew . . .
8. B: (a) The boss will hit the roof when he finds out. (b) Why the hell wasn't I told?
9. A: (a) Joe is responsible for absenteeism reports. (b) I didn't know you didn't know. (c) It's not recorded in the file?
10. B: (a) Obviously, there is no reason to change my decision. (b) He stays fired. (c) Good day.
11. A: (a) Right. (b) I'll talk to Joe about this. It must be a clerical omission. I suppose I underestimated the seriousness of the situation. He'll be better off with a long rest. Harry can continue to fill in for him. He's done a very good job so far. Uh . . . Uh . . . The account has picked up since he's taken charge. The boss will be happily surprised; I know he was feeling pessimistic about that account in particular.
12. B: (a) I'm glad to hear that. (b) Tell Joe to reprimand the secretary who fouled up the file. I don't want it to happen again.
13. A: (a) Righto. (b) Good day.

An ordinary conversation. Nothing special. Very commonplace. Yet we hope you can appreciate the extraordinary refinement of the transactional rituals involved. The levels of inferential processes performed by the two participants attains a complexity that is of an uncommon heuristic interest, and to us, at least, is of a rare esthetic beauty, especially since it is so ordinary. Here is a curtailed analysis of it:

1. (a) Pleads on the other person's behalf. Note he's appealing to two rules in the Transactional Codebook: I. Don't make hasty judgments in important decisions, and II. Don't be harsh in the treatment of others.
   (b) Strengthens his appeal to rule II by reminding him that, in this particular case, the strong form of it holds: II. Don't be harsh in the treatment of others, but especially to those loyal to you.
   (c) Baits him: You can change your position without having to lose face by claiming you weren't aware he was one of the loyal ones.
2. (a) Rejects the bait with a slap down: You are remiss in suggesting that I may not be totally competent.
   (b) Presents a reinterpretation of A's original formulation: you implied that I may be being harsh to a loyal employee, but there is a higher rule that relates to the security of the company; when it is endangered, it is obligated to protect itself.
   (c) Reiterates his previous decision.
   (d) Emphasizes its firmness.
3. (a) Reiterates his previous claim.
   (b) Baits him: there may be some considerations to the issue that you may have overlooked.
4. (a) Calls the bluff.
5. (a) Takes time out to process implications: did he call the bluff because he is attempting a counterbluff—not a bad move, or does he not know about the mental breakdown—which might spell trouble for me since he can then accuse me that I tried to hide it from him and that's a serious breach of the rule.
   (b) Presents information whose status is in doubt (*Note*: a more powerful DESOCS strategy would have postponed the presentation of this questionable information, or inhibited it altogether, and would have explored alternative routes: e.g., "Well . . . He was under great pressure."–capitulating without showing his hand.)
   (c) Attempts to minimize permanent damage due to irreparable deterioration: people often recover from such a blow.
6. (a) Delivers the *coup de grace*: now *you* are caught, at best, in possible negligence, at worst, in an irregular procedure.
7. (a) Takes the blow.
   (b) Admits defeat. (*Note*: to insist further would be suicidal; a practical DESOCS must have markers for repairing activities when a vital spot is attacked or wounded.)
8. (a) Wields deadly weapon: know, you, that I'm playing for keeps.
   (b) Demands the spoils of the victor. (*Note*: alternatives are available in a powerful DESOCS: e.g., "Listen, I'll try to cover for you, but I can't

promise anything"—more conciliatory; he doesn't want to antagonize him more than it's necessary, or "Let's hope he doesn't"—more friendly; I want him to retain his loyalty to me.)

9. (a) Prepares retreat.
   (b) Insures self-protection.
   (c) Buttresses his defense.
10. (a) Turns off attack (this is accomplished by relinquishing the pursuit of the defeated in retreat): I won't call your bluff involved in the claim that you didn't know it's not recorded in the files; I am allowing you to save face by not busting your claim.
    (b) Signals his victory.
    (c) Dismisses him.
11. (a) Acknowledges dismissal.
    (b) Engages in a number of repairing activities to reestablish their status as "in good standing" for further ordinary transaction in the future. (*Note*: this illustrates a particularly powerful DESOCS; note how he gives *B* an opportunity to reestablish cordial relations without making him appear too soft or lenient by claiming that his earlier intervention on behalf of the victim was not done at the sacrifice of the company's security.)
12. (a) Accepts offer: they are now back "in good standing."
    (b) Reasserts his authority by reminding him of his superior position (i.e., as one who has the right to give orders and act as a watchdog for the boss).
13. (a) Acknowledges *B*'s claim to authority.
    (b) Takes leave.

In ordinary conversational transactions, teller and listener are alternating roles that an individual is called upon to take on. The quality of his transactional competence is a joint function of the strength of the DESOCS controlling his ways of telling and the strength of the DESOCS controlling his ways of listening. In this example, both participants evidence a high degree of such competence. Conversational situations in which all participants exhibit a high degree of transactional competence tend to be authentic; everyone knows exactly what's going on, all bluffs are recognized, there is a minimum of the bumpiness that characterizes less competent, more inauthentic, less productive conversational episodes.

Authenticity and the Teaching-Learning Process

The more choices you make, the more authentic is your life. The more you're aware about yourself, the more authentically you can live, the more free you are, the more you can exercise your choices. Authenticity relates to awareness. It is self-actualization: the self is more itself; it is more authentic. More genuine. What it appears to be and what it truly is are together, one. Being together is authentic. Feeling right. Knowing what is.

Inauthentic is false. What it appears to be isn't what it is. Fake. Lack of genuineness. The more inauthentic you are, the less you are what you appear to be. You get faked out. The real you gets screwed. You're not together with yourself. You're ignorant of what is. You cannot make choices.

We are often being asked this question: How do you define "authentic" (authenticity)? As a result of the hundreds of instructional transactions we initiated in an attempt to comply with that request, we have discovered what appear to us some significant features about authenticity and the teaching process. We are referring to (personal) experiential discoveries. Most students we've had the privilege of teaching thus far have operated under a learning program (installed in their heads by the educational system) which has an obligatory procedural rule about "How to learn new things in school" as follows:

Step 1: find an authoritative source for a definition of the concept.

Step 2: memorize the definition, and accept it.

Step 3: you now know what the concept is. Proceed through Subroutine A9GX3. (*Note:* Subroutine A9GX3 includes, "What additional features does it have" and "What applications does it have.")

Our attempts to initiate the instructional transaction having "authenticity" as a topic kept bumping against the students' attempts to follow this obligatory procedural rule. Almost everyone involved corroborated the appropriateness of the description of our classes as "a bumpy ride." We are going to present to you an account of "What Happened?" during those bumpy rides.

Our proposed instructional transaction for "authenticity" as its topic has the following controlling DESOCS steps:

Step 1: Elaborate appropriately (for this particular class) the distinctions to be made between rote learning, experiential learning, and instructional learning. Propose and clarify the procedural rules whereby the participants are to interact for the next x minutes, or hours. In particular: (a) Be objective in your reporting; (b) Interrupt at any time when you wish to report an observation (viz., calling an ongoing transaction); (c) The immediate reporting of a felt insight (i.e., physical relief) is obligatory. (*Note*: See below for an elaboration of "Propose and clarify.")

Step 2: Develop and keep track of the structural analysis of the topic of "authenticity" in light of the data generated by the interaction governed by the procedural rules. This includes continual reformulations of the definition of authenticity and the nature of authentic transactions.

Step 3: Watch for evidence that participants are capable of replicating the first two steps when asked to initiate the instructional transaction with "authenticity" as its topic. Consider those participants passing this test as your colleagues and enlist their help with the remaining participants who have not as yet succeeded in passing the test.

Step 4: When all participants pass the test, this instructional transaction is successfully completed. The unit lesson is over. Do something else.

This is a typical DESOCS unit in the SAOROGAT method. Since this is a Look-See Method, outside materials are not used: textbooks, notes, definitions from somewhere else, guest speakers, and thought controlling precedents (e.g., outside authoritative sources, data, principles, and criteria). We start from where we are, which is not to say that we start from scratch: everything participants know up to that moment in time (including the proactive interferences of the prior outside materials) is there, present, to be dealt with, as the beginning point.

"Be objective in your reporting" is a crucial procedural rule in the SAOROGAT method, and we'd like to elaborate what is involved. An initial formulation of what it means to be objective in one's reporting goes something like this:

We're talking about the objective reporting of the here-and-now. From the point of view of the reporter, there are two components to the here-and-now: (a) his feelings: seen as a process that occurs within the self, a process to which he alone has direct access for observation: he is the only direct observer available for generating the empirical data on that topic; the other participants can only infer what the other's feelings might be; their subjective inferences do not have the same empirical status as the direct, objective, observation contributed by the reporter; (b) the ongoing transactions: seen as a process governed by a public transactional code that, when properly labeled, refers to what the participants are doing together seen from the perspective of one of the participants.

We are thus dealing with two topics of the reporting involved in this SAOROGAT rule: one's ongoing feelings and the ongoing transactions. The methods of adequate corroboration of the data within these two topics are different and must be understood. Corroboration of an observation dealing with one's ongoing feelings may be either direct or indirect. Direct sensual validation of another's feelings is possible through empathy: participants, in that case, must share, in common, a particular feeling, so that when A reports it, B can directly corroborate the observation by matching A's report. Indirect sensual validation is inferential and depends on B's ability to imagine, by recall or identification, what A's feeling is like, by "putting himself in A's position" and seeing what he would feel if he were there.

Corroboration of an observation dealing with the ongoing transactions is by consensual validation, a process that is always inferential. Consensual validation requires a common structural analysis of the topic: a common framework for transactional analysis, its components and syntax.

"Objective reporting" refers to a conversational register in which only factual statements are made which can be routinely corroborated by participants, either sensually (in the case of feelings) or consensually (in the case of transactions). When this condition is met, no disagreements are possible. The purpose of the reporting in this case is merely to point: Look-See, there goes another one. Its function is to guide the focus of attention, the locus of observation. The only legitimate response to an objective report is: "Yes, I see. Thank you."

When this condition is not met, the attempt to report objectively will have failed. Disagreements develop. Forward motion is blocked. Time is lost. Let us look at the nature of these disagreements and how they are to be dealt with when they occur.

Disagreeing: An Inauthentic Transaction

When we succeed in telling you what we know about Disagreeing Transactions you will be able to corroborate consensually the statement that disagreements can never be authentic. It is impossible to successfully play the game of "Let us agree to disagree," only that of "Let us agree to pretend to disagree." The latter refers to faked disagreements. A participant may, for various personal reasons, choose to initiate a Disagreeing Transaction at a particular strategic point in a conversational episode (e.g., to attract attention, gain time, etc.). Both participants, A and B, may know that they are colluding, pretending that they don't see through the game, but neither of them may wish to publicly acknowledge it, so they continue to disagree falsely, a fake disagreement.

If A and B are transacting a genuine disagreement, neither of them recognizes that they are disagreeing; instead, they mislabel the disagreeing transaction, believing it to be something else; criticizing, hurting, resisting, bulldozing, being pig-headed, inconsistent, recalcitrant, persistent, and so on.

Disagreeing Transactions form a significant proportion of ordinary human transactions, although they vary in frequency according to the conversational context. In our observations of all forms of teaching in mass education classrooms, the instructional register used contains a very high rate of disagreeing transactions. By the time students are in graduate school, they have had sixteen years of exclusive practice in that register, so we find in our own teaching that most of our time is spent attempting to diagnose and repair disagreeing transactions.

Disagreeing transactions block out experiential learning. They involve the participants in a sideways motion in which they persevere in a collusion whereby each of them tries to prevent the other from seeing what's going on: pulling the wool over the eyes, denying, invalidating, victimizing, conning, bluffing, trapping, giving a bum steer, and so on. Disagreeing transactions are thus participants' attempts at creating or maintaining inauthenticity in the interaction. They are conversational strategies made available by the transactional code which participants use to create inauthenticity, to maintain it, so as to hide from recognition some other transaction that is ongoing, simultaneously in time, at a different level.

Objective reporting is a strategy for counteracting disagreeing transactions, for reinjecting authenticity into the interaction. Objective reporting of feelings prevents the cover-up job, when, for instance, B reports a feeling of distress at hearing A's statement, it is more difficult to continue to maintain that they are merely "Exchanging Opinions" or "Having a Heart-to-Heart Talk." When you publicly call the shots that hit you, it is more difficult to pretend that the ongoing slugging match you're in is but a polite exchange: there is too much noise and blood to account for. Similarly, the objective reporting of ongoing transactions by the other participants makes it plain to all concerned that the cat is out of the bag, and it becomes difficult to continue to pretend genuine ignorance.

Under what conditions do participants collude in disagreeing transactions? When they have a stake in maintaining inauthenticity, when they wish to cover up. Bluffing transactions are often used for manipulative purposes, and their success depends on dissimulation, on introjecting inauthenticity in the interaction. Parents often bluff and trick their children into believing some things or adopting some values in order to better control their present and future behavior. Teachers often bluff their students and trick them into learning a particular set of facts and principles (see Castaneda, 1969, 1970; and Watts, 1969).

In the instructional register, the DESOCS strategy is so designed as to get the student to adopt a set of premises which, through a learned process of ratiocination, leads him to adopt the objective of the DESOCS unit: the acceptance of a principle, theory, or evaluation. The pedagogic process depends on the teacher being able to manipulate the teacher-pupil transactions, to engineer them in such a way that the student comes to adopt a view held by the teacher and which the latter has chosen to transmit. By the very nature of the instructional transaction, the pupil cannot know all that the teacher knows about the topic, recognizes that fact, and enters into a collusion with the teacher so as to be manipulated by him. The teacher's status further insures the process by giving him powers of reward and punishment. This is the case for traditional, ordinary teaching. Inauthentic teaching.

Authentic Teaching

Authentic teaching attempts to transcend the basic manipulative aspect of the instructional transaction. The teacher uses two pedagogic strategies in this: Transacting the Authentic Teaching Contract and Transacting Objective Reporting. The Authentic Teaching Contract is an agreement arrived at between teacher and pupil whereby the rights of the potential victim in the ensuing manipulative transaction are to be publicly and continuously reaffirmed. It entails a double responsibility: on the teacher's side, a responsibility to safeguard the best interests of the pupil and to engage in repairing activities should the pupil feel victimized; on the pupil's side, it entails the responsibility of attempting to remain authentic: to legitimize the teacher's statements by listening and to report all forms of reneging (failure to listen, engaging in bluffing, in disagreement). Objective Reporting insures, among other things, that the Contract is being publicly reaffirmed. We shall elaborate further on the notion of authentic teaching by considering next the following topics: Antidotes to Disagreements, the Teacher Paradox, and the Authentic Teacher's Profile.

Antidotes to Disagreements

Disagreeing Transactions are set up through the following means: withholding appropriate legitimization, attempting to victimize, and attempting to defend the self.

A. *Legitimizing Transactions*: When an individual is a participant in a conversation, he is performing transactions. When a participant talks, he is engineering a transactional exchange in which he receives (i.e., appropriately responds to) and initiates a number of transactions simultaneously. The transactional code in force specifies the manner in which these transactions are to be properly performed (initiated and responded to). In any particular conversational episode, the successful completion of transactional exchanges depends on the extent to which the participants share a transactional dialect. The participants themselves originate the specific ongoing transactions. To our knowledge, there exists no systematic account of this process: why does a participant initiate a particular transaction, and is he aware of what he is doing? Transactional exchanges can be successful even though the participants involved may not be able to report that they have occurred and may not even be aware that they occurred either because of their routine (unnoticed) status (i.e., code governed) or because of their hidden nature (cf., defense mechanisms).

When a participant initiates a transaction (e.g., Requests Support) the intended receiver must either comply with the request or reject it appropriately. The transactional dialect in force specifies the rules for appropriate rejection. Consider the following illustration:

> *contextual setting:* husband requests support from wife at a dinner conversation during a bluffing exchange with a colleague:
>
> husband: I don't think so, George. I know it was Thursday, not Wednesday, because 'Jane takes Joy to music practice on Thursday afternoons, and I was home babysitting on that afternoon. It couldn't have been Wednesday. Right, Jane?

Consider now the following alternative possibilities open to the wife in response to the husband's request:

(a) wife: That's right.

(b) wife: That's right. I remember that. Last Thursday I came home late, and you had set the table. Darling you.

(c) wife: Uh . . . uh.

(d) wife: Is it Thursdays or Wednesdays that I take Joy? I can never remember . . . .

(e) wife: No, you're wrong. It was Wednesday.

(f) wife: Actually, it usually is on Thursdays, but last week, Joy had a party to go to on Thursday, so I took her on Wednesday.

Independently of when the event in question actually occurred or the wife's own recollections of it, any one of the half dozen possibilities listed can occur. In (a) she is complying with the request in a minimal adequate fashion. In (b) she is elaborating upon this minimum which amounts to a stronger support. In (c) she fails to comply adequately and leaves a note of ambiguity. In (d) she elaborates upon her failure to comply which amounts to public recognition that she has thus failed. In (e), she not only publicly recognizes her failure to comply but, in addition, initiates a disagreeing transaction. In (f), she fails to comply, publicly recognizes it, but also, provides adequate justification for failure to comply—hence does not constitute the initiation of a disagreeing transaction.

The transactional dialect in force specifies what constitutes adequate compliance and appropriate rejection of transactional requests. A distinction should be made between the public and the private transactional dialect. The public transactional dialect is described in the code book of transactional etiquette: participants' exchanges are jointly interpreted (cf., "bidding" rules in bridge). The private transactional register specifies the significance of an exchange on the basis of rules known only to a subgroup of the whole group. When two intimates converse with nonintimates, the significance of a transaction may be different at the private and public level. Sometimes, the demand characteristics of these two codes are incompatible, in which case a Double-entendre transaction is performed, but here, unlike the theatre, it is the audience (the other conversational participants) that is the party being kept in the dark. For instance, response (a), in the illustration above, may represent adequate compliance according to the public code, yet it may be deficient on the basis of the private code between husband and wife (cf., response (b)). Similarly, response (e) may be deficient according to the public transactional dialect in force among the participants around the dinner table (cf., response (f)—which *is* adequate), yet it may be adequate according to their private transactional code which in fact contextualizes adequacy according to the topic at hand, as in this case where the topic is not crucial (relative to this colleague), less justification is insisted upon as necessary (a convenient rule since it does not interrupt an activity the other spouse is involved in, e.g., flirting with the husband's colleague).

What constitutes minimal adequate compliance with transactional requests is what is involved in the problem of initiating legitimizing transactions. This problem faces the participant at every talking turn. It is an obligatory transaction and has only two outcomes: he either complies adequately (viz., he legitimizes), or he fails to do so. Which of these two events occurs has momentous implications for the ongoing transactions and the whole ensuing conversational episode. Conversation is a series of steps in brinkmanship: at any point, a talker may fail to comply with a legitimization request, and in that case the participants are no longer on a friendly basis; depending on the felt importance of the breach, victimizing transactions may ensue in which case the face of one or more participants may have been injured (sometimes with severe emotional consequences).

In the Nonvictimizing register of the transactional code, legitimization requests may not be turned down without adequate justification. What constitutes adequate justification lies at the bottom of instructional strategies designed as antidotes to disagreements, as well as, more generally, the smoothness and efficiency of the transactional flow in a conversation. Only a brief and incomplete sketch will be given here.

Legitimization requests represent the fluid that oils the mechanism of the transactional machinery. During dry periods (e.g., after a series of victimizing exchanges) a request for legitimization is so serious that failure to comply disrupts the conversation to the point where participants quickly end it. Long before termination, however, many kinds of transactions become impossible to perform, among them the instructional transaction.

A common form of a legitimization request can be dramatized as "Did you hear me?" At the surface level, this legitimization request refers to the topic of the talker's statements and can be adequately complied with by paraphrasing the talker's remarks or by jumping that step and responding by a retort which implies that the remarks were understood. In cases where the retort leaves the status of the legitimization request ambiguous, the first speaker will point that out and try again (cf., "I don't think I made my point clear. What I mean is . . . "). Nodding of the head is a frequently used legitimization response necessitating no interruption. It is ambiguous, however, and in instructional transactions, as every teacher knows, it is quite deficient.

A serious problematic element involving legitimization requests is the fact that they are often requests for the legitimization of a nonsurface, nontopical ongoing transaction. In terms of depth, husband makes three simultaneous requests in the previous illustration ("Right, Jane?"); from surface down: Requests Information, Requests Support, and Demands Loyalty. In her response, the wife can comply with the first request through all the alternatives listed, save (c). She can comply with the second request only through alternatives (a) and (b), and it is solely through alternative (b) that she can comply with the third request. If the private transactional dialect contextualizes this particular interaction such that the third request (Demands Loyalty) is a legitimization request, the wife must choose alternative (b), otherwise she will have failed to legitimize with possible serious consequences (e.g., being victimized by the husband after the guests have left).

In the instructional register, the public transactional dialect governing authentic teaching (i.e., where the Authentic Teaching Contract is in force; see above) attempts to insure that all legitimization requests on the part of the students are complied with by the teacher. Without attempting to be exhaustive, let us list some of the legitimization requests typically made by students with which it is important for the teacher to comply:

1. *"Please, teacher, could we talk about* x, *not* y*":* teacher responses that fail to comply, hence impede the learning process, include: "That's not a relevant point," or "You shouldn't be doing that," or "I'll come back to that later," or "I want you to do it this way, not that way," and so on, all of which serve to invalidate the student's right to choose topics in the instructional conversation. Students with higher learning competence are able to learn under conditions where the teacher disregards some of their legitimization requests, but not all.

2. *"Please, teacher, could we engage in a Repairing Transaction before proceeding":* whenever there has been a failure to comply with a legitimization request, participants can set things right by engaging in repairing activities: apologizing, reaffirming the speaking contract, making the lack of compliance the next topic of conversation and justifying it more adequately, etc. Teachers who are faced with "pig-headedness," "anger," "resistance," and "uncooperativeness" on the part of their pupils may be in that position as a result of failing to engage in adequate repairing activities after repeated lack of compliance with earlier legitimization requests (cf., task- vs. people-centered teaching).

3. *"Please, teacher, could you stop requesting that I simultaneously comply with incompatible requests":* a teacher may say "You must listen to me to understand this" while at the same time he inhibits feedback necessary to succeed in listening to him by lecturing or colluding with the students in their silence or inauthenticity.

In the SAOROGAT method, the encouragement to report objectively the here-and-now of ongoing feelings and transactions minimizes the likelihood of Disagreeing, Victimizing, and Invalidating Transactions. In ordinary conversations, including the instructional register of inauthentic teaching, many syntactic and semantic devices are used to maintain inauthenticity and increase disagreeing and victimizing transactions. For instance, participants will say, "He is not a likeable person" when they mean, "I don't like him"; or, they will say "People would like to take a coffee break," or "It's time for a coffee break" when they mean, "I would like us to take a coffee break now." Collective pronouns such as "we," "they," "you" are used "impersonally" and inauthentically for "I," and the here-and-now events are displaced, in talk, to the past, the future, the general, the typical. When this inauthentic register is used, legitimization requests are more difficult to comply with and disagreements ensue more readily.

Consider the following illustrative cases and their analyses:

1. A: I like chocolate ice cream.
   B: I don't.
   B^1:   Oh, I don't.

Response B fails to legitimize A's comment in the absence of a clause in the private transactional dialect between A and B that frees B from the necessity of legitimizing within that topic. In that case, the "Oh" in B^1 succeeds since B shows thereby evidence that he has acknowledged A's statement as Giving Information. In the absence of "Oh" (as in B), B initiates a Disagreeing Transaction by turning down without adequate justification A's request for Exchanging Information.

2. A: Isn't chocolate ice cream delicious?
   B: ?!**?!*
   B^1:   Yeah!

Here, A requests agreement and if B does not share A's preference he cannot authentically legitimize (as in B^1).

3. A: Marriage is restricting.
   B: No, it is not.
   B^1:   You think so?
   B^2:   Do you mean, generally?
   B^3:   Yes, it can be very trying.

Note that A's statement may be a displacement of "I feel marriage is restricting me." On the surface, this is a transaction of Giving Information (*self* is the topic). Simultaneously, however, there is another transaction initiated by A. This is given by the fact that an utterance in a conversation does not ordinarily stand by itself: it has transactional significance by virtue of the fact that any particular utterance is embedded in an ongoing matrix of transactions from which it derives its transactional significance. In this case, B might ask, What is the point of A's statement: why does he perform this particular transaction of Giving Information at this particular time? What is the transactional context? Are A and B currently in a Victimizing Transaction? Legitimization Transaction? Disagreeing Transaction? Instructional Transaction? Each decision will select the patterned features of the several transactions that this one utterance initiates. "Marriage is restricting" is transformed into "I feel restricted by marriage," and the latter is transformed (by contextual selectors) into "I would like to vent my emotions on how I feel about marriage right now," which is a transactional request for sympathy and empathy. In that case, response B is inauthentic since it ignores the true request, while appearing to respond to the logical structure of the topic. In other words, A speaks impersonally while he means to be personal, and B responds impersonally ignoring A's personal request. B and A are exchanging a Disagreeing transaction while appearing to Exchange Opinions. Response B^1 succeeds in accomplishing a number of transactional events: it furthers the conversational exchange without disagreeing by pointing in the direction of A's underlying intent; it is minimally legitimizing (cf., "Yeah, I know what you mean," which complies fully with A's request for empathy). Response B^2 is an alternative way of providing minimal legitimization. We include it here to point out that minimally adequate legitimization responses in the instructional register may have different directional significance. In this case, response B^2 is less directive, more ambiguous than B^1: it fails to counteract productively A's inauthentic impersonality. Response B^3 is interesting because it matches A's impersonality in surface style while responding to A's personal request. This is an example of transactional smoothness between participants that share dialects: the surface transactional style (i.e., form of dramatization) and the underlying transactional exchange are jointly synchronized.

The Teacher Paradox

The teacher-student dyadic role contains an inherent inequality of status and power that is characteristic of many social role dyads (parent-child, boss-employee, doctor-patient, policeman-accused). Inequality of knowledge, power, and responsibility is a fruitful context for manipulative transactions. Some such manipulations fall in the "helping" category, others in the "victimizing" category, depending on social value definitions in force. Within the context of the classrooms of our current educational system, we can distinguish between manipulative transactions that are instructionally motivated and those that are personally motivated. The latter can be either victimizing or validating, both of which may be authentic or inauthentic, depending on the knowledge and awareness of the participants. Inauthentic victimizing transactions are frequent and personally damaging to participants (cf., "Student as nigger," "Teacher as enemy"). Authentic victimizing transactions often occur in the context of bilingual education where the Anglo teacher and the ethnic minority students are engaged in mutually victimizing transactions, both sides knowing just what is going on, and what the rules of the game are. Authentic validating transactions occur in the context of mature, competent learners helping the teacher present his instructional transaction at the authentic level. Given the public school context, a teacher interested in authentic teaching will be involved in inauthentic validating transactions. This is what creates the Teacher Paradox.

Given the inequality in knowledge between the participants of an instructional dyad, the teaching process is inherently manipulative. In the authentic teaching style, adequate safeguards are created to discourage the occurrence of victimizing transactions. Nevertheless, it remains true that, from the student's point of view, the mysteries of engineering instructional transactions remain beyond his awareness, and the exchange is perforce inauthentic. He submits himself to the inauthentic transactions in the hope that they will ultimately validate his request for a learning that is personally significant and useful.

In the meantime, during the laborious classroom hours, he is expected to abide by the rules of the instructional game: Listen! Do not interrupt! Do this exercise. Repeat after me. Answer this question. Correct your mistake. Consider this. Find the implication of that. Reverse the order. Paraphrase. And so on to a very large number of bumpy directives and restrictive imperatives. The student's compliance with these instructional requests is based on borrowed time. Sooner or later, depending on learner's competence in interaction with teacher's style, his goodwill (perseverance) runs out and the teacher is faced with learner resistance. How does he overcome it? Assuming he is not giving up when faced with that problem (e.g., continues to lecture or ends lecture), he must find a way to *trick* the recalcitrant learner. Excluded from the transactional register of authentic instruction are such inauthentic victimizing transactions as intimidating, duping, deceiving, brainwashing, corrupting. Perhaps some other types of inauthentic transactions might be less sanguinely victimizing yet equally effective manipulators: enticing, cajoling, bluffing, baiting, seducing. We were once asked, why not "convincing through rational exposition" or some such stylistic alternative in reference to the historic euphemism of the concept of "academic instruction." From the ethnomethodological point of view, the same heuristic device accounts for the sequencing of operative procedures of practical interactions in any transactional context: the Instructional Game, the Scientific Research Game, the Salesman-Customer Game, the Parent-Child Game. Thus, whether we deal with the strategic moves of opponents in a televised political debate, or that of Mommy toilet-training Baby, or that of the alphabet cartoonists on Sesame Street, we are faced in every instance with the con artist's implements: the end place having been adjudged Good-for-Him by the teacher and whom he represents, he then proceeds to get the student there by whatever means allowed to him by the context: asking, pushing, pulling, cajoling, intimidating, bulldozing, seducing, convincing, persuading, and so on. Whichever it is, it remains the fact that the authentic teacher is faced with an obligatory choice between inauthentic instructional strategies. The Authentic Teacher's Paradox.

Can it be transcended?

The Authentic Teacher's Profile

Transactional technology is an engineering problem. Intuitive and inadequately formulated descriptions of "the art of teaching" are transformed into the systematically precise register of educational psycholinguistics, of the transactional analysis of teaching. The charismatic inspirational performances of the Great Teacher are dissected into the components and subcomponents of ordinary transactional competence, the kind every ordinary teacher possesses, but may not ordinarily use. We give below a tentative semantic differential profile of the authentic teacher who struggles with adequate success in transcending the Teacher's Paradox. (See adjoining Table.) The halfway point between the defining opposite transactional labels separates the success from the failure zone of pedagogical endeavor. The successful teacher is capable of engineering classroom transactions so that he consistently finds himself on the left-hand zone of the transactional profile.

The Authentic Teacher's Transactional Profile

Success Zone		Failure Zone
Confirms		Disconfirms
Accepts		Rejects
Validates		Victimizes
Agrees		Disagrees
Supports		Undermines
Legitimizes		Disagrees
Encourages		Discourages
Enhances		Constricts
Creates		Destroys
Reflects		Deflects
Believes		Disbelieves
Admits		Denies
Receives		Initiates
Cooperates		Competes
Thwarts		Colludes
Inspires		Flattens
Interests		Bores

In his authentic teaching, he selects those inauthentic strategies that will validate the student's trust and will result in greater awareness of the self in relation to the instructional topic. Teachers ought to remind themselves that the deliberate, manipulative, pedagogic use of authentic teaching strategies (as specified by the left-hand terms of the profile) is an inauthentic manipulative device and as long as they remain teachers vis-à-vis the students, they cannot engage in noninstructional authentic transactional exchanges. Attempts toward the latter are not realistically possible on a general scale in the present educational system given the current sociopolitical setting. In our opinion, however, the noninstructional authentic transactional mode of relationship is not essential for experiential or instructional learning to take place. Parental figures can be teachers, or peers, or both at different times. Restriction to the first of these, teacher mode only, ignores many essential components of personal growth of the student, but it does not thwart it per se; only a specialization is set up.

Encounter workshops have helped us become more aware of the transactional dances we perform. Self-analytic observations during our teaching attempts revealed the mechanism of the transactional code in the teaching-learning process. Our teaching performance changed in accordance with this developing personal pedagogic model.

REFERENCES

Austin, J. L. *How To Do Things With Words.* (1955 Lectures, ed. by J. O. Urmson). New York: Oxford University Press, 1965.

Bales, R.F., *Personality and Interpersonal Behavior.* New York: Holt, Rinehart, and Winston, 1970.

Berne, Eric. *Games People Play.* New York: Grove Press, 1967. (First published: 1964)

Castaneda, Carlos. *The Teachings of Don Juan: A Yaqui Way of Knowledge.* New York: Ballantine Books, 1969.

————. *A Separate Reality: Further Conversations With Don Juan.* New York: Simon and Schuster, 1971.

Chomsky, Noam. *Aspects of the Theory of Syntax.* Cambridge, Mass.: M.I.T. Press, 1965.

Garfinkel, Harold. *Studies in Ethnomethodology.* Englewood Cliffs, N.J.: Prentice-Hall, 1968.

Gendlin, E.T. "Values and the Process of Experiencing." In A. H. Mahrer, (ed.), *The Goals of Psychotherapy.* New York: Appleton-Century Crofts, 1967.

Goffman, Erving. *Relations in Public: Microstudies of the Public Order*. New York: Basic Books, 1971.

Kochman, Thomas. "Black English in the Classroom." Department of Linguistics, Northeastern Illinois State College, 1969 (Mimeo.).

Laing, R. D. *The Politics of Experience*. New York: Ballantine Books, 1967.

Mitchell-Kernan, Claudia. *Language Behavior in a Black Urban Community*. Working Paper No. 23, Language Behavior Research Laboratory, 1969 (Mimeo.).

Sacks, Harvey. "Aspects of the Sequential Organization of Conversation." (Forthcoming, Prentice-Hall).

Searle, J. R. *Speech Acts*. Cambridge, England and New York: Cambridge University Press, 1969.

Watts, A. W. *Psychotherapy: East and West*. New York: Ballantine Books, 1969.

Wilkinson, A. M. (ed.). "The State of Language." *Educational Review, 22*(1), 1969.

8 An Empirical Study of the Development of Transactional Engineering Competence

A comprehensive study of human language must include a serious attempt to specify the relationship between what a speaker knows and what he can say. At a sufficiently abstract level of generality, the notion "what a speaker knows" includes that which a speaker says and can say as well as various other things, but it will be useful, for our present purposes, to consider the concept of "knowledge" at a less general level, even though we may not succeed in giving it a sufficiently precise definition so as to clearly exclude "what a person can say" from "what a person knows." This, however, is not crucial to our present intent, which is to show how a person's conception of reality is built upon and develops from the everyday conversational interactions in which he participates.[1]

It is not our intention to minimize the importance of physical manipulation of the environment and nondiscourse thinking[2] as factors that contribute to a person's acquisition of knowledge and discovery of reality. In fact, we have no idea what the relative contribution is between these various factors, or even that they can be separated observationally, but it appears evident to us that a significant proportion of that which is ordinarily ascribed to what a person knows is acquired via the intermediary of verbal interaction with others.[3] Formal education, as practiced in technological societies, is almost exclusively transmitted through the medium of verbal interaction, and the social and physical reality of the preschool child is similarly based on the category systems and methods of inferencing that govern linguistic and discourse structure as used in the home.

It is possible to adopt a strictly behavioristic approach to this problem by defining a person's conception of reality as the sum total of all the verbal interactions in the life history of a speaker. But we cannot reconcile ourselves to such a narrow approach inasmuch as we can find no theoretical justification for distinguishing between "what a person says" (or "understands") and "what a person can say" (or "can understand"). A nontrivial account of speaking and understanding will include processes of semantic analysis that will permit application to an indefinitely large number of verbal interactions, only some of which will have actually occurred in the history of any one speaker. We are convinced that a significant part of what a person evidences that he knows cannot be traced to actual verbal interactions that are observationally identifiable, partly on account of the fact that deep structure semantic relations and discourse rules are never verbalized overtly, and partly because some knowledge is self-generated in discourse thinking.

We are, furthermore, not concerned here with the "truth value" of what a person knows. Thus, a speaker can evidence that he knows x by uttering y and it matters not whether y is a true or false statement, a belief, a hypothesis, an illusion based on fantasy, or whatever. What a person can say is some function of what he knows, and this in turn will define a significant portion of that person's reality. Since what a person knows evidently varies from moment to moment, it is proper to say that a person's reality also varies accordingly. An individual may read a few pages of a book or listen to a speech and have thereby his reality changed. Similarly, he may have a dream, a "vision" or some nonparticipatory transcendental experience, and his reality may change in significant ways.

Our specific purpose in what follows is to show how the reality of a two-and-a-half-year-old boy, Rex, changes as a function of the nature of the verbal interactions he is exposed to. In its broad terms of reference, this is a study of the socialization process. The reality to which Rex is exposed in his home is the reality of his mother and father who are the principal participants in his verbal interactions. In important ways, the reality of Rex's parents is related to a standard, which is definable in reference to an ethnography of the subculture they belong to. Thus, whether Rex's reality will include a God that manipulates his environment, whether he assigns some of the events he sees on T.V. to "real things" versus "fantasy things," or whether his self-concept is diminished as a result of defecating in his pants, or whatever, will be traceable to what he is told about these things by his parents, and what he is told will depend on what his parents' reality is, which in turn will depend on their subcultural standards and their own previous socialization process.

There are numerous ways in which the socialization process can be seen to direct the etiology of a person's conception of reality. The pattern of interaction with others affects an infant's conception of the role of people in the world: who they are, what their rights and privileges are, what they do, what they consider proper and for which they are rewarded positively and what they consider improper and for which they are rewarded negatively, and so on. The home environment serves as a selective mechanism of exposure to specific things: what foods are eaten, what objects are present, which ones are "playable with," and which ones must be seen without being touched, their functional use, their break down and replacement histories, and for obscuring, ignoring, forgetting, dismissing, distorting purposefully, and so on. In all of this, verbal interaction plays a crucial role: what aspects of the physical and social world are selected for focus of attention, for topicality in conversational interaction, for interpretation, evaluation, analysis, elaboration, explanation, justification. The quality of the social adjustment of a child is reflected in the nature of the verbal interactions in which he participates. Does he whine and cry a lot? Does he know how to ask for what he wants? Do the parents have to scream, lecture, warn, threaten? Do they typically explain, justify, elaborate, evaluate, scold, express feelings, and do they place similar requirements upon the child? Who is Santa Claus? Why do we celebrate birthdays? Why is it bad to lie? Why must we brush our teeth every day? What's going to happen if I stick my fingers in the wall plug? Can Baby Joy die, and do cars eat? And on and on to a limitless number of verbal interactions that reflect the underlying structure of our everyday reality. As the child grows and matures—becomes socialized, the structure of his reality changes, and this is reflected by a change in the nature of his verbal interactions: the things he says, the questions he asks, the explanations he gives, the feelings he expresses, the reasons he accepts, change in direct measure to the changing picture of his reality. At first his world is populated with people, monsters, fairies, fantasy characters. Gradually, he begins to show—in his verbal interactions—the effects of the verbal socialization process: he comes to make distinctions between Yes and No, a lot and a little, real things and pretend things, what's alive and what isn't, I want to and you want to, and learns to use appropriately such expressions as I need, have to, must, because, which one, why, if . . . then, which reflect the particular processes of logical implication and inference making that are proper to the reality of the parental subculture. By the time the child reaches his third birthday he has acquired a significant proportion of the adult reality and evidences the rules of ordinary consensus in his conversational interactions.

Conversations with a two-and-a-half-year old

In what follows, we shall present samples of conversational interactions one of us has had with Rex (LAJ's son) at a time just prior to his third birthday, specifically during his 34th month of life. In general, Rex's motor and language development appear to have followed the typical pattern described by Lenneberg (1957, Table 4.1), although his motor development was somewhat slower and his language development somewhat faster than those norms would indicate. All conversational interactions presented here are based on verbatim records written down as they occurred or a few seconds after they occurred. We made no effort to be either comprehensive or representative, but simply wrote down interactions whenever it was convenient to do so, or whenever a particular interaction appeared at the time to be noteworthy for a number of reasons that are not particularly relevant for our present purposes. Although we have no documented evidence to support this claim, it is our strong impression, corroborated by his mother's judgment, that these recorded interactions were "typical" of Rex's utterances at this stage of development.

A cursory inspection of these verbal interactions (to be found in the materials appended to this chapter) reveals the general character of Rex's conversational rules at this stage of his development. One of the most striking aspects of these records is that, with virtually no exceptions, Rex's verbal interactions are one-topic conversations. This is not an artifact of the method of record keeping. At this stage, Rex shows no evidence of engaging in multiple-topic conversations typical of adults. If the verbal interaction is initiated by the adult, the child might participate in the ordinary fashion, but without making any attempt to pursue the interaction beyond the specific topic raised by the initiator, and will typically allow the interaction to lapse into silence unless the adult once again chooses to initiate a topic switch. The same holds true for interactions initiated by the child himself. One possibility occurs to us to account for this pattern. It may be that, at this stage, the child has not acquired any adult rules relating to topic switches in conversational interaction and thus allows the verbal interaction to lapse into silence. Adult conversational interaction under ordinary conditions contains a prohibition rule against silence, and various devices are typically used to move from one topic of discourse to the next (e.g., Incidentally . . . ; By the way . . . ; This reminds me of . . . ; So, what else have you been doing? . . . ; And how is . . . , or And how are you . . . ; I hear that . . . ; Did you read about . . . ; etc., etc.). There isn't a single occurrence of these topic switch devices in Rex's speech at this stage of his development.

The lack of topic switch rules either contributes to or is merely correlative with a number of other features of Rex's conversations that contrast with adult conversations. The sample interactions being considered here are dramatically single-minded and purposeful. There is no "beating around the bush," small talk, innuendo, or indirect expression of intent. These interactions are in a direct representational style, and Rex pursues his conversational intent with a striking bluntness that can appear to the adult embarrassing, if not sanguine, in its directness and unpretentious simplicity.

This directness also expresses itself in a total literalness in meaning that Rex attaches to utterances. One way in which this manifests itself is his extreme susceptibility to teasing. He will instantaneously switch from a happy, playful mood to crying when told he must do something he does not wish to do or when contradicted in a statement, even though the adult's intent was one of playful teasing. Conversely, he will switch from crying to demonstrative jubilation at the mere intervention of a verbal assent. His reality at this stage is determined as much by verbal fiats as it is by nonverbal contingencies in the environment. The promise of a cookie to be had later seems to be as effective a reinforcer for Rex as the actual receiving of it, and a verbal prohibition or threat has comparable effects to a physical intervention. He shows similar effects of fright when his father verbally play-acts a "monster," and when he puts on facial and bodily contortions in imitation of one. If it is true for the older child or adult that words have a magical power, for the two-and-a-half-year-old they assume truly awesome power.

Singlemindedness, directness, and literalness are further notable in an absolute egocentricity of participant interaction. Rex will interject himself in a conversation without any preliminaries whether or not he is a prior participant and whether or not he retains the ongoing topic of conversation. He has no rules against interruptions and acts as if he expects a response merely as a result of his making an utterance. He does not use, at this stage, any verbal attention-getting device but simply proceeds with his utterance.[4] If no response is forthcoming, he will merely repeat his utterance and proceed to do so a number of times until he gets a response or is otherwise distracted. Conversely, when an adult addresses an utterance to him, and he is not inclined to respond (for whatever reason), he will simply ignore it without showing any inclination to explain his silence. He also exhibits strong resistance to talking in the dark insisting that he must *see* the interlocutor, and he will similarly insist on face-to-face visual contact whenever possible. We noticed that when the latter is not possible (as in telephone conversations or talking loudly from another room), his comprehension shows considerable attenuation in a way that cannot be attributed to a mere hearing problem.

The absence of metalinguistic attention-getting devices and the lack of topic switch rules, coupled with an absolute egocentricity and literalness are thus some primary factors that contribute to the striking character of Rex's conversational interactions shortly before his third birthday of life. Yet despite these structural differences between his and an adult's pattern of interaction, it is evident that even this intermediary form of competence has sufficient power to enable Rex to discover the reality of his subculture: the intricacies of the social order around him, the nature of consensual validation, the appropriateness of justification, the semantic order and the culturally sanctioned conceptual syntax. It appears clear to us, and we hope we can make a convincing case for it in what follows, that the syntax of Rex's conversational competence at this early stage already approaches the awesome power of the full-fledged adult model despite the fact that his capacity for logical inferencing and the intricacies of his taxonomic semantic system are woefully inadequate when compared to the adult model. Sapir's analogy (quoted in Bruner, 1967) again comes to mind: "It is somewhat as though a dynamo capable of generating enough power to run an elevator were operated almost exclusively to feed an electric doorbell." But the waste implied by this analogy does not seem appropriate, for is it not the very power of this structural generator that affords the occasion for the acquisition in socialization of a conceptual structure as intricate as ordinary knowledge? A more efficient coupling between discourse syntax and conceptual thinking may not be able to achieve the same results. The acquisition of language does not seem to be a feat at all, not for the individual, even though it may be for the race, no more so than seeing, or hearing, or walking: the presently evolved structure of the brain makes it as inevitable and unproblematic as imprinting is for the greylag goose. If there is a feat at all, it is surely the use of this human capacity to discover the fortuitous peculiarities of the socially validated reality of the particular group of humans the child happens to be raised in.

There are many examples we can present to evidence the specific deficiencies in Rex's conversational interaction. He will repeat an utterance over and over again until acknowledged by the adult, rather than make a prior attempt to obtain the adult's attention. He apparently does not consider it criterial what the addressee is doing before addressing him (viz., whether he is available for conversation) and will proceed in a uniform manner whether the other person is engaged in play with him, is engaged in a separate conversation with a third party, or even is talking on the telephone. He will interject himself in a conversation in total disregard of his prior nonparticipation. He will merely disregard any utterance he does not understand rather than demand clarification. He might even start an utterance in the absence of the addressee as in the following recorded instance.

Father: Go tell Mommy to bring me an ashtray.
Rex: O.K. Mommy, bring an ashtray for Daddy. (Walking out of the kitchen. He kept repeating his utterance while on his way to find his mother and repeated it in her presence.)

Discovering Reality Through Questions

An analysis of the range of questions he typically asks at this stage gives an indication of the strategies he uses in discovering the consensual validation process of his parents' ordinary reality. Here is a near complete list of types as they occur in our records.

Why?

Where is X? $(X \longrightarrow \begin{cases} VP \\ NP \\ proper\ noun \end{cases}$)

Is there too much in here?

Where do I put this?

Can I X? $(X \longrightarrow VP)$

Pam?

In the sandbox? (elliptical for "Is she . . .")

What's X? $(X \longrightarrow N)$

O.K.?

Why don't you X? $(X \longrightarrow VP)$

Is this X or Y? $(\begin{cases} X \\ Y \end{cases} \longrightarrow NP)$

What? (elliptical for $\begin{cases} \text{What did you say?} \\ \text{What do you want?} \\ \text{What's the matter?} \end{cases}$)

What are you doing?

Can I X? $(X \longrightarrow \begin{cases} V \\ VP \end{cases}$)

Can Y X? $(Y \longrightarrow \begin{cases} NP \\ N \end{cases}$; $X \longrightarrow \begin{cases} V \\ VP \end{cases}$)

Will you X? $(X \longrightarrow VP)$

How many X's? $(X \longrightarrow \begin{cases} null\ element \\ plural\ noun \\ VP \end{cases}$)

Do you X? $(X \longrightarrow VP)$

What happened?

Which way you didn't look?

Are you X? $(X \longrightarrow VP)$

The X and the Y? $\left(\left. \begin{matrix} X \\ Y \end{matrix} \right\} \longrightarrow S \right)$

Am I X? $(X \longrightarrow VP)$

Huh?

Is X? $(X \longrightarrow S)$

Yeah or No?

Does X have to Y? $\left(X \longrightarrow \begin{cases} NP \\ N \end{cases} \quad Y \longrightarrow \begin{cases} V \\ VP \end{cases} \right)$

She wants to be nice to me so I'll be nice to her?

Why are you X? $(X \longrightarrow VP)$

About what?

Remember?

You are leaving those for me?

You like to eat some more corn?

Is Mommy finished?

Is that your paper?

Where?

Do you want it?

Who bought this?

Do all Mommies buy food?

What's gonna happen if X? $(X \longrightarrow S)$

What's gonna people say?

Why you X? $(X \longrightarrow VP)$

What are X's? $(X \longrightarrow plural\ noun)$

What's a Y? $(Y \longrightarrow N)$

Undoubtedly, a detailed linguistic analysis of Rex's questions would present a more coherent syntactic picture, but our purpose here is merely to illustrate the power of the conversational devices he controls for obtaining information about the socially given order in his environment. To do this systematically, it would be necessary to develop analytical techniques pertaining to discourse rules, which are not, at the moment, available to us. Inspection of the verbal interactions presented in the appendices do, nevertheless, reveal a number of elementary strategies Rex uses for obtaining information about certain aspects of the socially conceived order. In examples (8), (12), and (17) in Appendix I Rex poses questions that are satisfied by a neutral Yes/No answer, while in (10) and (30) it is clear that he has a hypothesis about the answer but wants confirmation for it. If he has sufficient information about a topic or understanding of the issue, he will ask a highly specific clarification, as in (16b), otherwise he will use a shotgun inquiry technique that is too general, intrinsically, but still succeeds because of the adult's willingness to guess what his specific problem is, as in (16a), (23) and (31). Note, however, that the latter technique is nonfunctional when the adult is uncooperative, as in (32), and presumably, when he makes a wrong guess about the child's particular interest, as appears to be the case in examples (20a) and (40a). Further evidence of the nature of Rex's discovery techniques will be found in the other interactions recorded in Appendix I. More specifically, example (14) in which he sets up a two-step problem for the listener in order to inquire about the latter's motivation for helping him in a task, example (15) in which he tests out the adult's reaction to a potentially improper action, example (13) in which he ingeneously sets up the frame for the adult's answer by analogic thinking, and example (18) in which he invents a counting game whose rationale resembles an instructional program. Example (11) shows that he can frame a request using an utterance that appears to be a neutral question, which is a stylistic variant of a direct request (cf., 22a).

Areas of Consensual Validation

The other examples in Appendix I are presented to illustrate the manner in which conversational interactions with an adult can serve to transmit consensual validation about the social and physical order of the environment. The following conceptual areas are evidenced:

(a) *the nature of logical implication in conversational interaction* dealing, in these examples, with functional use (1), counting (18), private events not directly accessible to the other (21), (37a, b), and availability for participatory interaction (39b, c; (b) *the definitional range* of concepts (2), (5), (18), (22b), (25), (27), (29), (35b), conversational situations (7), verbal (3), (4), (6) and nonverbal rituals (35a); (c) *accessibility of the other to verbal control* (34a), (35a);(d) *psychological implication about interpersonal intention* (9), (24); (e) *verbal interaction as an expression of phatic communion* (19), (34b), (37); and (f) *reporting events* (28). In addition note the child's behavior in practicing reporting (26) and description, the latter via a verbal monologue in the presence of an adult (38).

Discovering the Nature of Social Justification
Through Conversational Interaction

In Appendix II, we present 59 verbal interactions all of which contain a *Why*-question followed by a *because* statement. At the time these records were collected (viz., during the 34th month of Rex's life) a substantial proportion (possibly up to 50%) of the father's verbal interactions with Rex consisted of short, one-topic conversations revolving around the socially acceptable justification for verbal and nonverbal events. It is clear that this was an active period for the development of consensual validation for justifying socially relevant phenomena. Inspection of these conversational interactions reveals the wide range of events that are salient to a three-year-old child and the manner in which the socially sanctioned order can be transmitted through conversational interactions. In Table 1, we have attempted to summarize the topics of these interactions about ordinary justification by classifying them into ten types or conceptual areas about the socially relevant order as viewed from the adult's perspective. The numbers in the Table refer to the sequenced order of conversations as presented in Appendix II. The sequence approximates the order of their recording or occurrence in time. It can be seen that, by this stage of development, the child is capable of initiating *because* statements in every category used by the adult.

TABLE 1

**Types of Ordinary Justification Recorded
in Adult-Child Conversational Interaction**

Type	Initiator of Justification	
	Adult	Child
1. Consequence of personal preference	13, 21, 48, 18c	2, 5, 6, 31, 54, 18a
2. Antecedents to physical states of comfort	1, 29, 56b, 56c, 56d	32, 44
3. Manipulative consequences	41, 43, 55	8
4. Leading to desirable or undesirable consequences	14, 33, 51b	16, 38
5. Functional use	37, 56f	30
6. Genesis of feeling states	9c	28
7. Logical implication	9b, 17a, 18e, 45, 56, 52c, 56a, 56e, 57, 58a	9a, 10, 18d, 50
8. Definitional relation	17b, 39, 40, 47, 49a, 51a, 56g, 58b	25, 59
9. Obscure/incomplete	15, 19, 20, 36, 42, 49b, 52b, 53b	3, 7, 11, 12, 24, 26, 27, 34, 35
10. Pseudo-justification	18b	4, 22, 23, 52a, 53a

The general character of conversational interactions with an almost-three-year-old, as typified by the examples presented in Appendix II, differs in some crucial respects from adult conversational interactions. Perhaps the most salient differentiating feature about the data under consideration relates to the explicitness of social justification. Adult conversational interaction is highly elliptical in the sense that inferential processes that must form part of the interaction for it to be meaningful are never concretized in the observable data that form the phonetic shape of the utterances. An example, cited by Garfinkel (1967, pp. 25-26) will serve to illustrate our point. The following is an interaction that took place between a couple:

> Husband: Dana succeeded in putting a penny in a parking meter today without being picked up.
> Wife: Did you take him to the record store?
> Husband: No, to the shoe repair shop.
> Wife: What for?
> Husband: I got some new shoe laces for my shoes.
> Wife: Your loafers need new heels badly.

The elliptical nature of this interaction, typical of everyday ordinary conversations, renders it partly meaningful and partly meaningless to the uninvolved observer. It is obvious that the participants do not find it necessary to refer, in their overt verbalizations, to much information that they share in common as well as to the logical inferential steps that we must posit if we assume, as would be normal, that what each says is meaningful to the other. If we were to attempt to restore the full conversation by verbalizing overtly that which typically remains unexpressed, we might come up with the kind of awkward and atypical conversation suggested by one of Garfinkel's students. To wit:

> Husband: This afternoon as I was bringing Dana, our four-year-old son, home from the nursery school, he succeeded in reaching high enough to put a penny in a parking meter when we parked in a meter zone, whereas before he had always had to be picked up to reach that high.
> Wife: Since he put a penny in a meter that means that you stopped while he was with you. I know that you stopped at the record store either on the way to get him or on the way back. Was it on the way

Husband: back, so that he was with you, or did you stop there on the way to get him and somewhere else on the way back?

Husband: No, I stopped at the record store on the way to get him and stopped at the shoe repair shop on the way home when he was with me.

Wife: I know of one reason why you might have stopped at the shoe repair shop. Why did you in fact?

Husband: As you will remember I broke a shoe lace on one of my brown oxfords the other day so I stopped to get some new laces.

Wife: Something else you could have gotten that I was thinking of. You could have taken in your black loafers which need heels badly. You'd better get them taken care of pretty soon.

Garfinkel quite correctly points out that the elliptical nature of ordinary conversations cannot be restored by attempting to fill in the missing details, no matter how elaborate the restoration process is. Although it might be possible to render a conversation more meaningful to a third party by elaborating on certain missing information, as was done in this example, this gain is possible only because the third party is himself a conversationalist and can interpret the elaborated version on the basis of his prior knowledge of how to particpate in conversations. Were this not the case, as for instance if he were a stranger to the community or a not yet socialized child, it would be impossible for him to understand the elaborated version of the conversation, so long as he does not know the rules of ordinary talk: that people talk in order to say something, that certain types of information (what kind?) can be assumed to be known by the listener whereas other types (what kind?) must be supplied in the conversation, that the listener shares with the speaker certain methods of inferencing and that he can be trusted to follow those rules in the absence of their elaboration, that one can speak directly, indirectly, metaphorically, seriously, jokingly, by double talk, etc., and that the listener can be trusted to know which is the case in each instance, that the ongoing conversation is but a member of a sequence of conversations that extends from the past to the foreseeable future, and so on, and so on.

To render conversations comprehensible, therefore, it is necessary to deal with three sorts of things: (a) shared information relevant to the topic of the conversation, (b) common processes of inferencing in terms of what leads to what, and (c) knowledge about the rules of ordinary talk. The data presented here are not particularly enlightening with respect to the development of the competencies involved in each of these three areas. By the time Rex engages in conversational interactions with adults, his competence already includes the basic skills involved in talking ordinarily, even though there is evidence that his actual competence is deficient in various specific ways relative to the adult. An examination of these deficiencies may be instructive as to the developing nature of the child's conversational competence, while at the same time, it may be suggestive of the nature of the underlying structure of adult conversational ability.

The data in Appendix II are particularly useful for the present purposes because all the verbal interactions therein contain a *Why*-question followed by a *because* statement (sometimes not verbalized) supplied by the addressee. One of the most pervasive rules of ordinary talk is that everything one says must have a point. Another way of saying this is that a participant who produces an utterance thereby makes a claim that he is saying something, rather than just making noises or talking for the sake of talking. The question *Why*, therefore, does not ordinarily mean "Why are you saying that," but rather, "Please justify what you are saying since your logic for saying that isn't clear to me." Thus, the occurrence of *Why* in an ordinary conversation is evidence that there has been a breakdown in the shared inferential processes between participants that are ordinarily necessary for conversations to be successful. The verbal interactions in Appendix II show the specific deficiencies in Rex's inferential processes in conversations inasmuch as many of the occurrences of *Why* to be found there would not occur in ordinary adult conversations. The data are additionally illuminating in that Rex will accept particular justifications (*because* statements) as adequate explanations in places where an adult would not—where an adult would ask for further clarification, and the reverse, such that Rex would continue to ask for further justification after a place where an adult would desist, both of these anomalies serving as evidence for a deficiency in the structure of his conversational competence.

Let us start with verbal interchange number (1) (Appendix II). In the first place, Rex's opening question is anomalous, on the surface, if it is assumed, as we do on the basis of the context (Pam is a live-in babysitter), that he does not mean "Is Pam going to eat with us?" The father's straightforward answer in the affirmative demonstrates his willingness to engage in a conversation with Rex under less than ordinary conditions, by adult standards, for had his wife asked the same question, his answer no doubt would have been something like "What do you mean?" Similarly, the justification he gives, which Rex accepts as adequate, would be taken as facetious in an adult conversation with the probable merited retort of "Aren't you funny!," at the very least. Conversation (1), though not out of the ordinary for Rex, is an impossible interchange for adults.[5]

The next few interchanges ((2)-(16), with the exception of (3) and (8)) do not seem to depart unacceptably from adult standards, although some of these would have to be interpreted, in adult terms, as game activity, a dimension which, however, would not overlap totally with Rex's definition. For example, Rex's justification in (2), (I'm making a hole cause I like a hole) was said in all seriousness as if he was providing his father with relevant information he did not possess before asking the question. His justifying statement in (7), (Let's put Baby Joy in there cause I like her), is structurally more complex than (2), with which it has a surface similarity, since the argument contains three steps:

I want her to be in there
  1. because it's nice in there
  2. and I want her to enjoy it
  3. because I like her

The justification in (3) can be rendered meaningful if we're willing to make some inferences such as "It's dangerous to go in the forest, but it's all right now because there are no tigers or other dangerous animals in there at this time," but such an inferential process falls outside the specified boundaries of the type of inferences that are routinely called for in ordinary conversations by participants (unlike the three-step argument in (7), which follows expected rules of conversational inferencing). (8) is anomalous because, in the absence of a contextual indicator that places an utterance in the "rhetorical" style, it is odd to ask a question about the speaker's own motivation for doing something, and then proceed to specify that intention.

In (13)-(15) Rex poses *Why*-questions that indicate abnormal departure from ordinary rules of inference in conversations. In (13) it would be permissible to insist on immediate attention despite the adult's present reluctance, that would be merely a case of a conflict in wishes, but it is odd to ask a participant why his wishes should take precedence over the speaker's in such matters of personal preference. The *Why*-question in (15) is deviant in a different sense: it does not violate a conversational rule if it is assumed that Rex does not know that to playfully "throw pipi on the floor" is to be silly. This occurrence of *Why* can thus be interpreted as ignorance of certain commonplace rules of social propriety. On the other hand, in (18), it is odd to question the motivation of the other to be helpful in the absence of a prior existing reason for doubting either the propriety or sincerity of the other in wanting to be helpful.

In all of the subsequent interactions recorded in Appendix II, there do not appear to be any further major violations of the rules of ordinary conversational interactions. The oddity of some of the exchanges can be accounted for in other terms: the child's inadequate knowledge of interpersonal motivation and the socially sanctioned conception of the physical world, or in a few cases, to his clearly playful activity.

The Underlying Structure of Conversations

These analyses of the oddity of some of Rex's verbal interactions are suggestive of the kind of structural rules that must be posited to account for the successful accomplishment of participants in conversational interactions, the underlying rules of ordinary talk. The following exchange, which occurred three months after the time the earlier data were recorded, will serve as a departing point for our discussion on an initial formulation of some aspects of the underlying structure of ordinary conversations.

R: What's that? (holding up an animal cookie he took out from its container)

F: I can't see. Turn it around.

R: (turns it, the front facing me)

F: It's an ostrich.

R: No, it's a camel.

F: It's an ostrich.

R: No because look! (points to pictures of animals on box, one of which was that of a camel; subsequently I determined that there was no ostrich cookie or picture.)

Rex's "proof," *No because look!*, is an involved argument that contains in its underlying structure, at least the following four steps:

1. Cookie animals in box correspond to pictures on box, and only the animals shown on the box can be found in the box.
2. When cookie shape is ambiguous, you must match it with one of the pictures on the box.
3. Since there are no pictures of an ostrich, the cookie in question cannot be an ostrich.
4. The closest possible match between the cookie in question and one of the pictures is with the camel. Therefore, it must be a camel.

It is not our intention here to propose a hypothesis about the specific content of the mental operations that underlie Rex's statement *No because look!*, and no serious significance should be attached to the particular wording of the four-stage "proof" we have proposed. At this stage, we can offer nothing of importance as to the psychological reality of the underlying structure of conversational interactions. Nevertheless, it seems to us that hypothetical accounts of this type, when they succeed in being descriptively adequate, may ultimately throw some light on the nature of real mental operations that must form the basis of the observable data as given by records of actual conversations. At the moment, we shall limit ourselves to an examination of the character of the form of the underlying structure, leaving questions about content for subsequent inquiries. In this example, our task is to account for three discourse elements, namely, *No, because,* and *look!* In the following notation, the statement in parentheses refers to the hypothetical underlying structure, and the arrow points to the overt verbalized element that it generates:

(ia) (You said it's an ostrich, but it isn't)

No

(iia) (I am denying your assertion, and I justify my denial by the following)

because

(iiia) (If you looked here, you could see that there is no picture of an ostrich, while there is a picture of a camel)

look!

If one compares this account with the four-stage "proof" given earlier, it can be seen to be incomplete. In fact, the three hypothetical underlying statements in (ia) to (iiia) do not constitute a "proof" in the formal logical sense in which the "proof" was presented earlier. But now, let us present the underlying structure of the hearer's interpretation of Rex's statement using an equivalent notation in reverse order:

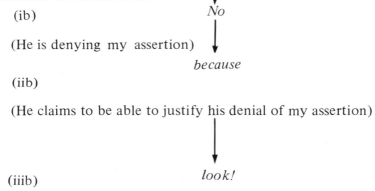

(ib)   *No*

(He is denying my assertion)

                                            because

(iib)

(He claims to be able to justify his denial of my assertion)

(iiib)   *look!*

(He is pointing to the picture of a camel. His denial would be properly justified if it were the case that the cookies in the box represent animals shown on the pictures, and only those animals. Since there is a picture of a camel and no picture of an ostrich, and the cookie in question looks more like a camel than any of the other pictures, it must therefore be a camel, and thus his denial of my assertion is justified.)

The underlying structures in (ia) to (iiia) taken jointly with the underlying structures in (ib) to (iiib), together constitute the equivalent of the four-stage formal "proof." This indicates that the logical structure of justification in conversations is a joint product of the interactional work of participants and is not a function of the statement of any single participant. By extention, we would argue that the formal structure of all conversational activities is a joint product of the interactional work of participants.[6] This outcome suggests that the analysis of the meaning of an utterance cannot be appropriately pursued by a semantic analysis of sentences, or by an analysis of a speaker's intention, or by an analysis of a hearer's interpretive inferences—all three of which have been attempted in isolation in previous studies, but must instead be pursued by an investigation of the joint cooccurrent interactional work of conversational participants .

NOTES

[1] We hope that when Rex grows up, he will not think unkindly of his father for revealing to the public eye those most intimate conversations with a Daddy who loves him so.

[2] We are using "discourse thinking" in the sense of thought processes whose structure has affinity with the discourse rules of ordinary conversational interaction. Further elaboration will be given in the text that follows.

[3] Under the notion of "verbal interaction" we mean to include all forms of language use: face-to-face conversations, being a listener in an audience or small group, reading and writing.

[4] Although he may, at infrequent times, preface an utterance by "Daddy . . . , " it is clear from paralinguistic features that it is not used as an attention getting device. Instead, it appears to be a stylistic variant of the adult pattern in which the address form occurs in the middle or at the end of an utterance.

[5] Even if, by cleverly supplying a special context in which this verbal exchange could plausibly take place between adults, its meaning within the context it took place with Rex, would be altered. (We're willing to wager on it!)

[6] The general thesis is that *all* conversational events are joint cooccurrent activities, a thesis ably defended by Sacks (cf. his discussion on when an utterance is complete or not complete in Chapter 3).

REFERENCES

Bruner, J. S. "The Ontogenesis of Symbols." In *To Honor Roman Jakobson: Essays on the Occasion of his Seventieth Birthday*. The Hague: Mouton, 1967.

Garfinkel, Harold. *Studies in Ethnomethodology*. Englewood Cliffs, N. J.: Prentice-Hall, 1968.

Lenneberg, E. H. *Biological Foundations of Language*. New York: John Wiley, 1967.

Sacks, Harvey. *Aspects of the Sequential Organization of Conversation.* (Forthcoming: Prentice-Hall).

9 The Psychology of Ordinary Language Use

The question of when a specialized area of study is, is not, or is not yet a 'scientific' discipline appears to us an interesting one. Whatever else science is, one of its important characteristics is that of being a social enterprise and, as such, it becomes a matter of definition, of social agreement or sanction, as to whether a particular activity or body of knowledge is to be considered a science, and its self-appointed experts or "mandarins" (Chomsky, 1969) as 'scientists'.

Parapsychology has associated with it all the trappings of a social or behavioral science—statistics, control conditions, the Null Hypothesis, Journals, and Chairmen of Departments, but the mandarins of the other sciences have so far successfully neutralized their claim to science-hood. Psychologists and sociologists refuse to acknowledge the science-hood claims of 'political science' (although, one must admit that the choice of the title was a nice exercise in one upmanship), but they in turn are looked upon with kind-hearted paternalism and tongue-in-cheek non-recognition by chemists and engineers.

The Claim to Science-Hood

The base for a claim to science-hood has always been that of being engaged in the study of 'natural' (real) phenomena by means of systematic discovery procedures, in conjunction with the claim that the body of knowledge thus accumulated will afford a considerable amount of predictability and control, these being socially useful skills, and it is here that the problem assumes its interesting characteristic. Although we believe it is possible to present a general argument in this connection, we shall restrict the following discussion to the 'language sciences,' a phrase which has come to include a number of currently flourishing scientific disciplines which include psycholinguistics, sociolinguistics, ethnolinguistics, as well as psychology, linguistics, anthropology, and sociology proper.

The interesting problem, as we see it, is this: Why and how does it come about that successful claims can be made in the sociopolitical sphere for the naturalness or real-ness of phenomena, and their predictability and control, when these alleged phenomena are neither natural nor real, and furthermore, when the claimed predictability and control are not only never achieved but could not possibly be achieved. In point of fact, the analysis of this interesting problem will show that it is precisely because the alleged phenomena in the language sciences are not natural and not predictable that it is possible to lay successful claims as to their naturalness and predictability. We were lead to this kind of a shockingly perverse conclusion through our readings in 'ethnomethodology'—the latest of disciplines to claim science-hood (see Garfinkel, 1968; Sacks, 1971). Let us proceed while we ask your indulgence and patience for a little while at least.

Lewis Carroll's *Alice in Wonderland* and Milne's *Winnie the Pooh* aren't usually on the required reading list in psycholinguistic courses and probably never will be, and we, at least, consider this most unenlightened, for here are two masterpieces in psychological insight and, incidentally, excellent treatises on ethnomethodology. The trick is to realize that the wonderland Alice has the good misfortune to fall into is in no ways different from the wonderland she fell from. "A rose by any other name would smell as sweet" is simultaneoulsy true and false. It is true because a "rose" and a "meigwei" smell and look equally sweet, this being a consequence of a cross-cultural coincidence whereby speakers of the English and Chinese tongues assign a similar conceptual and affective status to what botanists have come to refer to as "Genus Rosa." It is false wherever such a happy coincidence does not occur, as is well known by butchers and managers of supermarkets where "hocks" is considerably more marketable than "pigs' feet," and by furriers who sell a coat made of Zorina rather than South American skunk, and it's no longer good practice to publicly refer to sanitary engineers as garbage collectors. The rose dictum is flatly contradicted by the doctrine that has established the magical power of euphemisms throughout man's social history, whereby if something is unacceptable by one name, it becomes acceptable by another name, and vice versa.

Ordinarily, for euphemisms to be euphemisms, it is necessary to deny that they are euphemisms. Thus, it is the very denial of the thing that establishes the realness of it. Here we have another one of those perverse conclusions that we started out with, and thereby, another instance of the interesting aspect of the problem that interests us: why and how does it come about that the very denial of something is precisely what establishes that thing as real?

Speech Acts as Institutional Facts

Ordinary language philosophers have examined this problem in ways that we find instructive (see Austin, 1965; Searle, 1969; Vendler, 1967). They have drawn attention to acts within ordinary language use—speech acts that are 'illocutionary' in nature and these differ from non-illocutionary acts in specific ways whose analysis throws some light on the paradoxical conclusions of the type we are concerned with here. Take for instance 'promising' as such a speech act. Although there are socially appropriate ways of making promises, such as the prefacing of an utterance by "I promise that . . . , " the form of the expression of promising is not by itself what constitutes a promise. For one, one can make a promise without such a prefacing statement as for instance in "I will be there at six, sharp"; for another, one can preface a statement in that way without thereby establishing the utterance as a promise, as for instance in "I promise that it will rain tomorrow" or as in the threat, "I promise that I will kill you if you hurt him." Thus for an utterance to be a successful rather than a defective promise, it must have certain criterial features which, as Searle (1969, p. 57 ff) points out include, among others, the following: that the topic of the promising act be an act whose perpetrator must be the individual doing the promising act (cf. "I promise that he will do it" which is defective, vs. "I promise to see to it that he will do it") that the topical act in question be in the future, not the past or the present; that the listener to whom the promising act is addressed be knowledgeable about acts of promising; that the speaker believe that the listener would prefer his doing the topical act rather than his not doing it (this requirement distinguishes promises from other statements that are prefaced by "I promise" to indicate obligation or emphatic assertion, as in "I didn't do it, I promise you I didn't"); that the topical act of the promise not be an act that the speaker would do in the normal course of events—as Searle (p. 59) points out, "a happily married man who promises his wife he will not desert her in the next week is likely to provide more anxiety than comfort"; that the speaker claim that he intends to do it; and, that he claim that he intends that the promising act will place him under the obligation to do it. Thus, the successful performance of the illocutionary act of promising necessitates certain specificable conditions related to the speaker, the speaker's claimed intentions, the hearer, the hearer's alleged interests, and the knowledge of the rules of promising on the part of the speaker and the listener.

Now, if we examine transactions that socialized human beings execute, we find non-illocutionary ones such as staring, kicking, crying, making love, blushing, eating and so on, and these differ in a crucial respect from the illocutionary ones, as follows: that the criterial features that establish non-illocutionary acts are objectively and operationally definable in terms of a system of description that is independent of the very act whose status or reality we are trying to establish. The denial by the author of an illocutionary act that he has performed the act, is tantamount to establishing its non-existence, whereas this is not the case for non-illocutionary acts. Thus, if a person denies that he has made or broken a promise, it will do you no good to present evidence such as a witness or a tape recording, since then he can claim that he did not intend to make a promise, that circumstances forced him to act as if he was promising, but that in fact he did not promise. You may then call him a liar or a hypocrite, but you cannot reasonably claim that he broke his promise. The breaking of a promise is thus in itself another illocutionary act, and such an act can come into existence only with the cooperation of the originator of the alleged promise, as when someone admits to having broken a promise. There are of course social and legal sanctions one can impose on people who lie, but there is no way of establishing the making or the breaking of a promise without the consent of the alleged perpetrator. This is not true of non-illocutionary acts, and indeed if a person is presented with a film in which he is seen kicking someone, there is no reasonable way in which he can deny the fact that he has kicked the person in question, even though he may present alleviating rationalizations for having kicked someone, such as ("It was an accident" or "I didn't mean it" or "It was his fault" or whatever.)

Now we wish to show that the distinction between illocutionary and non-illocutionary acts just considered is an instance of a fundamental and general distinction that is just the distinction that we need to resolve paradoxes of the kind we mentioned above, namely, first, that the establishment of the language sciences rests on assertions about the realness, predictability, and control of phenomena that can't possibly have these characteristics and, second, that the establishment of euphemisms rests on assertions about their denial. Let us refer to a distinction Searle (1969, p. 33 ff) makes between systems based on "constitutive rules (like the illocutionary acts or the game of football) versus systems based on "regulative" rules (like the prohibition against murder or the laws of planetary motion). We shall eventually try to show that while many basic phenomena involved in language use represent institutional facts that belong to both regulative and constitutive systems, the traditional as well as current scientific concepts in the language sciences treat them as brute facts belonging to regulative systems only, and that therefore no adequate, productive, non-trivial accounts of language use phenomena are possible with these concepts.

Assuming for the moment that we can show what we claim we shall show, it is pertinent to ask what is it then that the language sciences are actually about? It seems to us that the language sciences actually deal with a hypothetical type of reification of what human language use phenomena would be like if they were of the type posited by these sciences (i.e., brute facts). In other words, if there were such a thing as a human language that is based on a system of natural regulative (as opposed to institutional) rules, then the language sciences now in vogue might possibly represent an adequate descriptive and discovery procedure for their study. Thus, in answer to the question of what it is that the language sciences are about, we would say that they are about non-existent and hypothetical phenomena that are proper to a non-existent hypothetical human language, that is, an artificial language rather than a natural one. The substitution of an artificial language as an object of scientific study in lieu of the natural one while simultaneously denying that that is precisely what is being done, is a process that becomes understandable when we view the enterprise of the language sciences as an instance of social activities that humans engage in within a constitutive system of rules, just as we have seen is the case with illocutionary acts like promising. In other words, the body of knowledge accumulated under the language sciences constitutes a set of statements that are illocutionary in character. Therefore it does us no good for advancing our argument to point out to the mandarins of the language sciences that what they are doing does not constitute a description of natural language phenomena, since they can claim that they never intended to study anything but what it is that they were studying, just as the person confronted with evidence of having made a promise can claim that he never intended to make a promise, and therefore no promise was made.

There are numerous examples of this sort in the history of psychology and we want to mention two that are well known. One is the counter claim to criticisms of the notion of 'intelligence' whereby psychometricians, in the face of evidence that what they had claimed intelligence was, did not appear to be that, then claimed that what they meant by intelligence was that which their intelligence tests measured, nothing more, nothing less. The other instance is the counter claim by verbal learning theorists to criticisms that their theories do not account for classroom learning whereby they then asserted that their laboratory experiments on rote memorization were not intended to be anything but experiments on rote memorization.

In the relatively short history of psycholinguistics, hundreds of experiments have been conducted on language phenomena such as the grammatical transformation of sentences, the speed and accuracy with which sentences were decoded and encoded, the efficiency with which specific types of information was being transmitted and received, the ease with which sentences of a particular type were recalled after given amounts and conditions of exposure, and the like. In the past few years an increasing number of critics have consistently pointed out the irrelevance of these phenomena to such everyday commonplace events as conversations. These criticisms, whatever their merit may be, can have no force since the "new scientists of language" as Miller (1964) has called these psycholinguist mandarins, can always claim that psycholinguistics consists of the body of knowledge adduced by these experiments and therefore one has no reasonable claims against the Pope for doing that which the Pope is sanctioned to do.

The Practice of Ordinary Science

Kuhn's revolutionary thesis in his *The Structure of Scientific Revolutions* was based on a survey of paradigm switches in the "natural sciences," mostly physics and chemistry, but his greatest influence may yet be not in those sciences, but rather in the social sciences.

According to Kuhn "Normal science, the activity in which most scientist inevitably spend almost all their time, is predicated on the assumption that the scientific community knows what the world is like. Much of the success of the enterprise derives from the community's willingness to defend that assumption, if necessary at considerable cost" (1962, p. 5). When anomalies occur, an extraordinary set of investigations begin which lead to a new set of commitments, "a new basis for the practice of science," a "scientific revolution." "They are the tradition-shattering complements to the tradition-bound activity of a normal science" (p. 6). A shift occurs in "the standards by which the profession determine(s) what should count as an admissible problem or as a legitimate problem-solution (p. 6). "For these men (the established mandarins) the new theory implies a change in the rules governing the prior practice of normal science. Inevitably, therefore, it reflects upon much scientific work they have already successfully completed" (p. 7).

We are particularly interested in Kuhn's use of the concept of "normal science" in its ethnomethodological sense, even though Kuhn himself does not explicitly discuss it from this perspective. The meaning of "normal science" that we see being of great interest is this: the behavior of scientists when they are being ordinary. We don't mean "ordinary" in the usual statistical sense of the mode or the most frequently occuring pattern of behavior. We mean it in the sense of the expected norm or the appropriate pattern of behavior under prescribed conditions. For instance, the way an academic psychologist at all of the well known universities can be ordinary, rather than nonordinary or special, is to conduct research and to publish in journals that have a reputation for high scientific standards in editorial policy. This is one of the things an academic psychologist is expected to do, and in doing so, he is being ordinary qua an academic psychologist. Knowing how to be ordinary in a particular social endeavour requires the acquisition of certain specialized competencies that are defined with reference to the behaviors that are expected and appropriate in those particular circumstances. Thus, we can view the function of graduate training in academic psychology as being that of facilitating the acquisition of a set of skills that will enable the graduate to later be ordinary as an academic psychologist.

One of the required rules for behaving ordinarily or being ordinary in one's practice of academic psychology has to do with following certain prescribed methodological procedures in research and theory building. In the field of psychology, the nature of acceptable methodological procedures have changed over historical epochs, so that what it was to be ordinary in Wundt's or in Titchener's time does not constitute the same pattern of behavior (in fact, they are contradictory) as the pattern of behavior that is associated with being ordinary in Watson's or our own time. When differences in what is being ordinary in two epochs involve the nature of the methodological procedures that generate data, we have reached an instance of what Kuhn refers to as a "paradigm switch." It is a fact in the sociology of science that the innovators of a new paradigm believe it to be superior to the old paradigm. For instance, American Behaviorism believed itself to be superior to Introspectionism. Similarly, generative transformational linguistics is believed to be by their proponents a significant advance over American structuralist linguistics. It is important to realize that the alleged superiority attributed to the new paradigm appears to be a self-evident truth to the innovators. In other words, the adoption of a new paradigm does not represent an "objective" decision on the part of impartial judges. The character of the arguments involved in this kind of a decision is that of an oriented to *operative*, by which we mean, along with the ethnomethodologists (see below), that type of situation in which the innovators reject the features which the old paradigmers are oriented to by prior agreement and training, and the new features they pick to be oriented to are just those features which the old paradigmers are not oriented to. For instance, in the recent revolution in linguistics, Chomsky and the new paradigmers chose as a central feature of language to be oriented to the underlying deep structure of sentences and to deliberately reject the fundamental significance as a source of input to theory of the overtly manifested surface features of language, precisely those that formed the foundation of structuralist linguistics. It was not the case that structuralist linguistics could either be the foundation upon which transformational linguistics could build upon, or that its findings and theories could be built upon cumulatively with the refinement of newer and stronger methodologies. If the facts of fifty years of structuralist linguistics were suddenly wiped out, current generative transformational linguistics would not be the worse off in terms of its development. This is the argument of non-cumulative increments of scientific revolutions that Kuhn has tried to develop for physics and chemistry, and it appears to be true in linguistics as well, and we would offer the generalization that it is probably true in all other scientific disciplines.

By proposing a paradigm switch in psycholinguistics, we are engaging in persuasive argumentation rather than in what would be considered in the old paradigm as "objective" ratiocination. This is necessarily so inasmuch as we are "advocating" that we become oriented to a new set of features, these features being in some crucial instances contradictory to the existing set of features. Therefore, we cannot present "scientific" arguments within the present paradigm in favor of the new paradigm. Kuhn tries to show that the direction new paradigms take is influenced not solely by rational or logical considerations but by social psychological, religious and philosophical ones as well. Part of being ordinary as a scientist is to resist changes of a certain sort, the sort that question fundamental assumptions, this resistance going under the vigilante activity of "maintaining high scientific standards," We would like to show how this resistance process in being ordinary as a scientist operates in psycholinguistics.

To do this, we would like initially to establish the concept of "askable questions" and its converse of "non-askable questions." Consider the following question: Does St. Peter admit to Heaven clergymen who have supported the principle of killing in religious wars? Cabell answers this question in the negative in the mythological fiction of *Jurgen*, but there is no way in which this question, or its equivalent, can be asked in the language of psychology. As soon as you think about it you realize that this is not a special or abnormal case, and that there must be an infinity of questions of this sort; in short, there is a set of questions in a scientific discipline that are "not-askable" and a set that are "askable."

Consider, next, a definition we propose for a new field to be called "ethno-methodology."[1] Ethnomethodology is the study of the discovery procedures used by scientists (the latter term is to be given a special definition in what ensues). By "discovery procedures" we mean the particular methodological steps (data collection and status of concepts) to be followed in being ordinary as a researcher in a particular field or sub-field of specialization. Thus, "types of methods" is to "ethnomethodology" what "types of cultures" is to "ethnolinguistics" (or "anthropology"). Furthermore, ethnomethodology restricts its perspective to "operatives," which is to say it will define all problems as "interactional processes," so that "scientific methods" becomes "the procedures carried out by various scientists in their activities qua scientists." These differences in what constitutes ordinary behavior in particular socially defined circumstances (e.g., scientific research) are ascribable to the rules of the ethnic subculture represented by a particular paradigm in a field of specialization. Ethnomethodology thus becomes the study of the subcultural rules of discovery of a particular group of paradigmers.

Thus far, we expect no special opposition from the psycholinguists. They would no doubt say "Well, if that's what you want to do, go ahead." and might add: "And, anyway, isn't that what the history or philosophy of science is supposed to be doing already." (The latter question we must answer in the negative, but we shall not elaborate at this point.)

Now, as we go on to elaborate our definition of ethno-methodology, in particular the term "scientist," we shall be stating what to us seems readily obvious, even self-evident, yet it will be non-evident and inacceptable to psycholinguists in the old paradigm.

Ethnomethodology studies the practices that constitute being ordinary as a scientist. Its interest in the scientist does not arise out of a special interest in the scientist, as traditionally identified, but in the fact that scientists, when behaving ordinarily, claim to subscribe to a set of explicitly stated discovery procedures. Both because his interest is not exclusive in any one social group, and because a comparative study of discovery procedures of other social groups sheds light on the scientists as well, the ethnomethodologist is committed to the general study of discovery procedures of other groups of individuals (including, of course, their own). But the concept of "social group" represents an outcome of and derives its meaning from the methodological procedures of existing paradigms in sociology and psychology. Therefore, the concept of "social group" remains an object of ethnomethodological study and is not a concept that can be directly incorporated as a working concept in it. So, in fact, ethnomethodology does not study the practices of any particular group of individuals, be they scientists or whatever. It studies the discovery practices of individuals in their social interactive setting. The only meaning "scientist" can have in the definition of ethnomethodology is that of an individual engaging in systematic discovery practices. The task of ethnomethodology is to show that the discovery practices of any individual when being ordinary are systematic and rule governed. Now, to get back to the psycholinguist in the current paradigm.

We have already pointed out that many questions, such as St. Peter's admission practices at the gates of Heaven, fall in the category of non-askable questions in the old paradigm. This leads to a proper and interesting question in ethnomethodology, an askable question as follows: How does it come about that in the language and conception of current psychology, the St. Peter question falls in the non-askable category? To study this question the ethnomethodologist will compare the practices of two "groups" of individuals: those for whom the St. Peter question falls in the non-askable category (this will include academic psychologists) and those for whom it falls in the askable category (this will include theologians, classical scholars, mythologists, many ordinary people, and the like). Ethnomethodology is the study of the discovery practices of individuals when they are being ordinary. What is here the proper sense of "discovery practices?" Among all the practices that individuals engage in which one contains the sub-set of "discovery practices?" Once again we are not permitted to give a traditional definition since that is precisely what forms the object of study, viz. how does it come about that individuals classify different items of practice into the category of "discovery practices?" The answer to this question, and other questions of this sort, must lie in an elaboration of what constitutes "being ordinary" in various interactional circumstances. Our original definition has now been transformed to read as follows: Ethnomethodology is the study of the transactional practices of individuals when they are being ordinary. Our subsequent discussion will clarify the following additional points that can be made about this definition: that "transactional" refers to joint cooccurrent interaction that stems from coordinated work of individuals who are oriented to the same features of the interaction; that "practices" refers to operatives, viz. that it is the doing of the activity that constitutes the activity; and that "being ordinary" refers to the set of operatives whose oriented to features are jointly defined by interactants as ordinary, not special.

To summarize these points we shall attempt one final definition as follows: Ethnomethodology is the study of those joint cooccurrent operatives which participants in a transaction are oriented to in circumstances they describe as ordinary. Now there remain three points for us to argue in order to show the inadequacy of the old paradigm in psycholinguistics. These are as follows: (1) that the set of operatives thus defined is not made up of unusual or special cases, but that they constitute a large and significant body of the social practices of individuals in conversational interaction; (2) that the study of this important set of verbal interactions falls in the nonaskable category in the old paradigm; and (3) that it falls in the category of askable questions in the new paradigm. To accomplish this task we shall have to consider first what it is that ethnomethodologists mean when they talk about "ordinary commonplace conversational interaction." Because the exposition of this concept is fairly long, we would like to reassure the reader that this is not an irrelevant digression and we promise to return to these three points in due course.

Some Features of Ordinary Talk

We begin with the commonplace observation that ordinary talk is partly made up of talk about talk. For instance, you can say "Did you see George, yesterday?" and some utterances later you can say "Why aren't you answering my question?" The latter utterance is no less a part of ordinary talk, yet in relation to the first utterance, it is an utterance about an utterance, talk about talk or metatalk. That metatalk is part of ordinary talk appears to be a fundamental aspect of human conversational interaction that allows its present constitutive character. In other words, we are claiming that this is a nontrivial feature of ordinary talk whose absence would fundamentally alter the character of ordinary conversations and would become immediately noticeable to participants leading to their qualification of talk without the possibility of metatalk as nonordinary or abnormal.

All illocutionary acts belong to the metatalk set of the full set of ordinary talk. In general, acts that belong to the class of metatalk are just those acts that are mentioned when in ordinary talk someone asks "What is he doing?" by which they intend to mean "What is he doing in his talk and through it?", such as: promising, complimenting, lambasting, flattering, joking, being smart-Alecky, polite, obtuse, fastidious, imaginitive, sweet, supportive, cold, immature, opinionated, incomprehensible, thankful, electrifying, vulgar, and so on. This is, as you no doubt realize, an open set, and it may be an interesting problem to look into as to why and how it comes about that it is an open set.

To inquire into this problem it might be useful to recall certain distinctions in types of speech acts which Austin (1965) and Searle (1969) among others have explicated, in particular the difference between illocutionary, and perlocutionary acts. An 'illocutionary' act, as we have discussed, involves such things as promising, criticizing, requesting, approving, apologizing, objecting, commenting, questioning, and so on. A 'perlocutionary' act involves having an effect on the intended listener such as persuading, inspiring, surprising, misleading, confusing, alarming and so on. It seems to us that there exists another set of locutionary acts that are different from propositional, illocutionary, or perlocutionary acts, a set that is exemplified by such qualifiers as being polite, pompous, immature, opinionated, supportive, warm, cold, sweet, understanding, creative and so on. In ordinary talk we sometimes use these terms to refer to 'personality traits' although we do not necessarily insist that they be permanent or even characteristic. For instance, we can be polite in one conversation and impolite in another, pompous and opinionated in one context, and supportive and understanding in another. What the members of this set seem to have in common is the attribution of a descriptive trait to something the speaker is doing in a specific conversational circumstance or episode, but unlike so-called personality traits, the description refers to the conversationalist's work qua conversationalist in a particular conversational interaction. Note that it is not the traits of the speaker that are being qualified, but rather the speaker's conversational acts in the particular interaction. This, we think, is precisely the difference that exists between "He is so-and-so" and "He is being so-and-so," as for instance, "George is opinionated" (i.e., generally and characteristically), versus "George is being opinionated" (i.e., now, as he is acting in this part of the conversation). We propose to call these locutionary acts, translocutionary acts (for locutionary plus transactional), to distinguish them from propositional, illocutionary, and perlocutionary acts.

Translocutionary as well as perlocutionary acts differ from illocutionary acts in the criteria that must hold for their successful performance. As we have seen, illocutionary acts cannot reasonably be defined independently of the speaker's definition of what it is that he is doing. A speaker cannot properly promise without claiming that he intends to promise, but he can be opinionated or offensive without claiming that he intends to be so. The reason for this difference is that participants treat translocutionary and perlocutionary acts as acts that are to be evaluated by a regulative system of rules. These rules are stated in terms that are independent of the speaker's claimed intentions.

Searle (1969) claims that all institutional facts belong to a constitutive system, and that all facts belonging to regulative systems are brute facts. We think this is an oversimplification that eliminates certain distinctions that are useful to make. For instance, we would say that both illocutionary and translocutionary acts are institutional facts, but the latter belong to a regulative system while the former belong to a constitutive system. In other words, we wish to distinguish between two sorts of facts that yet belong to regulative systems: brute facts such as kicking or caressing someone and institutional facts such as being opinionated or impolite. This distinction is necessary for specifying the nature of the observation procedures that are capable of establishing the existence of institutional (regulative) facts and brute (regulative) facts. An independent observer armed with a camera can establish the brute fact that one native aborigine kicked another member of the tribe, but never could he establish the institutional fact that a native was being opinionated or offensive with nothing but a camera or tape recorder. Facts of this sort have no meaning or existence independently of the system of (regulative) rules that governs interpersonal interaction among the tribesmen. A psychologist or anthropologist armed with a universal descriptive system of behavior could never discover a single institutional fact, whether regulative or constitutive. The reason for this is that institutional facts are all "operatives," which is to say that it is the doing of the activity that establishes them as instances of that activity, and this establishment procedure may be done in two ways: by appeal to the joint cooccurrent oriented to features of the ongoing activity (constitutive systems), or by appeal to a standard of reference that is usually practiced in situations of the sort that the present activity is claimed as being an instance of (regulative systems). These relationships are illustrated in Fig. 1.

To summarize what we have said thus far, ordinary talk is made up of locutionary acts of various types that are identified by participants in answer to the question "What is he doing in his talk and through it?" Now, a second question that can ordinarily be asked about talk is "What is he talking about?" and the answer to this question ordinarily refers to what participants call the 'topic' of the conversation or utterance. Topic refers to the set of things that are talkable about and this set is defined in reference to the conversational circumstance. Not any topic is appropriate within a particular conversational circumstance. Thus, when we ask in any particular conversational circumstance "What did he talk about?" we specifically mean to exclude from the answer that set of topics that are not talkable about in that circumstance. Should someone want to talk about a topic that isn't talkable about, he must preface the doing so by some statement that indicates to the participants that he is not engaging in an ordinary conversation. For instance, he might say "I know I am not supposed to talk about that but . . . " or "Hey, Dad, I am doing an experiment for my Psych 100 course. What is your name, please." In the absence of such a prefatory statement he will not succeed in talking about what he wants to talk about; in that case, the other participants would not say that he is talking about something; instead, he would be sounding off, being smart, complaining, insulting, going mad, talking for the sake of talking, imitating, fooling around, being obnoxious, talking nonsense, or whatever, but not talking about something.

Talking ordinarily restricts not only what you can talk about in a particular conversational circumstance, but also the sequence of the

Fig. 1. The nature of facts that form the object of investigation

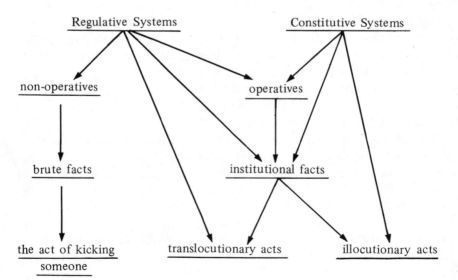

things you can talk about. For instance, you cannot transact an ordinary conversation by performing the illocutionary acts of greeting and leave-taking in the middle of the conversational episode as opposed to the beginning and end, respectively. Should someone attempt that, the conversation will either come to an abrupt end or the act will be treated according to the conversational rules for handling interruptions, in this case probably by a topic switch that makes the interruption the next topic of conversation as in "What's the matter with you, anyway" or "What are you trying to do. Have you been feeling all right lately?" or whatever. Goffman (1961) has made the observation that the reason inmates of an asylum strike us as very odd is not so much due to the fact that they say or do very odd things, but rather because they break the most ordinary rules of talking and behaving publicly, and it is the doing of that that strikes us as very odd.

While it is possible to talk about a number of different things in any particular conversational circumstance, it is not possible to do so without performing the illocutionary act of announcing a topic switch every time you wish to change topics. Such acts may take the form of "Oh, by the way, . . ." or "Incidentally . . ." or "That reminds me of . . ." and so on in which the illocutionary act of announcing a topic switch is accomplished by an utterance, or alternately, by the vehicle of a lull in conversation. In the latter case, it cannot be just any silence; it must be a silence that participants recognize and identify as the type that constitutes an occasion for topic switch and not some other kind of silence such as pondering an answer, or refusing to participate in the conversation, or seeing the effect of a perlocutionary act, or whatever.

It may be useful at this point to introduce some additional terms and distinctions that are involved in the successful performance of an ordinary conversation. A conversational circumstance is an interactional episode that is made up of a structured sequence of conversational events being transacted within the framework of an identifiable background context. By 'interactional' episode we mean to indicate not merely the trivial feature that more than one person must be involved, but the nontrivial fact that it is cooccurrent oriented to operative work (see Sacks, 1971) in which the listener contributes to the joint interaction just as crucially, definitionally or constitutively as the speaker in ways that shall become clear later. By 'identifiable background context' we mean to indicate the fact that it matters critically who the participants are, where they are talking and for what purpose. The nature of conversational events that make up an episode needs to be examined. Basically, we are dealing with silences and utterances in a structured sequence. Silences can be distinguished by length and locus of occurence (within and between utterances). Utterances themselves vary in syntactic type, locutionary type, communicative function, and integrity level. By *syntactic type* we mean to refer to their syntactic value within the structured sequence that constitutes the episode. For instance, an interruption is an utterance that prevents the completion of an ongoing utterance; an opener marks the beginning of a conversational sequence, either at the beginning of a conversational episode or during the introduction of a topical switch; a repartee is an utterance that is appropriate during a talker switch and serves to continue or maintain a conversational episode; and so on. *Locutionary type* refers to the type of locutionary act it is, namely propositional, illocutionary, perlocutionary, or translocutionary, as discussed earlier. The *communicative function* of an utterance relates to the purpose or motive of the conversational interaction as defined by the set of socially legitimate uses of talk: reporting an event, instructing, problem solving, being sociable, describing something, expressing an opinion, making a judgment, establishing one's status vis-à-vis participants, laying claims for some special competence, and so on. The *integrity level* of an utterance refers to its status vis-à-vis it being what it appears to be on the surface. There appear to be at least five levels of talk in addition to "direct representational " talk, namely "indirect representational" talk (as in making allusions or talking around the subject when participants know what it is but agree tacitly not to mention it directly); "misrepresentational" talk as in propaganda, dissimulation and other manipulative situations); "tactful" talk (in which, like in indirect representational talk, the topic is not mentioned directly, but in this case, one or more of the participants can claim that they are unaware of the topic); "non-representational" talk (in which the expressed topic is incidental to another underlying topic with which the participants actually deal, knowingly or unknowingly, such as in beating around the bush or, in instances where a participant wishes to change its non-representational character would say "Come on, what is it really that you want to tell me" or some such thing); and finally, "other directed" talk (in which the effective audience is other than the addressee, as in "loud-talking" (see Mitchell-Kerman, 1969, or in statements to reporters made at press conferences).

The characteristics of utterances that we have elaborated thus far, namely syntactic and locutionary type, communicative function, and integrity level belong to considerations about the syntax of conversations (for additional observations on the syntax of conversations see the recent and stimulating work of Harvey Sacks, 1971). Now we wish to make certain comments on the semantics of conversations.

The Meaning of an Utterance

When in ordinary conversations we wish to inquire about the meaning of an utterance, we normally ask four sorts of questions: "What did he say?", "Why did he say that?", "What did he mean?" and, "What was he trying to do in saying that?" That these represent different questions, rather than being paraphrases of one another is evidenced by the fact that different kinds of answers are appropriate to each of them, and an answer that is satisfactory to one question is not satisfactory to another, as shown by the following illustration:

A1: What did he say?
B1: He said he is not satisfied with Helen.
A2: Why did he say that?
· B2: He doesn't think she is suited for that kind of work.
A3: What did he mean?
B3: She doesn't show sufficient initiative.
A4: What was he trying to do?
B4: He wanted me to try to get her fired.

Note that B's answers are different for each of the four questions and furthermore, they are not interchangeable: B1 is an indirect quote or a paraphrase; B2 is a justification; B3 is an elaboration and B4 is an explanation. Thus, the 'meaning' of an utterance in ordinary conversation is to be given in terms of a paraphrase or quote, a justification, an elaboration, or an explanation (see McCawley, 1971). Note that B's answers can be tied into one utterance as follows:

> "*He said* he is not satisfied with Helen *because*
> she is not suited for this kind of work *inasmuch*
> *as* she doesn't show sufficient initiative and *therefore*
> he wants me to fire her."

Expressions like "He said that . . . , " "because," "inasmuch as," and "therefore" are discourse hinges which underlie the structure of utterances whether or not they are actualized in surface structure (see Jakobovits, 1968). The semantics of utterances in ordinary conversation must take into account the contextual structure in which they occur no less than the meaning of a word in an utterance must be derived from the underlying structure of the sentence. What constitutes the contextual structure of an utterance in ordinary conversation? Let us attempt a preliminary formulation to this basic problem in the theory of communicative competence.

Consider once again the four questions that seem to be involved in what people mean ordinarily when they inquire about the meaning of a locutionary act:

1. What did he say?
2. Why did he say it?
3. What did he mean?
4. What was he trying to do (in his talking)?

Except in the case of a direct quote the answer to the first question involves paraphrasing. Paraphrasing is a selectional and creative process and, with the possible exception of the paraphrasing of a single sentence, it involves inferences about what kind of information the questioner may have an interest in at the moment. The ability to make appropriate selections in answer to the question "What did he say?" is part of the competence participants need to have to engage in ordinary conversations. There are rules of conversational interaction that tag topical information of conversations in some such terms as: reportable information, non-reportable information, reportable to so-and-so and not reportable to so-and-so or in such-and-such a place, and so on. Thus, if a participant is asked "What did he say?" (e.g., "What did the President say at his press conference yesterday?"), his answer will vary in significant and nontrivial ways depending on the conversational circumstance in which the request occurs: who the questioner is (child or adult, friend or foe, peer or subordinate, etc.), what the social setting of the request is (e.g., are there other listeners present, etc.), what the interpersonal import is of the participants' reaction to his choice of information to select, etc.). It is the non-trivial specification of these various "etceteras" that needs to be done if we are interested in describing the semantics of ordinary conversations.

The Inadequacies of the Old Paradigm

Earlier, we claimed that we shall argue the following three points: (1) that joint cooccurrent oriented to operatives constitute a significant core set of phenomena that cannot reasonably be excluded from a theory of communicative competence; (2) that this significant set is yet excluded from study in the old paradigm; and (3) that it forms the central focus of the new paradigm. We believe we have adequately dealt so far with the first and third questions. What the ethnomethodologists call ordinary commonplace conversational interaction cannot reasonably be excluded from study and still claim an interest in communicative competence. Our discussion on the nature of these phenomena, as studied from the perspective of the new ethnomethodological paradigm, constitutes a partial argument to point number two, as well, but it might be best to elaborate further at the risk of being tedious.

The central issue has already been stated: the facts that constitute the data for the study of locutionary phenomena, whether regulative or constitutive, are institutional in character (i.e., oriented to operatives). The facts that constitute the data for the study of language use phenomena in the old paradigm are (regulative) brute facts (i.e., independently observable). Facts that are oriented to operatives and facts that are independently observable are worlds apart and separated by an insurmountable chasm. The discovery of oriented to features cannot be accomplished through objective observations by an independent investigator. When we think of what is needed in psycholinguistics today, we have in mind a reversal of the choice made by "scientific" psychologists, one that is in favor of substance and against methodology.[2] We are using 'against' advisedly because there is strong professional pressure to maintain the present choice in favor of current conceptions of methodology. The pressure takes the form of the maintenance of so-called 'high' scientific standards sanctioned by the established mandarins: the journal editors, the book reviewers, the research evaluators of granting agencies, the senior personnel in academic departments, the officers of professional organizations, the graduate curriculum in psychology. The people who maintain these standards are people who helped define and establish them, who are 'achievers' in them, and believe in them. We are faced with the necessity of a 'paradigm switch' and in such a situation, as Kuhn (1962) so convincingly documented for the physical sciences, there is left no contact point between the 'old' and the 'new' paradigms.

An analogous necessity has faced the field of linguistics at the beginning of the Chomskian 'revolution' and it exists now in the field of education as well. Theoretical and experimental psychology has disqualified itself from the task of explicating the instructional process, both on account of their practical failure in enabling us to deal effectively with the current problems in education, as well as on account of the disclaimers of some of their foremost spokesmen (e.g., Postman, 1961). On the other hand, we do not believe that the problems encountered in education, psychotherapy, human communication, are beyond the reach of systematic study, but we need to make them the focus of our concern, the departing point of our study rather than the elusive and ideal goal of it.

It seems that we are in search of an explanatory theory; where do we begin? It seems to us a reasonable strategy to begin at precisely the point the 'old' paradigm tried to get away from, namely common sense. We have in mind the 'commonness' feature of this strategic goal rather than its 'common sensical-ness.' Humans strike us as marvelously complex and powerful organisms when we focus on all the things they can do 'ordinarily.' Think of the intricacies involved in the successful completion of a conversational episode, and yet this is a very ordinary, common competence most, if not all humans, have. At the same time, the scientific competence needed to successfully complete a trip to the moon is most certainly not ordinary or common. Wherein lies the difference? Man is the creator of constitutive systems and the institutional facts in them; he is a master at it. But he is not the creator (in the same sense as above) of the universe and the brute facts in it; the so-called physical world is a regulative system, not constitutive, and man feels himself being regulated by it. Here he is a child, not a master. And so, the flight to the stars is one he has to take on the wings of those amongst us, the Newtons and the Einsteins, who have very special, non-common, competencies.

But here we are concerned with very common competencies, in fact, the more ordinary they are the more they point up the superb and admirable mastery which we possess. Should we then not trust our common synthetic powers for creating constitutive systems just because they are of little use in the analysis of regulative systems? We believe one of the important reasons psychologists have come to disdain popular wisdom is that the language of folk theories and popular writers has remained inaccessible to the scientific language. In the field of philosophy, for instance, many traditional epistemological problems that have been debated by scholars for centuries, have been resolved as soon as a few philosophers got the unusual idea of looking for their solution in ordinary language, and today, "ordinary language philosophy" is the most influential and powerful development in the field of philosophy. One of the most crucial innovations of transformational generative linguistics was to begin using in systematic and non-trivial ways the linguistic competence of the ordinary native speaker as opposed to relying exclusively on the non-ordinary special competencies of the linguist. It is to the competence of the ordinary conversationalist that we entrust the beginning of our search for a theory of communicative competence.

Our previous discussion on the analysis of the meaning of an utterance has taken such a frame of reference. We have asked how the participant in an ordinary conversation construes the problem of utterance meaning and using our own ordinary conversational competence we have adduced four queries that focus on that which we might mean when we ask about what an utterance might mean. These were: What did the speaker say? Why did he say it? What did he mean? What was he trying to do through his talking?

We do not necessarily expect, nor do we think it important, that should any one else consider this problem he would come up with the same set of questions that we have adduced. The relevant consideration here would be, not that the two sets are different, but rather how they are different. Suppose, for instance, that someone, perhaps an old paradigmer, would list the following queries when considering the problem of the meaning of an utterance:

1. Was he wearing a hat when he said what he said?
2. Were the listener's hands in his pocket at the time the utterance was made?
3. Did the utterance in question contain a word that was of low frequency according to the Thorndike-Lorge count?
4. Was the syntactic form of the utterance in question left-branching, right-branching, or something else?

It is conceivable that the meaning of an utterance may be affected by conditions of the sort that this new set of questions refer to, but to claim that they tap in a general way that which we mean when we inquire about the meaning of an utterance sounds totally implausible. Our rejection of this second set would thus not constitute merely an arbitrary and idiosyncratic decision. We have publicly statable and verifiable grounds for rejecting these questions as a general paradigm for how people determine the meaning of an utterance.

Suppose, as a third instance, that someone proposes the following questions as a general solution:

1. When did he make the utterance in question?
2. Was the speaker in a normal state or did he seem disturbed?
3. Who were the other people present when he said it, if any?
4. Did he seem to be aware of the effect his utterance had on the other participants?

Now this third set is also different from the first set we suggested but this difference can be seen upon examination to be of another sort than the difference between our first set and the second one. If we went on to elaborate the implications of the third set, we would be led to considerations about the meaning of an utterance which would be similar to those we discussed earlier, namely a specification of the characteristics that relate to joint, cooccurrent oriented to interactive operatives that constitute conversational work and the specific background context of the conversational circumstance in which the utterance in question was embedded.

We are considering this methodological problem in some detail in anticipation of methodological criticisms that a traditional psycholinguist might raise in connection with an approach to the theory of communicative competence such as the one we are proposing here. The specific form that common explanations or accounts take is not of critical importance. The elaboration of these implications, however, does constitute a critical problem. Those elaborations that seem to run against what is common knowledge and practice as to the meaning of an utterance, become ipso facto suspect.

Some General Characteristics of the Nature of Concepts in a Theory of Communicative Competence

The process of elaboration of paradigmatic questions in this kind of inquiry needs closer scrutiny. Let us first point out what seems to us evident in this connection, which is that, though the formulation of the questions themselves are dependent on ordinary conversational competence, their elaboration into a systematic framework is dependent on non-ordinary scholastic competence of the type we fancy ourselves as having, along with other people with similar interests and experiences as ours. This is in no way different from the linguist's task in formulating an adequate descriptive grammar for the linguistic competence of ordinary speakers. At the present time, since this is a novel enterprise for us, we can only make certain very general and simple-minded observations about the form or character that such an elaboration process might take. To wit:

(1) Whatever specific form the analysis of the meaning of an utterance will eventually take, its general character must be such as to take into account the contextual background structure of the conversational circumstance in which it is embedded. For instance, the elementary problem of the identification of a complete utterance (where it begins and where it ends) is not possible without considering adjacent utterances on the part of the same speaker or other participants (see Sacks, 1971). The notion "a complete utterance" does not necessarily overlap with the notion of one speaker or with that of one sentence. An utterance begun by speaker A may be completed only after one or more other speakers have talked (as for instance when speaker A introduces a newcomer to a group of individuals), and an utterance begun by one speaker may be completed by and through the intervention of one or more additional speakers.

(2) Whatever specific working concepts are additionally specified in the analysis of the meaning of an utterance, there must be some that have the character of being operative acts, by which we mean that it is the doing of them that constitutes what it is that they are. This is the sense in which we have discussed the notion of institutional facts, both regulative and constitutive.

(3) The fact that an utterance has meaning and what that might be must be explicated within a framework that views an utterance as a sequential step within a larger interactional sequence that has the character of cooccurrent oriented to work on the part of two or more participants. While the phonetic concretization of an utterance is attributable entirely to the speaker, its meaning is the joint responsibility of the speaker and one or more other participants. An utterance is, thus, not a response a speaker makes which then constitutes a stimulus for a listener, but rather a specification of the condition in which two or more people find themselves vis-à-vis each other when talking. It is for this reason that we find the notions of decoding and encoding unproductive and misleading for our present purposes. In this connection, we are following the lead of Goffman, Garfinkel, Sacks, Austin, Searle and others in the use of ordinary commonplace interaction, not as a statistical conception whereby "ordinary" behavior would mean a conglomerate or average, but rather in the sense of a characterization of that type of behavior which people would consider ordinary, not special. Knowing how to be ordinary comes about through enculturation and socialization within a cultural peer group. The rules for being ordinary vary subculturally and must be specified on a grid of "available" or "socially doable" events. It is to be emphasized that the independent 'objective' description of an event or behavior as is traditionally done in psychology is not the same as the description of what is ordinary behavior since the latter is not defined by frequency distributions or occurences of events but rather by its being treated as ordinary by the participants involved in accordance with the operative rules within a subculture. If we analyzed interactions solely in terms of "observable features" we would have no way of identifying those features that are relevant to, say a conversation, and those that are not (e.g., the shirt color of the participants). The relevant data for the analysis of social interactions are not the

"observable features" but rather the "observably oriented to features," viz. those features that are marked for interactional work by the participants—whether their presence or absence is noticed or is given overt interpretive significance. Most people spend most of their time being ordinary; they are masters at it; it means being socialized; it means having communicative competence. A person who tries to render the ordinary as nonordinary will be pegged as odd and treated as such by his peers (see Garfinkel, 1968). Furthermore, as Sacks (1971) points out, when a person is being not ordinary (e.g., commits illegitimate acts) the feelings and interpretations associated with these acts are as they are expected to be, i.e., ordinary. A theory of communicative competence will include the analysis of the "interaction rituals" (Goffman, 1967) performed by members of a community when they are being ordinary with each other. Once again, the emphasis will not be on "observed performances" but on "possible performances" whether or not they occur since the absence of an event is as significant as its presence. For instance, the fact that greetings usually occur at the beginning of our interaction must be interpreted within a framework that recognizes that importance of its absence when it does not occur; both presence and absence are conversational events and contribute to the description of "what happened."

(4) The analysis of conversational interactions, rather than being neutrally descriptive, must take the form of "prescriptive rules," which is to say that every event in a conversational circumstance either follows a prescribed rule or violates it, and if the latter, then the event that follows it is further prescribed by rules for handling violations. For instance, an interruption in a conversation constitutes a conversational event that has violated the rule of speaking whereby no more than one participant talks at a time. An interruption thus implies not only that a violation has occured and who the violator is, but also that the participants are expected to do something about it: apologize for it, deny it, or ignore it. If it is ignored, it still does not mean that no violation has taken place but only that there are rules for ignoring, not-noticing, violations. This is the proper meaning that is to be attached to the notion that every conversational event is rule governed.

The Indeterminacy of the Meaning of an Utterance

We would like now to return to the problem of the meaning of an utterance as stated earlier in terms of the four paradigmatic questions: What did he say? Why did he say it? What did he mean? What was he trying to do in his talking? It seems to us that the general problem of the meaning of utterances does not permit a determinate solution. This seems like a paradoxical conclusion since it states that an utterance does not have a meaning, strictly speaking, but if this is true, how then is it possible to communicate with utterances? This paradox to which our analysis leads suggests to us that the notion that we communicate via utterances is not a sound one. In other words, utterances viewed as events in a conversation are not to be interpreted as units of communication, or vehicles for the transmission of information, or any such thing. To say that language is a means of communication, or that we communicate via language, though it seems like a reasonable thing to say, turns out to be not so reasonable after all in view of the state of indeterminacy of the solution to the problem of what an utterance means. At least one well-known contemporary philosopher (Grice, 1957) has expounded a similar thesis, and his solution to the problem of the meaning of a statement is given in terms of the intention of the speaker and the determination of his intention by the listener through some sort of inferential reasoning. Curiously enough, this solution is also favored by the foremost contemporary behaviorist psychologist, B. F. Skinner, (1957), although his insistence that intentions be reduced to behavioral consequences puts him in a bind at another place so that his solution becomes as unsatisfactory as any of the others thus far proposed (see the discussions in Jakobovits, 1970; 1969; 1968).

The notion that a word, a sentence, or an utterance has no determinate meaning, though paradoxical, is thus certainly not new. Actually, it is precisely because an utterance does not have a determinate meaning that we are faced with the problem of the meaning of an utterance, for would it make sense to ask "What did he mean?" when a person makes an utterance if utterances had a determinate meaning?

Consider the following commonplace conversational episode around the family dinner table:

Housewife: Would you like some more potatoes?

Guest: No, thank you.

What does the guest's utterance mean? First, what did he say? He said that he doesn't want any more potatoes. Second, why did he say that? Perhaps because he is sated. Perhaps not because he is sated, but because he is on a diet, or because he doesn't think it's polite to have a second serving, or because he wishes to give the impression that he is the type of person who doesn't take second servings, or because he wants to save room for dessert, or perhaps because of some other reason. Third, what did he mean? Did he mean that he doesn't want any more potatoes or did he mean that he doesn't want a second serving if queried only once by the housewife, but that he does want a second serving should the housewife ask a second time. Fourth, what was he trying to do by saying that? Was he trying to influence the housewife's actions in connection with her serving activity or, was he trying to get her to insist on a second serving immediately or some time later? Or what?

That the guest's utterance is an event that must be responded to in some way by the housewife is clear, but what her actual reaction is going to be is not determined by any such thing as the meaning of the guest's utterance. To describe this conversational episode in terms of a communication event in which information was encoded by one and decoded by another, or in terms of the meaning of the utterances composing it, does not shed much light on what transpired.

You might wish to say that we are confusing two problems here: one is the determination of the meaning of the utterances in question and the other is the reactions or adjustment of the participants to the utterances in the context of the episode. Thus, you might say that the guest's utterance "No, thank you" means "No, I don't want any," giving a determinate solution to the meaning problem, but the purpose or motivation that led him to say what he said is indeterminate.

This traditional approach separating the problem of the meaning of an utterance from the problem of the state of mind of the speaker is entirely unsatisfactory. It is a solution that raises more difficulties than it solves. In the first place, recall that conversational events are cooccurrent oriented to interactive work, which is to say that an utterance means what the participants agree it shall mean and not some other thing that a psycholinguist might declare it means, and the process whereby participants jointly agree what an utterance event shall mean when it is used in a particular instance is not a process that can reasonably be separated from the state of mind of the participants such as their motive, intention, or purpose, or the characteristics of the cooccurrent interactional work to which they are jointly oriented. In the second place, the traditional separation solution leads to very odd states of affairs such as that encountered by "Alice in Wonderland," wherein an utterance such as "Yes" means the affirmative while the speaker means the negative, and vice versa. It is less odd to say that the utterance "Yes" is indeterminate in meaning, and the participants may mean by it either the affirmative or the negative or neither depending on what it is they have agreed to do in that situation. Alice's confusion comes about not because she does not know the meaning of the utterances, but because, being a stranger in Wonderland, she has not learned the cooccurrent oriented to features of conversations of the inhabitants. And we submit that a Martian armed with a linguistic analysis of English and a set of objective discovery procedures from the old paradigm and looking for the meaning of utterances, would be equally confused as to what it is that goes on in ordinary conversations.

Recapitulation, Implications, and Conclusions

When we first read Skinner's *Verbal Behavior* (1957) we were struck by the goal he set for himself, which was no less than account for every verbal utterance a speaker makes over a lifetime, a goal we considered utterly fantastic yet beautiful in its classic simplicity. Behind this attitude was the characteristic behavioristic total and exclusive emphasis on overt performance: the stated problem was to account for verbal utterances as operants. This attitude ran against the prevailing philosophy of the new developing field of psycholinguistics in the early 1950's which was neo-behavioristic or mediational, at first, and later added an increasing interest in abstract, underlying, linguistic concepts and processes, drawing away totally from functional behaviorism.

We felt dissatisfied with both these trends. The psycholinguists interpreted their task in terms of Chomsky's initial formulation of the competence-performance dichotomy: linguists concern themselves with the abstract, underlying (invisible, nonobservable) substratum of knowledge of a language, while psycholinguists concern themselves with overt performance. The latter, however, was not seen in Skinnerian terms, which was every verbal utterance in the course of daily life, but rather the artificial manipulative skills involved in learning, memory, perception, concept formation, inference making, problem solving, and other cognitive tasks performed under experimental conditions of observation and control. It seemed as if the more psycholinguists gained knowledge about these artificial, special uses of language, the less interest they retained in the operants of verbal behavior which constitute the ordinary use of language.

Our initial attempt at formulating a theory of communicative competence (Jakobovits, 1968; 1970) was significantly influenced by the behavioristic attitude towards the functional (interpersonal) bases of verbal utterances and we relied heavily on Skinner's functional taxonomy of utterances in terms of their interpersonal and communicative function. The discussion in this chapter represents a further extension of the theoretical significance we attach to the interpersonal function of verbal operants as modified by recent developments in ethnomethodology. However, instead of "operants" we use the term "operative," in the ethnomethodological sense, but there is still a great deal of affinity between Skinner's concept and our own and the underlying attitude that ascribes a particular theoretical significance to them. The relationship between them is subcategorical and unidirectional such that the investigation of operants is included as part of the investigation of operatives, but not vice versa. The reason for this nonsymmetrical relationship is methodological more than theoretical, if indeed such a distinction makes sense. That is, verbal operants are operatives whose occurrence is conditioned by the functional, interactive characteristics of their environmental context. The investigation of this context, viz. the functional properties of the utterance, however, involves the notion of "oriented to features" which refers to the constitutive system of rules that generate institutional facts. The latter task must, in our present judgment, assign a bona fide (non-reduced) theoretical status to the mentalistic notion involved in "x counts as y" (e.g., saying "Hello" counts as a greeting, or, we are going to treat your previous utterance as an apology, etc.). This necessary methodological device, without which the functional context of speech acts (What people do when they talk) cannot be specified, is however precluded from an objective functional analysis, to the extent that we understand this problem. We qualify this methodological device as 'mentalistic' since it is this feature that is likely to be unacceptable to the behavioristic experimental approach in psychology, but this does not mean that we agree with the justification that is ordinarily given in behavioristic psychology for the argument against the mentalism involved in this instance. The mentalistic feature involved in the methodological device of "x counts as y" retains the characteristics of replicability and empiricism, but not "objectivity" (i.e., the capacity of being independently observable by an investigator). Thus, the functional controlling elements of verbal utterances lie not in an independently describably environmental context, but rather in the constitutive system supplied by participants according to rules such as "x counts as y." To put in another way, the conceptual order of components that constitute the taxonomy of oriented to operatives is composed of a different species of conceptual-theoretic things than that given by the environmental reinforcement contingencies of verbal operants. It is for this reason that we argued in this chapter for a methodological paradigm switch from the current psycholinguistic tradition to the new ethnomethodological approach that is involved in our proposal for a psychology of ordinary language.

Methodologically, our proposal is more congruent with the current work in linguistics, philosophy, and cognitive anthropology than with psycholinguistics and psychology; however, the interest in utterances in their ordinary context in terms of their interpersonal function is more congruent with the goals of a functional analysis of verbal behavior than with the goals of current psycholinguistics and linguistics. We find the neo-behaviorism of much of current and past work in psycholinguistics wrong headed in both method and goal.

We will not elaborate here on the empirical investigation of the problems we raise from a theoretical and commonsensical point of view. Our main task is to suggest that the following three claims be made: (1) locutionary acts in ordinary commonplace conversational interaction are operatives and are describable only in terms belonging to a constitutive system of rules to which participants are oriented cooccurrently by a common, subculturally specified contractual arrangement; (2) the scientific investigation of locutionary acts cannot be pursued solely, or even to any relevant and significant extent, within the old paradigm as long as it continues to exclude institutional and other constitutive facts as a result of its insistence on objective, independently definable observation criteria, (3) the method of the empirical investigation of operatives (as in ethnomethodology) can provide an adequate and powerful means of analysis of conversational phenomena.

Fig. 1 illustrates the relationships between various observational facts that require different investigatory procedures. The syntax of conversational interaction is summarized in Fig. 2. The successful performance of a conversational episode is predicated on participants' knowledge (or communicative competence) of the subcultural rules of conversational interaction. The use of this knowledge by participants in a conversational interaction is identified with their performance of the procedural steps in the operative order of conversational events. The acquisition of this knowledge takes place in the context of socialization and the

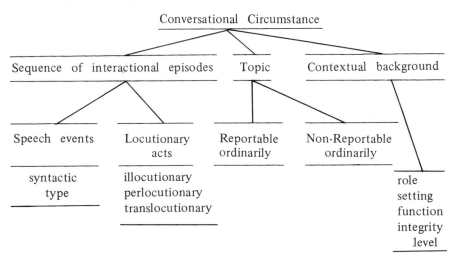

Fig. 2. Structural elements in the syntax of conversational interaction

development of linguistic, social interactional, and communicative competence. The scientific description of this knowledge is accomplished by means of a syntactic analysis of conversational events and a semantic analysis of locutionary acts. Such analyses are designed to provide nontrivial answers to questions such as these:

> At which stage is the conversational sequence? (e.g., What is the syntactic type of the utterance?)
> What topic is being talked about? Is it reportable under ordinary circumstances or not?
> What kind of locutionary act is it?
> What is the role relationship between participants?
> What is the conversational setting?
> What is the communicative function of the interaction?
> At which integrity level is the conversational event being transacted?
> What are the oriented to features of the interaction (status; distance; games people play)?

Each of these questions represents a significant problematic element in the analysis of conversational interactions; note at the same time that independent objective analyses of these empirical phenomena cannot escape being arbitrary or trivial or both. To escape the arbitrariness and circularity of the analysis inherent in the objective, independent observation techniques to these phenomena—techniques that are criterial in the old paradigm, it is necessary to adopt ethnomethodological practices of analysis, and these investigatory practices constitute that which we have called the new paradigm in psycholinguistics. All observation techniques derive their validity and specific pragmatic implications from a preexisting state of consensus. Scientific investigation is made up of an operative procedure within the context of a particular preexisting conceptual order related to a disciplinary field of specialization. Thus, current scientific practices in the objective analysis of language behavior (Behaviorist, Neo-Behaviorist, Cognitive) represent in their totality a special consensus about the operative and conceptual order of language phenomena. This special consensus, developed through apprenticeship in graduate training and through the selective practices of the profession in sanctioning the illegitimacy of certain procedures as "unscientific," acts to perpetuate itself by excluding from its range of admissible facts all those that are not encompassed by the preexisting conceptual order.

The maintenance of a preexisting conceptual order and the perpetration of a particular operative order by means of special consensus appears to us to be a general characteristic of discovery practices and, hence, would be an ethnomethodological universal.

A question now arises as to the characteristics of the interplay between two sorts of discovery practices each belonging to a different conceptual order and operative procedure. This is the problematic element that confronts us in our task to show the interesting nature of the phenomena of language use that are obvious and evident in the new paradigm while they have no conceptual status in the old paradigm. A principal point of difficulty resides in the tendency to alter in an unacceptable way the conceptual meaning of a bona fide component element in the new paradigm. For instance, the reduction of the meaning of the concept of "intention" as the most likely response in a divergent S-R hierarchy (e.g., Osgood, 1953; 1971) represents such an unacceptable redefinition (see Jakobovits, 1970). Another instance is the insistence that all conceptual categories in the system have an objectively and independently definable status, either in terms of the establishment of environmental contingencies for operant behavior or in terms of overt verbal reports about internal mental states (e.g., questionnaire responses, the semantic differential technique, overt verbalizations). Both of these difficulties are illustrated in the dramatic account by Castaneda (1969) of his efforts to adopt a new conceptual order for the phenomenology of ordinary reality, and we have noted similar difficulties in our efforts with students to validate for them the special consensus needed for the scientific conceptual and operative order in psychology (and no doubt other disciplines which substitute a special consensus for the ordinary consensus of everyday life).

The empirical investigation of the phenomena of ordinary conversational interactions, as we see this task from our current perspective, must include the following two steps: (1) a taxonomic classification of the components of the conceptual order of ordinary conversational interactions, and (2) a description of the organizational structure of the operative order of conversational events. Note that that description relies on the inherent characteristics of ordinary consensus rather than on the special consensus of psychological research and this avoids the first difficulty of reductionism mentioned above. Another task at this level is the specification of the criterial features of the notion of "topic," including the notion of "appropriateness" in terms of contextual features of the conversational interaction.

Because this second step is based on the classificatory scheme derived in the first step, it avoids the other difficulty mentioned above, that of having to validate the observations in terms of an independent, objective system of behavioral responses. The two steps together constitute the necessary and sufficient conditions for the systematic description of ordinary consensus and the empirical investigation of the operative order of commonplace conversational interaction. The problem of the meaning of a verbal utterance and the notion of communication via language become understandable in terms of these two steps. Hence, they constitute necessary and central activities in the investigation of communicative competence.

REFERENCES

Austin, J. L. *How To Do Things With Words*. (1955 Lectures, Ed. by J. O. Urmson). New York: Oxford University Press, 1965.

Bever, T.G. The cognitive basis for linguistic structures. In J. R. Hayes (Ed.), *Cognition and the Development of Language*. New York: John Wiley, 1970.

Castaneda, Carlos. *The Teachings of Don Juan: A Yaqui Way of Knowledge*. New York: Ballantine Books, 1969.

Chomsky, N. *American Power and The New Mandarins*. New York: Pantheon Books, 1969.

Garfinkel, H. *Studies in Ethnomethodology*. Englewood Cliffs, N.J.: Prentice-Hall, 1968.

Goffman, E. *Interaction Ritual*. Garden City, N.Y.: Doubleday, Anchor Books, 1967.

———. *Asylums*. Garden City, N.Y.: Doubleday, Anchor Books, 1961.

———. *The Presentation of Self in Everyday Life*. New York: Doubleday, 1959.

Grice, H. P. Meaning. *Philosophical Review*, LXVI, 1957, 377-88. (Reprinted in Steinberg and Jakobovits, 1971.)

Jakobovits, L.A. Prolegomena to a theory of communicative competence. In R.C. Lugton (Ed.), *English as a Second Language: Current Issues* (Vol. 6). Philadelphia: The Center for Curriculum Development, 1970.

———. Rhetoric and Stylistics: Some basic issues in the analysis of discourse. *College Composition and Communication*, December 1969, 314-328.

———. The act of composition: Some elements in a performance model of language. Proceedings of the Conference on the Composing Process, November 1968. (Unpublished.)

Jakobovits, L. A. and Miron, M. S. (Eds.) *Readings in the Psychology of Language*. Englewood Cliffs, N.J.: Prentice-Hall, 1967.

Kuhn, T. S. *The Structure of Scientific Revolutions*. Chicago: University of Chicago Press, 1962.

Miller, G. A. The psycholinguists: On the new scientists of language. *Encounter*, 23, 1964, 29-37.

Mitchell-Kerman, Claudia. Language behavior in a Black urban community. Unpublished doctoral dissertation in Anthropology, University of California, Berkeley, 1969. (Working Paper No. 23, Language Behavior Research Laboratory. Mimeo.)

Osgood, C. E. *Method and Theory in Experimental Psychology*. New York: Oxford University Press, 1953.

———. Where do sentences come from? In Steinberg and Jakobovits, 1971.

Postman, L. The present status of interference theory. In C. N. Cofer and Barbara S. Musgrove (Eds.), *Verbal Learning and Verbal Behavior*. New York: McGraw-Hill, 1961. (pp. 152-179)

Sacks, H. *Aspects of the Sequential Organization of Conversation*. (Forthcoming Prentice-Hall publication, 1971).

Searle, J. R. *Speech Acts*. Cambridge, England: Cambridge University Press, 1969.

Skinner, B. F. *Verbal Behavior*. New York: Appleton-Century-Crofts, 1957.

Steinberg, D. D. and Jakobovits, L. A. (Eds.), *Semantics: An Interdisciplinary Reader in Philosophy, Linguistics, and Psychology*. Cambridge, England: Cambridge University Press, 1971.

Vendler, Z. *Linguistics in Philosophy*. Ithaca: Cornell University Press, 1967.

NOTES

[1] As far as we know, Garfinkel (1968) was the first to use the term in any such sense that we are proposing here. We believe his definition and our definition have compatible underlying structures, although we have no idea whether this will appear to be so to Garfinkel (or to Sacks).

[2] cf. David McClelland's comment in *Psychology Today* (January 1971, p. 35): "Academic psychology in America has sold out to process . . . It is odorless, colorless and idealess . . . "

10 Review Study Questions and Discussion

Q.   Drs. Gordon and Jakobovits, in this book you sometimes use the expression "communicative competence" and at other times "transactional competence." Is there a difference? And if so, what?
A.   This book was written over a three-year period. The parts written earlier use the expression "communicative competence" while, more recently, we've preferred to use the expression "transactional competence." [*Note:* The chapter orders do not reflect relative order of writing over the three-year period.]

The reasons for our preference for "transactional competence" are discussed in the early parts of Chapter 7. We find communication theory too restrictive since the ordinary uses of language are not chiefly oriented to the transmission of information but rather to the structured display of rituals in the form of transactional moves and replies.

Q.   Why does the language teacher have to concern himself with the theoretical sophistications outlined in Part III of your book?
A.   We discuss this problem in Chapter 5. As long as the language teacher is a consumer of the basic research generated by psychologists and linguists, he must defer to their authoritative conclusions since the register of their research reports are too esoteric and technically specialized to permit evaluation by the teacher. We have argued that basic research techniques are not effectively productive for generating applied knowledge. The latter must be produced by the person who is going to use it and is closest to the data, namely the teacher himself.

Therefore, an essential competence of the language teacher must include a pedagogic register about the use of language for displaying transactional moves in ordinary conversations. This register allows him to be more effective in engineering instructional transactions in the classroom, as well as providing the structured components to be taught in the language course.

We have tried to outline the pedagogic register in Part III of this book. We have found that after some initial discomfort due to the unfamiliarity of the language, students and teachers begin readily to function in the new mode.

Q. Is there a connection between your "transactional engineering analysis" and Eric Berne's "Transactional Analysis" or "T.A.?"

A. No connection whatsoever. Transactional engineering analysis or T.E. derives from Erving Goffman's work on the transactional rituals of everyday interactions and its approach is based on the ethnomethodological perspective as developed by Garfinkel, Sacks, Schegloff and their coworkers.

Q. What, then, is "educational psycholinguistics?"

A. The ethnomethodological perspective is offered as a new paradigm in contrast to the traditional psycholinguistics of the old paradigm. Because our focus has been on the investigation of the instructional register, we refer to this new paradigm as "educational psycholinguistics." The chief premises that this new perspective entails include the following.

1. Teaching as conversation.
2. Conversation as transactions.
3. Transactions as moves and reply moves.
4. Transactional moves as generated by a register.
5. Register as a subsystem of rules appropriate for specialized functions.
6. Classroom interactions as governed by the instructional register.
7. Analysis of the instructional register through observation of ongoing classroom activities.

Q. What is the relevance of educational psycholinguistics for FL teaching?

A. There are two relevant aspects. On the one hand, the FL teacher *is a teacher*, and, therefore, must concern himself with the effective engineering of appropriate instructional transactions. On the other hand, the *topic or content* of the FL course involves the transactional components as displayed in the target code. Thus, the

FL teacher must be familiar with the methods of educational psycholinguistics in order to teach the content and structure of transactional performance in the target code.

Q. What is the relevance of "authenticity" for FL teaching?

A. The authenticity of a transactional move depends on the shared awareness on the part of coparticipants of the interpersonal significance of the move beyond its visible content. Thus, expressing compliance to a request, for instance, may signify, beyond the compliance itself, a dependency role relationship, or it may not, and to the extent coparticipants are aware of these implications to that extent the transaction has an authenticating context. Inauthentic contexts cooccur with manipulative, competitive and victimizing moves in ordinary settings.

In specialized settings, a different contractual basis is set up by mutual consent or by authoritative precedent. That is the case, for instance, in the psychotherapeutic role dyad, where one coparticipant (the therapist) is seen as having more knowledge and authority, and the other (the client), as having less. The inauthenticity in the relationship is seen as due to the lack of awareness of the client rather than due to the dissimulative intent, of the therapist. Hence, the therapist's manipulative attempts are seen as benign rather than victimizing.

The classroom represents another instance of a specialized setting. The teaching-learning contract, established by precedent and enforced by practices and sanctions, assigns to the teacher a role which helps him manipulate the student's environment in ways that are not being justified adequately to the student. Here again, the inauthenticity of the instructional manipulation is seen as benign since it derives from the student's defined incompetence which is being remedied by the teacher.

In practice, observation shows that both ordinary and specialized (instructional) registers cooccur in the classroom. Now, because the teaching contract is often seen by both teachers and pupils as assigning a permanent role distinction, the teacher's special powers, derived from this role position, create an inauthentic relationship that often spills over to the ordinary (noninstructional) transactions in the school. When the teacher's manipulative attempts are seductive for benign reasons, his successes are seen as the qualities of being gifted and inspiring. When his manipulative attempts are insidious for competitive or defensive reasons, he is seen as being victimizing, prejudiced, critical, or unfair.

Transactional Engineering Workshops are designed to train teachers to use self-analytic observational techniques for the analysis of classroom interactions between teacher and pupil. This can help teachers evaluate the level of authenticity of classroom interactions, engineer more effective instructional transactions, and authenticate the teaching contract. As a result, there is a greater possibility for growth and self-actualization on the part of both teachers and students.

Q.   Where can one obtain information about Transactional Engineering Workshops for FL teachers?

A.   By writing to: Transactional Engineering Corporation, 48 Palm Island, Miami Beach, Florida, 33139.

Q.   What is the relevance of the concept of "authenticity" to the teaching of a second language?

A.   There are two relevant aspects. One derives from the fact that FL teachers are *teachers,* therefore their instructional manipulations can gain in efficiency through the greater awareness obtained when using techniques of transactional engineering. But in addition to this, the FL teacher stands to profit from this approach in a special and unique way because transactional engineering analysis provides him with a taxonomy of transactional moves and registers that he can use as content for his lessons on the target code. This notion was specifically elaborated in Chapter 4.

The concept of authenticity, furthermore, clarifies for the FL teacher, the nature of desirable conversational practice in the FL course. Simulated restricted dialogues and an exchange of directed replies constitute insufficient conditions for practicing the authentic use of language. Knowledge of transactional engineering analysis allows the FL teacher to engineer conversational interactions in the target code that are real and genuine uses of language, hence promoting faster learning.

Q.   How does a teacher, trained in the traditional mode, become a transactional engineer, how does he become free, and how does he learn to apply the register you advocate?

A.   A teacher already is a transactional engineer. A teacher already is free. A teacher already knows how to apply the instructional register we advocate. In this book, we are attempting to convince the teacher that he already is a free person—if he chooses to affirm that fact to himself, and that he already possesses all the knowledge and instruments and knowhow that he needs to become a master at his art. What's missing? Two essential things, both of which are to be supplied by the teacher himself for himself: one, the belief that he is free if he so decides; two, the belief that he can become a master teacher through his own self-training efforts.

In this book, we have tried to strengthen these two beliefs by providing the teacher with arguments, rationalizations, interpretations and demonstrations which might seem relevant and convincing.

The teacher who, by an act of spirit and will, decides that he is, after all, *free*, begins to act like a free person. Now, if he should be young, inexperienced, impetuous, and well socialized, the existential crisis may afford a context for his actions which, to others, may appear unstable, risky, dubious, even threatening. The problems he runs into are therefore a consequence of his "immaturity" as a person, some might say, though we would prefer "his lack of effective transactional engineering techniques." To that we must attribute the frustrating blocks he runs into, and not to his self-affirmation of freedom.

Now, if he should be less young and impetuous, more aware of the necessary inertia of institutional bureaucracies, the existential search for self-affirmation will be explored within a realistic perspective of actual possibilities within the particular setting he finds himself. Thus, after deciding that he is free, he must decide that there are no known limits to his potential competence as a teacher.

Our observations show that the sheer act of making this decision creates a tremendous momentum for altering one's previous mode of operation. The teacher now begins to reformulate his problems in a personally relevant way, rather than in general terms as represented by teaching principles and slogans. In Chapter 7 we refer to the teacher's "personal pedagogic model" as representing this reformulation. In this manner, the teacher gradually evolves from a position of "being supervised" and "being trained in the latest methods" to a position of independence and mastery where he begins to generate himself the seeds of his continued growth as an artist and technician.

Q.   What is your belief on the relative advantages of structured and unstructured teaching?

A.   To us, the expression "unstructured teaching" is a contradiction in terms. The activity of teaching, if the term is going to retain a meaning that distinguishes this activity from other activities, implies structuring a sequence of instructional activities. Now, of course, there are innumerable ways of structuring instructional activities, and the question arises "Which way is best?"

A first sort of reply to this kind of question is to point out that the question as it stands is incomplete. Perhaps a more useful question might be, "Which way is best for me and my students at this time?"

Next, it might be useful to break up the question into separate queries that appear relevant to a particular teacher's condition. How can we formulate more explicitly what our present practices and beliefs are? Adopting the SAOROGAT technique of analysis, as described in Chapter 7, will allow the teacher to become more explicitly aware of the specific transactions going on in his classrooms on a day-to-day basis. This kind of objective self-analytic feedback is essential in the initial formulation and continued evolution of a personal pedagogic model.

The liberated teacher uses teaching methods and standard materials to further his self-defined pedagogic goals. The ordinary teacher, lacking an explicit personal pedagogic model, is a slave to the methods he is assigned or adopts. To the latter, "Which way is best?" becomes a cry of help addressed to the expert, and the answer is accepted in ignorance. To the former, "Which way is best for me and my students at this time?" becomes the self-directed empirical search of a master teacher at work.

Q.   What does the master FL teacher know which the run-of-the-mill sort doesn't know?

A.   We would change the emphasis from "know" to "do," for it is not necessary for an effective teacher to "know" wherein his effectiveness lies. The master FL teacher places his confidence in the actuality of the instructional transactions that are ongoing rather than in the alleged power of the method he uses or the alleged learnability of the materials. He views FL learning, not as exercise or practice or homework or study or anything else, but, specifically and sufficiently, as the on-going transactions in the target code during his interactions with the pupils. The other usual activities associated with FL study are products or concessions to a particular approach to FL teaching which has evolved by precedent in the public educational system.

Thus, the master FL teacher never forgets that the goal of FL study is the acquisition of transactional competence in the target code, and all other aspects of FL study constitute helpful or unhelpful strategies for promoting that goal.

The master FL teacher does not rationalize failures to achieve that goal by blaming them on the inadequacy of the method, or student motivation, or supervisory interference. Neither does he blame himself. For he sees "failure" or "blame" as nonproductive conceptions of the situation. Since he always remains a student of his craft, learns by experience (not failure or success), and is constantly involved in the continued progression of his competence, he always does his best in every situation, and that is sufficient for his self-respect.

When the master FL teacher walks into the classroom, he ascends the stage for his performative teaching. Each period is worth only itself. He sets the stage by establishing the terms of the contractual arrangement. Each student is to enact himself. "You are student Johnny." Now, student Johnny needs to understand the instructional directives given by the teacher so that he may be able to enact himself within the activities proposed by the teacher. So, she gives Johnny the opportunity to perform following directives, so that he may come to do it effortlessly, by routine. "Let us practice. Johnny, turn to page 66. Very good. Now, Johnny, do the last exercise on p. 19. Very good. Now I want you to go to the blackboard and write down your name. No, no. Not on the paper. The blackboard. Blackboard. Over there. Very good. Now, I want you to talk to René over there. Go shake hands with him. That's right." And so on.

The master FL teacher may or may not rely on a predefined sequence. For instance, in situations where he expects to work with a group of students until they have reached a specified demonstrable level of transactional performance, he may feel more at ease with very little predefined structure, analogously to the natural acquisition of a second language outside the school. If, however, his defined contribution within an organized curriculum is set and evaluated jointly with others, then he might find it more useful to follow sequentially structured lesson plans. But in either case, the master FL teacher will create a classroom interactional climate that maintains a sufficient level of authenticity for the ongoing activities.

Q. How does the master FL teacher promote the authentication of classroom activities?

A. Every ongoing activity must be authenticated properly by insuring that the participants have an explicit awareness of its instructional function. We call this "performative learning," and it is the counterpoint to performative teaching.

For instance, if the students or the teacher are involved in a practice exchange and the student's contribution is to be evaluated as reflecting upon his intelligence or worth as a person, the transactional climate is inauthentic instructionally. If the student's contribution is to be authenticated, it ought to be seen for what it is, not a test of intelligence or whatever, but a one-time performance of himself enacting himself practicing an exchange. Both teacher and students must share this authentication process. Since students have been trained in the inauthentic context, the master FL teacher must engineer a more authentic climate in the FL classroom by establishing in clear and explicit terms the content of the teaching contract.

Q. You have questioned the traditional classification of FL teaching into the four basic skills of listening, speaking, reading and writing. What's wrong with it and what's a better way of classifying it?

A. The so-called four basic skills remind us of the Holy Roman Empire that was neither holy, nor Roman, nor an empire. True, tests of "listening comprehension" continue to be widely used, along with tests of the other three alleged types of skills, but this practice only reflects the past as well as current curricular orientation of language tests, which is what these tests were designed to do, given that course grades and achievement were used in their preparation and validation.

But, now, if we allow ourselves some freedom of inquiry, unencumbered by the precedent setting orientation of the past, and we begin to look at some recent work in sociolinguistics and ethnomethodological psycholinguistics (as, for instance, the arguments we have presented in Part III), it becomes readily apparent that the conception of language teaching must be reoriented to include the basic notion of the context of an utterance. As we have argued in Chapters 7 and 9 particularly, the meaning of a display in a conversation is given by the locus of the utterance (or gesture) within the ongoing transactional sequence. Evidence shows that transactional competence is tied to the notion of register and mode, and that a performance in one setting is not necessarily matched by the performance in another setting.

Thus, "listening comprehension in French" is a global expression that derives meaning from the arbitrary way in which tests of listening comprehension have been prepared, and does not reflect the reality of language use. The same goes for "a speaking knowledge of French," or reading or writing.

Q.   How would you define the basic skills to be learned in a FL course?

A.   We do not find the notion of "basic skill" a productive one. It begs the issue unnecessarily and we can get along better without it.

If we look upon the problem of FL teaching as the teaching of transactional performances in the target code, then it is only necessary to have an adequate taxonomy of transactional components as the target achievement, and in that case, everything is as important as everything else. True, there may be particular sequences that are easier than others, but such a learnability scale would vary from learner to learner and cannot be predetermined. Instead, it can be incorporated in individualized techniques of instruction. Individual differences in the learnability of sequential materials should not, however, be confused with "basic-ness."

Q.   You advocate a change in orientation for the FL teacher, from applied linguistics and psychology to transactional engineering analysis and ethnomethodology. What is the basic difference in these two orientations and how is the teacher to accomplish the switch?

A.   The first personally practical step the FL teacher can do to understand the direction of the new orientation to adopt, is to bring a tape recorder into the classroom and record some ongoing interactions in the classroom. Next, he should record some conversations in everyday settings on his daily round. Next, he should transcribe his tapes and study them. He will immediately get a feel for what we mean when we talk about register differences and how natural conversations differ from structured classroom exchanges.

Now this is just the beginning in the reorientation procedure. At this point the FL teacher becomes personally and intuitively convinced that the classroom interactions based on principles of applied linguistics and sequencing do not lead to practice of the relevant target performances.

The next major step is to acquire technical facility in analyzing the structural components of natural conversations. We have found that undergraduate students in our courses can develop this kind of technical competence in one semester's work. The FL teacher should have an advantage, in this respect, over the average college student, since he is already familiar with the technicalities of linguistics. Careful study of this book, and a few collateral readings to be found in the References, should suffice to enable the FL teacher to feel familiar with the kind of analysis that we have proposed, much of which relies on the intuitive knowledge of the academically oriented person.

Q.   Since the school represents a restricted social environment, is it then possible to engineer authentic transactions that duplicate the outside settings? And if not, is it possible to develop natural conversational ability in the classroom?

A.   It is obviously not possible to replicate outside settings in the classroom and still maintain authenticity. Fortunately, authenticity in classroom interactions need not depend on the duplication of outside conditions. After all, the child of three is a skilled transactional performer, even though his direct contact with the outside is drastically limited. This would not be possible were it not the case that the child's use of language is consistently authentic within the home environment.

Similarly, in the teaching of a second language under classroom conditions, one only need to insure that the language use is made in the context of authentic practice, as discussed specifically in Chapters 3 and 4.

Q.   You have stated that FL study should not be compulsory, and that more options should be available to the student in terms of mini-specialization of courses along a dimension of functional use. Do you think students are enlightened and wise enough to make these kinds of decisions?

A.   It does not take wisdom, but freedom and authenticity. The unwilling student does not learn of much value. Instead, the FL teacher must convince the student of the desirability of FL study, and only when he is successful in this task, should he begin to teach. Furthermore, he must continue to counsel the learner in his difficulties so that he continues to be propelled by self-interest rather than by submission to authority. With willing students in an atmosphere of freedom and authenticity, there is no language teaching problem. It goes without worry, though not without effort.

Q.   Would you advise FL teachers to join and participate in encounter groups?

A.   It may be relevant for some but not necessarily for everyone. But some form of more authentic encountering is necessary to replace the current competitive, risky, and inauthentic basis of interaction in the school context. We have observed that teachers feel most uneasy having colleagues or supervisors present as observers in their classroom. Why is that? We have also observed that consultation among teachers and administrative school personnel is formalized in style and content, and not particularly authentic. Why? There definitely exists a climate of mutual distrust and threat which is not productive for self-exploration and creative experimentation.

In some way at some point this threatening climate must be de-gelled, dissolved, and recrystallized into a more humane and reasonable transactional milieu. Encounter-transaction workshops and transactional engineering workshops for the entire school personnel represent possible techniques for a change towards greater freedom and authenticity.

Q.   You have presented an analysis of the teaching-learning process (particularly in Chapter 7) which appears to be a significant reformulation of the current widespread view. What is the significance of this reformulation for the FL teacher?

A.   The reformulation is based on the ideas of Carl Rogers, to whom we have dedicated this book. The self-authentication of the teacher's role affects not only his self-evaluation and feeling of wellbeing but also alters the basic contract between teacher and pupil. The most visible aspect of this change is a new orientation towards the student, one that is centered in the individual learner, not in the instructional task or the topical content of the acquired knowledge.

The FL teacher who adopts this new conception of teaching places emphasis on the facilitation of enacted transactional performances in an authentic context rather than on pacing or visible demonstrations of skills for test purposes. His style of teaching changes. He becomes more tolerant of incomplete or incorrect utterances and is more aware that the practicing student is involved in the execution of his enacted performance as well as in the acceptability of his display. He finds dull practice intolerable and avoids it in favor of the integrity of the ongoing authentic interaction trusting that each individual student will react according to his own timetable of acquisition and attempted performance. He avoids the loud-talking register whereby he tries to teach others a point of lesson under the guise of talking to Johnny in the presence of others. Thus, he avoids inauthentic directed questions like "What is your name?" "Can you tell me who threw the ball to Jane?," "Can you repeat after me . . . ," and so on, which are fake questions that have no part in the target skills to be learned. (Can you imagine ever asking those questions in a noninstructional setting?)

Instead, the authentic FL teacher performs in the classroom the authentic use of the target code, thereby providing the relevant learning opportunity for practicing the target skills. "What is your sister's name?" is an improvement over "What is your name?" "With whom did you play ball during recess this morning?" is preferable to "Who did Jane throw the ball to?" "What did you and Johnny talk about on your way to school today?" is more authentically relevant than "What did Mr. Jones eat for breakfast?"

The authentic FL teacher avoids emphasis on the cognitive aspects of FL study in favor of its experiential aspects. Thus, he minimizes linguistic explanations (except where the student has a specialized interest in it) and linguistic practice exercises and assignments. Instead, he finds ways of increasing the student's performative practice of authentic language use. He does this in a number of ways.

By talking to each student in a personally relevant way (vs. loud-talking or practicing). By splitting the class into dyads or triads so that each student has the opportunity to perform. By enlisting the help of student-aides, parents, and paraprofessionals. By making use of the mass media and audio visual aids as stimulants for subsequent authentic interactions (discussions, projects, games).

The current dilemma of the FL teacher is not the lack of opportunity for creating authentic transactions within the school context but the rigidity with which she tends to adhere to the necessity of linguistically oriented practice, an attitude that is reinforced, often demanded, by the administrative setting. The latter orientation is supported by existing institutional procedures including teacher training, curricular program that become well entrenched, commercially produced packages of materials, standardized norms on a small number of widely used tests, the literature and ongoing research, the convention speeches, and so on, and so on. It's the heavy machinery of enmeshed institutional gears creating the inertia of precedent and organized control over progressivist innovations.

Fortunately, all of this need not *necessarily* impede the FL teacher from engineering authentic instructional transactions in the classroom. The increasing use of behavioral objectives as a predefined assessment program can readily be employed in the service of authentic FL teaching by defining behavioral objectives in terms of specified transactional performances, thus providing the FL teacher with a convenient substitute for the current despotic influence of nationally standardized discrete-point tests of knowledge of a second language.

We believe that FL teachers are going to play a special and unique role in the innovation of novel and creative forms of authentic teaching. The future of FL teaching, seems to us, is even brighter than its distinguished past.

Appendix I

(1) Rex: I am hot. Put this on. I want to be warm. (points to air conditioner)
    Father: You mean "cool," You want to be cool.
    Rex: Yeah. I want to be cool.
    Father: (turns unit on)

(2) R: I *love* my paintings. (looking at his recently completed samples)
    F: I like them too.
    R: But why don't you love them too?
    F: I do love them.
    R: But . . . you said . . . (Mother walks in and R. gets distracted)

(3) R: Oh! We forgot my coloring book!
    F: How did you know?
    R: Fine. Forgot my coloring book.
    F: (laughs)

(4) Mother: (to F.) I wonder if next time I *will* take the nitric oxyde.
    R: No, you wouldn't!
    M: You're probably right. But how do you know?
    R: Fine. (laughing)

(5) F: Everyone has to die sometime. (to other adult during dinner conversation.)
    R: (picking up conversation) Can I die?
    F: Yes. Everything that's alive can die.
    R: Can hard things die?
    F. Only living things can die.
    R: Can cars die?
    F: No. Cars are not alive. But they can break down!
    R: Leaves can die. (seriously)
    F: Yes. Leaves can die.
    R: Can part of a tree die?
    F: Yes.
    R: Can the hard part of a tree die?
    F: Yes. The bark can die.
    R: Can a stick die?
    F: Yes.

(6) R: Can I dip my cookie in there?
    F: If you want to.
    R: I want to. (proceeds to do it)

(7)   R: Look at me. (making gestures)
        F: (continues talking on the phone)
        R: Look at me! (insistently)
        F: (interrupting his telephone conversation) I *am* looking at you!
        R: I am flying.
        F: (resumes his telephone conversation)
        R: (walks away as he continues to gesture)

(8)   R: Is some people gonna put some clothes on me?
        F: (taking R.'s wet pants off)
        R: Yeah or No?
        F: No.

(9)   F: I'm gonna go eat breakfast now. Would you like to come to the
           kitchen and talk to me? Keep me company?
        R: (watching T.V. in living room) No.
        F: Do you prefer the cartoons to talking to me?
        R: Huh?
        F: Do you like the cartoons better than me?
        R: But then I won't be able to see the cartoons!
        F: I see. Well, I see you later, Champ.

(10)   R: I want to go with you Daddy. (whining)
        F: O.K. We'll go together to pick up Mommy.
        R: O.K. (smiles happily)
        F: (picks up keys)
  (a)   R: Am I going with you Daddy?
        F. Yes.
        R: (smiles happily)

(11)   R: Where is my spoon?
        F: I don't know. (writing at his desk)
        R: It's in the drawer. (pointing)
        F: (gets up, finds and gives him spoon)

(12)   R: Are you tired?
        F: No. Are you?
        R: No.

(13)   R: The pipi comes out from my penis, and the stinky poo comes out
           from what?
        F: The anus.

(14)   R: Are you helping me paint?
        F: Yes.

R: Why?

F: Don't you want me to?

R: Yeah, I want to.

(15)   R: Are you gonna be mad, Mommy?

M: Why?

R: Are you gonna be mad?

M: What are you doing?

R: I'm putting the apple on my toes.

M: (laughing) No, I'm not gonna be mad. So long as you're not going to leave any pieces on the floor.

R: (nodding) Yeah, I'm gonna leave pieces on the floor.

M: (laughs)

R: I'm finished with the apple. I don't want any more.

(16)   F: (walks into bathroom)

(a) R: What happened? (referring to crashing sound coming from Baby Joy's room)

F: I don't know. I didn't look.

(b) R: Which way you didn't look?

F: The room where the baby is.

(17)   F: That's David Frost. (looking at T.V.)

R: Do you know him?

F: No, but I've seen him on T.V. before.

R: (appears to consider answer, but no further response)

(18)   R: How many pieces? (playing at table with pieces of an apple)

F: Ten. (joking)

R: No.

F: Five.

R: No.

F: Two.

R: Yeah . . . How many now? (after eating one)

F: Five. (joking)

R: No. How many?

F: Two.

R: No. How many?

F: Zero.

R: No. It's zero over here (points to where the other piece was lying before he ate it), but one over here. (pointing to piece that's left)

F: Oh, I see.

(19)   R: Daddy, I love you Daddy.

F: I love you too. (kisses him)

R: Your nose looks like an apple. (they both look at each other for a second then burst out laughing together)

(20) (a) R: Where is that shirt? (pointing to F's shirt)

F: Those are flower designs. Someone painted the flowers on it.

R: Where is this?

F: (puzzled, doesn't answer)

(b) R: Where is this from?

F: That's a shirt Zeidy brought back from Israel.

(c) R: Is it Daddy's day?

F: Yes, that's right. I got it for Daddy's day.

R: And where is *my* day?

F: (laughing) You have your *birthday*.

(d) R: Where is it?

F: In two months. Soon your birthday will be here, then you will get presents too.

R: (smiles happily)

(21)   F: What were you gonna say Rex?

R: What? (intonation and smiling expression indicating "What was I gonna say?", and not "What did you say?")

F: I don't know—What was it?

R: What? (as above but more emphatically)

F: I don't know. What could it have been?

R: Tell me.

F: (laughing) *I* don't know! I don't know what *you* want to say.

R: But *you* tell me what I wanted to say.

F: I *can't*. *You* are the one who knows that.

R: But I don't want to! (with a slight whine of frustration)

F: (kissing him) O.K. O.K.

(22) (a) R: Will you carry me, Daddy? (from the car to the house)

F: Oh, sure. You're my son, and I will do that for you.

(b) R: But . . . I want to be Mommy's!

F: You're both Mommy's and Daddy's. Let's go. (lifting him)

(23)   R: What are you doing? (F is writing while talking to R)

F: Writing down what you're saying. All the things you're saying.

R: (talks gibberish)

F: I can't write that down. It's too difficult.

R: Write this.

F: Oh, you're going to dictate something for me to write down. O.K. Go ahead.

R: (talking gibberish of the following approximate form: Pick a backa. Ponty. Picky, siky. Burndy. Ptiggy. Birdy. Gondy and biggy and giddy. B. D. Birdy. Dego dammer. Enger beinger, denger.

F: O.K. I've got it all. Thank you.

R: (walks away with smug expression)

(24)   R: Baby Joy spilled water on my bed!

F: Oh, really? Why?

R: Cause she wanted to.

F: Are you sure she wanted to or was it maybe an accident?

R: Yeah, es was an accident. (pauses, then looks up) No. Es wa not an accident. She did it on *purpose*.

F: No, not really.

R: Yes. She did it on purpose.

(25)   R: I made a stinky poo after my bath. No. Uh . . .uh . . . uh . . .

F: Before?

R: Yeah. I made a stinky poo before my bath.

(26)   R: (very excitedly) I saw a little boy!

F: Oh. And then what happened?

R: (excitedly) I said Hi to him.

F: And then what happened?

R: (laughs excitedly) He said Hi to me!

(27)   F: Rex, you're holding it upside down. (his coloring book)

R: Is this right-up-side or down? (as he rotates book)

F: Right side *up* and upside *down*. *Right* side *up* and upside *down*. Can you say that?

R: Right down upside down (smiling, aware of approximate nature of his imitation)

F: No. Say, right-side-up. That's this way. (straightens book)

R: Right-side-up.

F: Good. Now, this is upside down. (rotates book)

R: Upside down. Right side up. (rotating book)

F: Good.

(28)   R: Daddy, Daddy. The cake spilled on the floor. (as F was coming home from the office)

F: Oh, my God! (playfully exaggerating)

R: The cake spilled on the floor.

F: And what did Mommy say?

R: *Brendaaah!* (calling loudly)

F: (laughs) And what did *you* do?

R: I cried. (taking on a very serious look)

F: (laughs)

(29)   R: Hey, I have no black chips.

F: There are no *black* ones.

R: Yeah there are. Look. These.

F: Those are blue.

R: Oh. (the chips R called "black" were replacements for some missing blue chips and were of a much darker blue, hence the mislabeling)

(30)   R: Is there some juice in here?

F: No.

R: Yeah, look!

F: Oh, Yeah.

R: Is there some juice in here?

F: Yeah.

R: Is there some juice in here?

F: No.

R: Yeah, look!

F: Oh.

R: Is there some juice in here?

F: Yes. (this continued for about a dozen repetitions as R was pouring juice from one cup to another and checking my answers)

(31)   R: What are you doing?

F: I'm buttoning up your pants so they don't fall down.

R: But I'm not gonna fall down!

F: Not *you*! Your *pants*.

(32)   F: Excuse me. (to Rex)

R: What?

F: (no answer; walks towards door)

R: What? (as he looks around, puzzled)

F: I'll be right back.

(33)   R: Is this a finger or a brush paint? (showing a work he did recently)

F: Brush paint. (after examining it)

R: No. It's both.

F: Oh, you used both. It's a combination finger *and* brush paint.

R: Finger. Brush. Finger-brush. Pinger brush. Pingerbrush. (continues gibberish (?) as he walks away with a smile)

(34) (a) R: Daddy, show me how to do it. It's too hard for me. (hands bottle of soap bubbles to F)

F: (proceeds to demonstrate)

(b) R: O.K.?
    F: (continues to blow) O.K.? You try it now.

(35)   R: Shake hands. (extends left hand)
  (a) F: No, the other hand. Peace. (they shake hands)
  (b) R: Yeah, Peace . . . What's *war*?
        F: War is killing.
        R: War is shooting people.
        F: Yeah.

(36)   R: Pam? (looking for her)
        F: Pam is not here.
        R: Where is she?
        F: In the park.
        R: In the sandbox?
        F: Yes. (this took place a few minutes after he refused to go with her and Baby Joy to play "in the sandbox")

(37)   R: (runs into room, jumps into F's lap, smiles, and talks gibberish)
        F: What are you doing?
        R: Ta-ta-ba-ta-ta-ta? (imitating F's intonation pattern)
        F: You're happy, hey?
        R: Ta-pa-ta-ba-ba? (ditto)
  (a) F: You're happy I'm here, hey? (It was unusual for F to be home in midmorning.)
        R: Tapa kata, taka pa. (holding on to F's neck)
  (b) F: I like you too.
        R: Ma ma mu mu.
        F: I'm gonna kiss you now. (kisses him; R reciprocates—rather unusual for him to do so)

(38)   R: (playing with two cups of juice and pieces of bread) Put this one in there. Then in here. Then mix it together around. Is there too much in here? No. Where is my spoon? Oops. I didn't spill it. I just dripped. I'm making mushy juice. I'm gonna put it in here. Is there too much in here? I'm gonna hold it. Don't worry. I'm gonna mix it around with the spoon. I'm gonna be careful. I'm gonna pad it. See what is it. I'm making it mushy. There is more sugar in the paper. I'm finished. Where do I put this? Can I put this in the sink? (to F)

(39) (a) R: Where is Daddy?
        M. Daddy is in there.
        R: But I can't open the door.
  (b) M. He is busy.

R: But I want to see my Daddy! (begins to cry)

F. (coming out, picking him up) I have some work to do now.

R: But I want you to come here.

(c) F. But I have some work to do (apologetically)

R: (cries harder)

F. See you in a few minutes. (puts him down, closes door behind him. Rex cries for one minute, then leaves)

(40)   R: Look Daddy! (showing him painting he just finished)

F: Oh, it's the sign of the big bad monster! (low tone)

(a) R: Why? (examines sheet)

F: You made it!

(41)   F: See, we're driving down the hill.

R: Is this east or west?

F: It's north.

R: But which way is east?

F: That away. East, west, north, south. That way is east. That way is west. That way is north. And that way is south. Get it?

R: (nods)

(42)   F: (to M) Rex said the other day that he'd like two Mommies and two Daddies.

R: (interjecting) Yeah. I want two Daddies and two Mommies.

M: Oh?

R: If you do like this there is two Mommies. (presses finger against his eyeball)

(Note: F had shown him the eyeball distortion trick several weeks before this exchange. Its application to the present context is Rex's invention.)

Appendix II

(1)   R: Does Pam have to eat also?
        F: Yes.
        R: Why?
        F: Because she is hungry.

(2)   R: I'm making a hole. (playing in the sandbox)
        F: Why?
        R: Huh?
        F: Why?
        R: Cause I *like* a hole.

(3)   R: Come in the forest. (indicating bushes behind sandbox)
        F: Why?
        R: Cause there's no tigers in there.

(4)   R: I can't do it with two hands. (raking leaves)
        F: Why?
        R: Cause I can't do it.

(5)   R: Can I sit on the sandbox? (standing outside)
        F: Why?
        R: (after a long pause) Cause I like it dry.

(6)   R: Put all the toys in there. Please. (pointing to sandbox)
        F: Why?
        R: Cause I like them in there.

(7)   R: Let's put Baby Joy in there.
        F: Why?
        R: Cause I like her.

(8)   R: Look what I did! (setting up dominoes fixed to a slab)
        F: Yeah, I see.
        R: Why did I did that? Because I wanted to see what it did?
        F: That's right.

(9)   R: No, Baby Joy is taking away the chalk! (pushing her away)
        F: It's O.K., Rex. She's just trying to help you draw on the blackboard.
   (a) R: She wants to be nice to me so I'll be nice to her?
   (b) F: Yes. If you're nice to people, they will be nice to you.
        R: I was not nice to you today? (referring to an incident earlier that morning)

F: No, you weren't. You made me very mad.

R: Why?

(c) F: Because I asked you not to smear your peanut buttery hands on the back of the chair, and you deliberately did it anyway. And I got very mad.

(10)   F: You wanna climb this tree?

R: No.

F: Why?

R: Cause it's *high*.

(11)   R: I'm gonna hit the wood here. (as he hits tree with shovel)

F: Why?

R: Cause the wood is bad. It has glue here.

F: Is there glue in there?

R: (no answer as he continues hitting)

F: Why do you think there is glue in there?

R: (no answer)

F: Why do you think there is glue in there?

R: (no answer)

F: Why do you think there is glue in there?

R: (no answer)

(12)   F: What are you doing? (R walks around in back yard)

R: Nothing.

F: Why?

R: Nothing! (emphatically)

F: Why?

R: *NOTHING!* (very emphatically)

F: Why?

R: Cause . . . (pause) I'm a little boy.

F: Oh, I see.

R: That's right.

(13)   R: I wanna paint.

F: O.K. After I finish breakfast.

R: But I wanna paint now.

F: After I finish my breakfast.

R: Why?

F: Cause I want to finish eating. O.K.?

R: But I want to paint. (as he walks away)

(14)   R: I am tired. (feigning lassitude)

F: (no answer)

R: I want to go in the playpen. Can I?

F: No. You're too heavy for it.

R: Why?

F: (no answer)

R: (walks away, showing discontent)

(15)　R: There is a fish in my pipi. (pointing to potty he just used)

F: (no answer; empties potty in toilet bowl)

R: Throw the pipi on the floor.

F: No! Don't be silly.

R: Why?

F: (no answer)

(16)　R: No, don't put it there, Daddy.

F: Why not?

R: Cause Baby Joy is gonna get it.

F: It's O.K. She is in bed.

(17)　R: Open the lights! (whining in bed)

F: You don't need the lights.

R: But I can't *see!*

F: You don't need to see.

R: Why?

(a) F: Because you're going to sleep, and you don't need any lights when you're asleep.

R: Why?

(b) F: Because, when you sleep, your eyes are closed.

R: (gets up, goes to the bathroom, and squints into the mirror)

F: What are you doing?

R: I'm trying to see if my eyes are closed.

F: (laughing) Go back to bed.

(18)　R: Are you helping me? (picking up toys)

F: Yes.

R: Why are you helping me?

F: Mmmm.

(a) R: Because you want to be nice to me?

F: Yes.

R: Why?

(b) F: Because I want to.

R: Why?

F: Because I *want* to.

R: Why?

(c) F: Because I like to.

(d) R: Because then I'm gonna be nice to you?

(e) F: That's right. If I am nice to you, you're gonna be nice to me.

(19)   R: I want to tear it out to show it to you. (referring to top sheet of drawing pad)

F: No, leave it in the book.

R: Why?

F: It's better that way.

R: But I don't want it better that way. I want it better this way. (as he attempts to remove the sheet)

(20)   R: Let's put it on the wall. (referring to putting up one of his paintings)

F: No. These are for the book. (drawing pad)

R: Why?

F: Some are for the wall and some are for the book.

(21)   R: Read (gloss: tell) a story about a truck.

F: No, not now.

R: Why?

F: Cause I have to think.

R: About what?

F: About what we are going to do soon.

R: (after lull, long silence) There is the truck. Read me a story about it.

F: No, not now.

R: (no answer)

(22)   F: Rexy, is this daytime?

R: Yes.

F: Why?

R: Cause it's daytime.

(23)   F: Uh, uh . . .

R: What? (without looking up from play)

F: Are you a boy?

R: (looks up and smiles) Yes.

F: Why? (with exaggerated intonation, mimicking one of R's styles of asking "Why" as a game)

R: Cause I am a boy. (looks away back to play)

F: *Why?* (exaggerated)

R: Cause I am a *BOY!* (without looking up)

F: O.K.

(24)   F: Are you throwing sand?

R: Yeah.

F: Why?

R: Cause the boat is crashing. (moves boat in air making noises with mouth)

F: Oh.

R: It likes that.

(25)   R: There was a kitty cat here. (playing in sandbox)

F: Ah. Did she make . . . uh . . .

R: Pipi?

F: Yes.

R: Yeah.

F: Why?

R: Cause she is a kitty cat.

(26)   R: Paddy. Baddy. Daddy. Baddy.

F: Am I a baddy?

R: Yeah.

F: Why?

R: (no answer; makes silly mocking noises as when he seems frustrated or doesn't know what to say)

(27)   R: You're messing up my hair!

F: I am messing up your hair.

R: *Don't!*

F: Why? (mockingly)

R: Cause then I won't be a boy.

(28)   R: Are you so happy, Daddy?

F: Oh, yes. I feel pretty good.

R: Why?

F: Uh . . .

R: Cause you have my paintings?

F: Yep. That's right.

(29)   F: (making swallowing noises while driving car)

R: What are you eating?

F: Nothing.

R: Why are you making like that?

F: Because my mouth is dry, and that helps to make it wet.

(30)   F: What are you doing?

R: I'm looking for a pencil.

F: Why?

R: Cause I want to write something.

F: Here, I'll give you a pencil. Do you have paper?

R: Yeah.

(31) R: How many on your side? (playing with poker chips)

F: Six.

R: They are for you.

F: Why are you giving me only six?

R: Cause I like to give you six.

F: Oh.

R: Here. I give you one more.

F: Thanks.

(32) F: Do you want to go for a drive when you finish eating?

R: No. (with dramatically serious expression)

F: Why not?

R: Cause I am lazy. (with same expression)

(33) F: No! Don't splash. You can splash in the swimming pool and the lake, but not in the bathtub.

R: Why?

F: Because you are making everything wet . . . that's not supposed to be.

R: (desists)

(34) R: I'm a sleepy boy. I need two beds.

F: Why?

R: Cause . . . cause . . . I wanna be a baby.

F: Why?

R: Cause I like to. (F was dismantling Baby Joy's bed in which R was playing)

(35) F: Rex, let's go make pipi.

R: No, I don't want to.

F: Yes. I can see it by the way you jump around. Come. (they go, and R urinates) Oh, oh. You fooled me! (jokingly)

R: (laughs)

F: Why did you fool me?

R: Cause . . . (laughs) cause . . . (makes funny noises and runs away)

(36) F: Babby (gloss: grandma) has a bubu (gloss: pain, hurt) in the back. You have to call her to ask how she is.

R: She has many bubus or just one?

F: Just one. In the back. Here.

R: She has just one bubu?
F: Yes.
R: Why?
F: Because. Do *you* have a bubu here?
R: No. I have a bubu *here*. Es was yesterday. Remember?
F: Do you have a bubu here too?
R: No.
F: Why?
R: Es was here, remember?
F: Yeah, I remember.

(37)   R: Why did you throw out the pink one? (pen)
F: Because it wasn't writing any more.
R: Is this one writing? (he has been drawing with it for the previous few minutes)
F: Yes. This one is still good.

(38)   R: How many chips are there? (placing poker chips in front of F)
F: (counting aloud) Twelve.
R: Now how many are there? (removing a few)
F: (counting aloud) Five.
R: These are for you.
F: You are leaving those for me?
R: Yes.
F: Why?
R: Cause we gonna play a game. These are for you.
F: O.K.

(39)   R: (setting up a familiar game) Here, Hair, you like to eat some more corn?
F: Yes. (with high pitched voice)
R: Here, take some. (extends spoon)
F: No. Hair don't eat! (ordinary voice)
R: Why?
F: Because Hair don't have a mouth!

(40)   R: Is this a pencil?
F: No. That's a pen.
R: But is it a *pencil*?
F: No, not pencil, *pen*.
R: Why?
F: Because. That's what it's called.
R: But I want a pencil.
F: O.K. I'll get you one.

(41)   R: (pours juice from one cup to another) Is there some more in here? (looking at second cup now containing the liquid)
F: I don't know. I can't see.
R: Look. (shows F the first, now empty, cup)
F: Yep. It's empty.
R: Why?
F: Because you poured it all in there. (indicating other cup)

(42)   R: You want to drink this?
F: No!
R: Why?
F: (no answer)
R: Why?
F: No.
R: Why?
F: Because you washed your fingers in there!

(43)   R: (protesting) Why you put it in there? (rest of meat pie in plate)
F: Because there was too much in there. I didn't want you to spill it.
R: But now it's not good any more!
F: I'll buy you another one.
R: But I want a cake! (gloss: meat pie)
F: It's a meat pie.

(44)   R: (whining) I don't want to go outside.
F: Why not? It's so nice outside.
R: But I am tired. (whines)

(45)   R: Is Mommy finished with stinky?
F: No.
R: Why?
F: She is still in there.

(46)   F: I'll get you something to drink . . . Do you want . . . I'll give you some milk. Milk is good with peanut butter sandwich. (goes to refrigerator)
R: (whining) I want *juice*.
F: O.K. I'll give you juice. Juice is good with peanut butter sandwich.
R: I want *milk*.
F: I'll give you both. Milk *and* juice.
R: Why?
F: Because you don't know what you want. (during the following two minutes, R samples both cups)

(47)   R: Is that your paper? (referring to white writing pad)
          F: Yes. (interrupting his writing)
          R: But I don't have a paper? (normal question intonation)
          F: Yes, you do.
          R: Where?
          F: In the living room.
          R: Is this the same paper as mine?
          F: Yes.
          R: But where is the yellow paper? (referring to yellow writing pad)
          F: It's all used up.
          R: Why?
          F: There is no more room on it to write.
          R: You gonna turn the page when you finish this page?
          F: Yes.

(48)   R: Do you want it? (offering a piece of bread he soaked in orange juice)
          F: (shakes head)
          R: Do you want it?
          F: No.
          R: Why?
          F: Cause I don't like that. I don't feel like eating now.

(49)   R: Who bought this? (eating grapes)
          F: Mommy. Mommy buys all the food we eat.
          R: Why?
   (a)   F: Because Mommies buy food. That's one of the things Mommies do.
          R: Do all Mommies buy food?
          F: Yes.
          R: What's gonna happen if a Mommy doesn't buy food? What's gonna
             people say?
          F: People might say that she is not a good Mommy.
          R: Why?
   (b)   F: Because that's the way people think.

(50)   F: Rex, why are you switching on all the lights?
          R: Cause it's dark in here.
          F: Oh, all right.

(51)   R: What are you doing? (to the maid)
          F: She is cleaning up.
 (a, b)   R: Because that's her work. Because the house will then be neat.
          R: Why?
          F: (no answer)

(52)   R: I don't need the sunglasses.
          F: Why not?
    (a)   R: I don't need them.
          F: Your eyes are getting stronger. You can see without them.
          R: (sneezes)
          F: The sun makes you sneeze.
          R: Why?
    (b)   F: I don't know. I'll have to ask a doctor.
          R: Why?
    (c)   F: If you want to know why.
          R: (alarmed) I don't want to know.
          F: O.K.

(53)   R: (R is playing quietly in room. Radio is on. F is present) The news is
             over. It's French now. I don't like French.
          F: Why?
    (a)   R: I don't like it.
          F: Why?
          R: I don't like it!
    (b)   F: Because you don't understand it?
          R: No, I don't understand it.

(54)   F: What are you doing? (seeing R handling Kleenex tissue)
          R: Taking something out of my nose.
          F: What?
          R: Stuff.
          F: Why?
          R: Because I don't like it in my nose.

(55)   R: (coming into bathroom) What are you doing?
          F: I am giving my face a massage.
          R: Why?
          F: Because it's gonna make it look nice.

(56)   R: Why you put that on your face?
          F: It's Solarcaine. The sun burned my face.
          R: Why?
  (a, b) F: I stayed too long in the sun, and it burned my face. Solarcaine helps
             take the pain from the burn.
          R: Are you tired?
          F: No . . . .
          R: You're closing and opening your eyes?

(c) F: Well, that's because of the vapor in the Solarcaine. The vapor hurts

(d)   my eyes if I keep them open.

R: Why?

(e) F: Because Solarcaine is made with vapor, Uh . . . , mentholated vapor.

R: Why?

(f) F: Because mentholated vapor takes away the pain from the burn.

R: Is the sun mad at you?

(g) F: (laughs) No. The sun is not a person. It doesn't get mad.

(57)   R: Pipi! (urgently)

F: (Jumps up, helps him)

R: Why you not say to go make pipi?

F: You mean: Why didn't I tell you to go make pipi by yourself?

R: Yeah.

F: Because I thought your pants have straps and you have trouble with that.

R: But it doesn't.

F: Well, I *thought* it did. I made a mistake.

(58)   R: Look, I made some tracks.

F: Yeah, I see.

R: What are tracks?

F: A place where a car goes.

R: Are these tracks?

F: Yes.

R: Why?

(a) F: Because you made it that way.

R: What's a car?

F: A moving vehicle.

R: Why?

(b) F: Because that's what it is.

(59)   F: Did you give the car something to eat today?

R: No!

F: Why not?

R: Cause cars don't eat, Daddy.

F: Yeah, that's right. I'm just joking.

Index